The Entrepreneurial Society

The Entrepreneurial Society

David B. Audretsch

OXFORD
UNIVERSITY PRESS
2007

OXFORD
UNIVERSITY PRESS

Oxford University Press, Inc., publishes works that further
Oxford University's objective of excellence
in research, scholarship, and education.

Oxford New York
Auckland Cape Town Dar es Salaam Hong Kong Karachi
Kuala Lumpur Madrid Melbourne Mexico City Nairobi
New Delhi Shanghai Taipei Toronto

With offices in
Argentina Austria Brazil Chile Czech Republic France Greece
Guatemala Hungary Italy Japan Poland Portugal Singapore
South Korea Switzerland Thailand Turkey Ukraine Vietnam

Published by Oxford University Press, Inc.
198 Madison Avenue, New York, New York 10016

www.oup.com

Oxford is a registered trademark of Oxford University Press

Library of Congress Cataloging-in-Publication Data
Audretsch, David B.
The entrepreneurial society / by David B. Audretsch.
p.   cm.
Includes bibliographical references and index.
ISBN 978-0-19-518350-4
1. Entrepreneurship—United States.   2. United States—
Economic conditions—1945–   I. Title.
HB615.A933 2007
338'.040973—dc22   2006026797

1 3 5 7 9 8 6 4 2

Printed in the United States of America
on acid-free paper

This book is dedicated to Christopher, James, and Alex.

Preface

On November 9, 1989, the television program was abruptly inter-rupted. Inexplicably, East Germans were pouring unencumbered through the checkpoints into West Berlin, where I lived at that time. Joining the hoards of astonished on-lookers at the suddenly porous Berlin Wall, we could all sense this was one of history's great turning points. Not only did the fall of the Berlin Wall trigger the reunification of a divided Germany and the end of the Cold War, it fostered an expec-tation of an unprecedented peace dividend. Liberated from the finan-cial, military, and emotional burden of the Cold War, America and her European allies looked forward to a new era of not just peace but also unprecedented prosperity.

It didn't work out that way. In Europe, growth dwindled and opportunities were few. A stagnant economy in Europe triggered a seemingly unstoppable increase in unemployment that began in the early 1990s. Meanwhile, the United States enjoyed vigorous economic growth generated by one of the strongest and most dynamic expan-sions of the entire post-war era. However, accompanying the 1990s expansion was an increasing and worrisome gap between the haves and the have nots. Unlike other economic expansions, not all boats were lifted by the rising tide of national prosperity.

Something had changed. That something was globalization. With the fall of the Berlin Wall, vast expanses of previously inaccessible parts of the world, principally Eastern and Central Europe but also China and other parts of Asia, were swept up into the family of economic trading partners. Watching the Berlin Wall crumble that cold, dark November evening, I was amongst the thousands of Berliners witnessing firsthand not just the end of the Cold War but also the roots of contemporary globalization. At that point, no one had heard that word, yet within just a few years it would become a buzzword. Workers, businesses, industries, regions, and entire countries were suddenly exposed to relentless economic competition from not just Eastern European countries like Hungary and Romania, but also the new Asian giants, China and India.

Globalization has already left an undeniable imprint on society. What once worked so well, providing a sure-fired prescription for success, prosperity, and security for previous generations, stopped working. It stopped working not just in the United States but throughout the developed world, leaving a generation wondering exactly what had happened to them. The whole pattern of work, careers, and the vehicle that had provided citizens their livelihoods—the stalwart corporations of the Cold War era—were no longer delivering.

My father graduated from college, fought in the Pacific during World War II, and returned to a job with IBM. He kept that job for some forty years. Essentially, he had one job and one employer his entire adult life. There was a sense that the jobs were there, provided by the country's great corporations. The lesson imprinted in a generation of economists by John Maynard Keynes was to ensure sufficient demand to induce the country's great firms to fill those jobs. The great Keynesian insight was that if public policy made sure the demand was there, everything else—firms, jobs, and standard of living—would fall automatically into place.

But it was not falling into place anymore. Anyone looking to the great industrial stalwarts, such as General Motors, or even IBM, for anything approaching the security of the lifetime employment that was so prevalent in my father's generation would be disappointed. As the younger generation will tell you, the formulas of my father's generation, let alone mine, don't work anymore. The world has changed.

Even as many were shaking their heads, bewildered at what would have seemed incomprehensible just a short few years earlier, some people, businesses, industries, and even entire regions were thriving in this new global environment. The common denominator for success in rising to the challenges afforded by globalization rather than falling as yet another victim of globalization is what this book is all about.

In identifying the entrepreneurial society as the positive and productive response in this new global era, I have chosen to explain it in a way that is understandable, interesting, and valuable not necessarily only to my colleagues at the university, but perhaps more important, to the broad span of people engaged in the myriad spectrum of activities comprising our modern contemporary world. Individuals who understand the basic forces shaping both their choices and the consequences of those choices are better equipped to make those choices wisely. Business leaders and policymakers who are painfully discovering that the frameworks and theories they learned in school may no longer provide the path to success in the global era will similarly make better choices with a clear understanding of what the entrepreneurial society is, why it emerged, and why it is likely to hold the key for a prosperous future in the global era.

The writing of this book has benefited from the assistance of a number of people. The Ewing Marion Kauffman Foundation provided generous support of the research and writing of this book. Betty Fiscus, Paul Jackson, and Diana Black at the Institute of Development Strategies at Indiana University provided steady and reliable help with numerous aspects with the manuscript. Similarly, Taylor Aldridge, Melanie Aldridge, Iris Beckmann, Norman Bedtke, Max Keilbach, Anja Klaukien, Mathias Langner, Becky Mai, Erik Monsen, Lydia Nobis, Ilka Ritter, Mark Sanders, Madeleine Schmidt, Kerstin Schueck, Stephan Schütze, Uta Seydenschwanz, and Jagannadha Tamvada at the Max Planck Institute of Economics in Germany provided expert assistance in compiling background material and assisting with the writing of this book. I would also like to thank Sara Norwood for her outstanding work with the graphics in the book, as well as Naomi Lederer and Cathy delos Santos for their assistance. A special thanks goes to Adam Lederer, my student who threw himself into assisting with the writing of this book. He not only provided significant amounts of material and ideas, but he also exhibited extraordinary patience and tenacity while working through the numerous and varied earlier drafts of this book. Without his help, this would have been a very different and lesser book.

Finally, I would like to express particular gratitude to several people at Oxford University Press. Catherine Rae has been very helpful at moving the project from inception, through the writing, and finally into production. I have known Terry Vaughn since first publishing a book with him in 1983 and have always been proud and grateful to work with him. When the idea for this book emerged during a telephone conversation in 2003, he advised, "Understanding how the world has changed and how to deal with it is too important to be restricted to just a few scholars at universities. Write it for someone waiting at a bus stop in Indiana, the way you are telling me on the phone." So I did.

Contents

The Entrepreneurial Society

1

The Times They Are A-Changin'

Every generation has a defining moment. Perhaps the moment that defined the baby boom generation's voice, direction, and identity occurred in *The Graduate*. A (startlingly) young Dustin Hoffman is seen celebrating his college graduation. When he confesses his indecision about the future to an experienced family friend, the answer, whispered in his ear, shaped the consciousness of an entire generation: "Plastics." It could have been steel, autos, or tires as well. The point was that, back in the mid-1960s, as it had for some two decades, the future for ambitious young men lay within a large manufacturing corporation.

This belief was prevalent throughout the developed world during the post–World War II era. Just as the best and the brightest wanted to work for Philips Electronics in the Netherlands, Siemens in Germany, or Ericsson in Sweden, those without the same educational advantage were assured of a comfortable middle-class life by accepting employment on the factory floor at General Motors in Detroit, US Steel in Pittsburgh, Volkswagen in Germany, and Renault in France. It did not matter whether you were educated or not. The large corporation was the key to the American Dream—ownership of a home in the suburbs, and a car to drive.

If you fast-forward forty years into the contemporary world, few people, if any, would say plastics. Nor would they say autos or steel either. Today's icons are rooted in a very different and diametrically opposed image.

This image was famously forged in a television advertisement by Apple Computer during Super Bowl XVIII in 1984. The ad depicted a large congregation of homogeneous, listless, expressionless men wearing identical suits and carrying identical briefcases. An authoritative figure speaks on a massive screen in front of them, an allusion to Orwell's "Big Brother" that, without any doubt, symbolized IBM. Suddenly, a slender figure with long, unkempt hair, wearing running shorts and shoes, broke through and hurled a hammer forward, shattering the image on the screen, introducing Apple's new Macintosh personal computer.

It was symbolic of a seismic shift. The established, large corporation lost its omnipotence as the engine of economic growth—instead, action shifted to unheard-of start-ups like Apple Computer, Microsoft, Ben and Jerry's, Dell Computer, and Starbucks. While they are now large companies, what was most amazing to the entire world is that these companies had only recently been started by people like Steve Jobs, Bill Gates, Ben and Jerry, and Michael Dell. This is what would be whispered in the ear of a contemporary "Graduate."

It took some time before people began to recognize that these small, entrepreneurial startups were anything more than an interesting oddity, reflecting lifestyle choices that seemed to be incompatible with the more conservative norms in large corporations. No one could have imagined, say, the creators of ice cream flavors like Cherry Garcia would be ideal corporate men. In fact, IBM wrote off Bill Gates because he lacked the credentials—a college degree—to work for IBM. Similarly, Steve Jobs never made it through Reed College, and his subsequent time in India with a spiritual leader did not seem to compensate for the lack of an MBA.

During the post–World War II era, the direction, energy, and pulse of society remained fixed on the large corporation. Individuals, particularly young people, viewed large corporations as the source of jobs and opportunities—white-collar jobs if you were lucky enough to have a college education, blue-collar jobs if you did not. The union-protected blue-collar jobs in the auto, steel, and tire industries were a ticket into the middle class—just as the paper pushers, albeit without dirty hands, held dependable white-collar jobs. The large corporation was the source of well-paying jobs and security. No wonder America believed Charlie "Engine" Wilson, chairman of General Motors, when he declared "What's good for General Motors is good for America."[1] Postwar Americans knew who buttered their bread—the large corporation.

Until recently, most of my students' parents held one job their entire lives. They spent the majority of their work lives with one company, doing more or less one thing. My students often report their parents' bewilderment when not only do their children not know exactly what they want to do, they certainly don't plan on doing it for one employer their whole life. Being a loyal employee used to be highly valued and rewarded. Not anymore. Now, it's important for young people to nurture their networks to ensure they always have an outside option. A previous generation considered work to be something you did for money, for material gain. Nobody went into plastics because they loved plastics. My sense of young people today is that while they want a comfortable, materially secure life, just like generations before them, they also want to feel passionate about what they are doing. They want to believe that what they are doing connects something inside them-selves with the external world. Parents shake their heads and wonder why their offspring don't simply get a job. Why do they have to be so passionately involved with their work? Since when did work stop being something you did for money and become a means for self-fulfillment and self-development? To be involved in producing something you could touch and sell, like automobiles or refrigerators, had always been preferable to the "softer" services, yet today few young people want to be involved in the production of cars, steel, or almost any manufactured good for that matter. It is not surprising that to older generations the world has gone topsy-turvy. What was good and valuable only a few years earlier is now better avoided.

Something changed. And that something—the driving force of the economy—is the subject of this book. For my parents' generation, whom Tom Brokaw praised as the "greatest generation,"[2] the driving force of the economy were the large corporations. My father, like his entire generation, returned victorious from World War II, apprehensive about what lay ahead. After all, thanks to the war, an entire generation had been plucked from the worst economic disaster the United States had ever experienced, the Great Depression, during which as many as one in four Americans were unemployed.

How happy returning veterans must have felt to discover that the postwar American economy was entirely different. This economy had conquered the decade-long depression of the 1930s and come roaring back, because the nation had one thing that mattered most for an economy, at least at that time—factories, plants, and machines, or what the economists like to call physical capital. With education from the GI Bill and cash from their veteran benefits, these men and their new brides hungered for a house in the suburbs, a car to put in the driveway, and a collection of household goods to make their house a home. The demand was there, but, as a result of the nearly total destruction of not just German cities, but much of Europe, no other country had anything approaching the capacity needed to meet that demand.

America had spent the previous century struggling to learn how to make this large-scale type of production work efficiently. It took more than machines and factories; it took unions, schools, and government policies that provided an external environment that accommodated and facilitated the effectiveness of large corporations. It also took people who were able and willing to devote the better part of their days for most of their lives to running and maintaining those machines and factories. This was not much fun. If you were a blue-collar worker, you learned to numb your mind and devote yourself to life after work. If you were lucky enough to be educated for a white-collar job, you became what William H. Whyte penned into infamy, the "organization man."[3] Whether your collar was blue or white, one thing was the same: you were a cog in the machine of the large corporation, and it wasn't fun. Image after image from that period reinforces that life may have been wonderful but work was dull, tedious, and not to be discussed in front of women and children.[4] Baby boomers will never forget Fred Flintstone cheering "Yabba-Dabba Do." But did he ever shout this on the way to work? For poor Fred, work was drudgery, just as it was for members of the "greatest generation," who manned American corporations and factories, pouring out record numbers of automobiles and tons of steel. A more thoughtful critique of the emptiness of the workplace is portrayed by Gregory Peck in the film based on the best-selling novel from the 1950s *The Man in the Gray Flannel Suit*,[5] or in David Riesman's penetrating analysis of the alienation of working for the large corporation, *The Lonely Crowd*.[6] But the men and women returning victorious from war were thankful to have a good job that provided a middle-class life. If work was less than fun, it was certainly preferable to the war and the Great Depression before it. This was the American dream, at least the postwar 1950s and 1960s version.

William H. Whyte called the typical person who was required to run the factories and corporations of the postwar economy the "organization man." This economy was driven by the efficiencies and power of large corporations, like General Motors and US Steel. It required massive interventions, regulations, fine-tuning, and support from not just the government but from all facets of society, spanning a broad array of institutions, ranging from schools to, as Betty Friedan was quick to point out in *The Feminine Mystique*, marriage and the family.[7] It took what I will term *the managed economy* to provide the right institutions and policies to create a workforce and external conditions that could make an economy centered around the large corporation work the best.[8] Learning how to live with the beast of big business and how to get the most out of it was neither easy nor trivial, as a century of at times twisted and tortured history has shown us.[9] By the 1950s, the lessons had been learned, all of the institutions and policies were in place, and the Americans, who had saved the world from fascism and dictatorship, were well positioned to enjoy the fruits of their sacrifices. America's century-old investment in creating the managed economy was finally paying off.

However, it did not keep paying off. Maybe it couldn't. At first glance, it would seem that the culprit was the 1960s. The protests, the social movement, and the "cultural revolution" affronted and challenged everything that was sacred to the managed economy. The restraint and self-discipline inherent in that economy gave way to spontaneity and going with the flow. Conformity and strict adherence to the rules was replaced with "doing your own thing" and self-realization. Civility and deference were replaced by confrontation and challenge. Order and decorum gave way to chaos. As Bob Dylan sang in "The Times They Are A-Changing," perhaps the most penetrating song characterizing the great transition of the 1960s, "The first one now / Will later be last."[10]

I was a child at the zenith of the managed economy. I was a teenager as that economy began to fade, and a young adult as it started its great descent into a downward spiral. Was this eclipse and decline inevitable? The famous 1960s song by the Byrds "Turn! Turn! Turn!" quotes the Bible,

"To everything there is a season" (Ecclesiastes 3:1). To middle-aged people in the 1960s, not just the managed economy but also civilization as they had known it must have appeared to be going into eclipse. An entire popular culture, that of the 1950s, was swallowed up and disappeared into the vortex of the chaos and whirl that was the 1960s.

But it was not just the 1960s alone that led to the demise of the managed economy. By the 1970s, something unanticipated and unexpected happened. The country lay paralyzed by an oil crisis, triggered by the quadrupling of the price of crude oil from $3 a barrel in 1973 to $12 a barrel. At the same time, what had been a barely noticeable trickle of manufactured imports turned into a flood of automobiles and steel pouring into America's ports and harbors, more often than not bearing the tags "Made in Germany" or "Made in Japan."

In an issue in 1987 devoted to the question "Can America Compete?" *Business Week* concluded that the options facing the United States were either "a surge in productivity—or a lasting decline."[11] To the American public the crisis was as difficult to recognize as it was painful. After all, in the first several decades following World War II,

> the U.S. was virtually unchallenged as industrial leader. Americans could make anything, and because their products were the best, they could sell whatever they made, both at home and abroad. But somewhere around 1973, the gravy train was derailed—and it has never really gotten back on track. U.S. producers met fierce competition from foreign industries that churned out high-quality goods made by low-wage workers.[12]

The managed economy's days were numbered, at least in the United States. By the 1970s, Europe and Japan had caught up. When it came to physical capital—plants, factories, and machinery—America was no longer the only kid on the block. Rather, thanks in part to its own generosity in helping restore the defeated Japan and Germany back to their feet through the Marshall Plan and other programs, the United States now faced serious international competition. The Japanese and German institutional and policy approach to their respective managed economies was proving to be superior to America's approach.[13] After all, when it came to manufactured goods, the Germans and Japanese knew what should be produced, how it should be produced, and who should produce it. When it came to having a trained, disciplined, and dedicated workforce, the Japanese and Germans simply could not be beat. The Japanese and Germans, along with other European countries, like Sweden, had developed an elaborate institutional structure and government policies that made their large companies even more efficient and competitive than their American counterparts.

This is not to suggest that the playing field was always level. Both the Japanese and Europeans deployed industrial policies to compete against and beat the Americans in industries like automobiles and steel.[14] America's competitors were finding more ways to benefit from their investments in plants and factories than America could ever dream. The United States had missed the boat.

Arrogance and complacency in the United States had kept Americans from realizing that the nation's assumed position of superiority in manufacturing, in having a competitive advantage in the production of goods involving large-scale assembly, was not a given. Other countries had developed an understanding of and commitment to what it would take to push their economies and societies ahead of, and perhaps even past, the mighty United States. After all, if they could beat Great Britain, what was to keep them from achieving in the peace of the postwar era what had eluded them though militarization?

The demolished countries had recovered, and America was worried. Just as the Soviet threat alarmed the country during the Cold War, Japan and Europe now threatened America's economic dominance. President Jimmy Carter's failed 1980 reelection bid was attributable to both the dismal employment prospects in American stalwart industries as well as the Iranian hostage situation. Just as he lacked effective solutions for the Iranian hostage crisis, President Carter was unable to offer any substantive solution to the American *competitiveness crisis*. The American managed economy lay in shambles. The United States had been fooled into thinking that, by being the first to develop a postwar managed economy, by virtue of its victory in World War II, its lead would always be there. That proved to be a delusion.

I moved to West Berlin in 1985. As the 1980s rolled on, bringing year after year of breathtaking increases in German prosperity, the Germans increasingly shook their heads wondering what had happened to their partner on the other side of the Atlantic. Even while Germany was growing rich and prosperous, America was bogged down in a myriad

of plant closings, downsizings, and layoffs—particularly in the industrial heartland that became known as the Rust Belt. Germans, like their
Nordic neighbors to the north, seemed to have it all. Not only were these
countries growing wealthier with each passing year, but their social
welfare states provided health, retirement, and education benefits as
well as job security, provisions that were unimaginable in the United
States. The managed economy no longer delivered for the United States,
and had perhaps even become a burden. No wonder the Germans,
Swedes, and Japanese shook their heads in sympathy for the once-
mighty Americans. It seemed certain that economic domination, or at
least leadership, was shifting from the United States to its competitors.

The evolution from the internationalization of markets—involving
trade among the United States, Europe, and Japan in the postwar era—
to what Thomas Friedman proclaimed as the start of contemporary
globalization,[15] triggered by the fall of the Berlin Wall in 1989, spelled
an even worse future for America. After all, if American companies had
trouble competing against the high-wage countries like Germany and
Japan, how could they hold their own against the new low-cost
competition from central Europe, eastern Europe, and southeast Asia?

While America's future prospects looked even dimmer with the
advent of globalization, Europe and Japan licked their chops, anticipating still greater prosperity around the bend. Germany, like most of
western Europe and Japan, had developed sophisticated and subtle
social systems to support its version of the capital-driven managed
economy. This enabled it to enjoy what seemed to be unlimited success
in international markets. Germany and Japan had quickly ascended as
the leaders in exports, even though the United States was considerably
larger. The new globalization held the promise of even greater prosperity for these nations. If the Japanese and Germans could beat the
Americans in international markets, surely they could also beat the
Czechs, Poles, Hungarians, Chinese, and Indians.

A host of scholars, pundits, and business leaders bemoaned the
decline of the once proud and mighty economic power. Lester
Thurow, dean of the prestigious Sloan School of Management at the
Massachusetts Institute of Technology, lamented that the United States
was "losing the economic race"[16] because "today it's very hard to find
an industrial corporation in America that isn't in really serious trouble
basically because of trade problems. . . . The systematic erosion of

our competitiveness comes from having lower rates of growth of manufacturing productivity year after year, as compared with the rest of the world."[17] In one of the most widely discussed books of the time, *The Rise and Decline of Great Powers*, Paul Kennedy explained that economic decline was all but inevitable.[18] This pessimism ultimately led to the election of Ronald Reagan in 1980 and, twelve years later, Bill Clinton. The burning question emerging in the 1970s remained, more poignantly than ever, "how to get it back."

Regaining the lead was generally perceived as the way into the future. For the United States to do this, it needed to regain international competitiveness in the industries that mattered—especially the ones most devastated by Japanese and German international competition: automobiles and steel. This strategy suggested rethinking and revamping America's managed economy in order to win back ground that had been lost in these key industries. In 1989, an influential study called *Made in America* was directed by Michael L. Dertouzos, Richard K. Lester, and Robert M. Solow, the leaders of the prominent and prestigious Massachusetts Institute of Technology (MIT) Commission on Industrial Productivity, which consisted of a "dream team" of twenty-three top MIT scholars whose knowledge spanned a broad range of scholarly disciplines and backgrounds. The study argued that the way into the future was to restore productivity and international competitiveness.[19] For the United States to restore its international competitiveness, it had to regain primacy in manufacturing plants and equipment, that is, physical capital. In addition, America had to adapt its policies to target and promote its leading corporations, as had been done with formidable success in Japan and Germany. If you can't beat them, join them. Primacy in manufacturing would also secure American leadership in the world. It was time to restore the American managed economy. If this meant compromising and adjusting fundamental institutions and policies in the United States, like the antitrust laws, or introducing more heavy-handed industrial targeting to level the playing field in industries like steel, so be it. The United States had been blind-sided before—the sneak attack at Pearl Harbor, for example. Surely, if the nation could win that war, it could muster the will and resources to win this new war for manufacturing prowess.

Winning back economic supremacy is exactly what the United States did in the 1990s. By the middle of the decade, economic growth, productivity, and job creation were at record levels. Unemployment had nearly disappeared throughout much of the country. This was a new golden era for America. The stock market started climbing and would not stop until the end of the century. So did real estate prices. Meanwhile, Japan and Germany—in fact, virtually all European countries—were bogged down in economic stagnation and unemployment levels that ratcheted higher and higher throughout the decade.

So had America, in the end, won the battle for manufacturing? Had it adjusted its managed economy, perhaps developed a neo-managed economy to take back its manufacturing lead? Had it reversed the trend of industrial erosion and the hollowing out of its great corporations that had been taking place for the better part of two decades?

Not exactly. What had saved America, or at least what had saved its economy, was not the managed economy; rather, it was the demise of the managed economy and the emergence of something entirely different. The job and wealth machine that America had wondrously become in the 1990s was not, in fact, based on the great corporations and industries of the managed economy. Those industries continued to decline. Their eclipse was hardly retarded by the now-booming economy of the Clinton era.

What, in fact, saved America was the emergence of a broad host of new industries. These new firms and industries generated unprecedented wealth, income, and job creation for Americans. These industries ranged from the high-tech sectors—computers, software, information technology, and biotechnology—to services, especially financial, health, and educational services.

How did all this come about? Was it some enlightened plan of the Clinton administration? Hardly. The roots lie much deeper and also much earlier. It is true that the 1960s was a decade of excess, extremes, self-absorption, and decadence. But it was also a decade that broke down barriers. It was difficult to escape from succumbing to the social forces channeling people into the mold of the "organization man" in the 1950s, as William H. Whyte, and Sloan Wilson in *The Man in the Gray Flannel Suit*, suggested.[20] It would have been at least as difficult to become such a person by the end of the 1960s. Everything the 1950s represented, the 1960s seemed to be against. Whether you liked it, detested it, or viewed the 1960s as a mixed bag, one thing was for sure: the possibilities available at the end of the decade were much more vast and numerous than when it started. For example, it became possible for blacks to attend the same schools as whites, to sit on the same buses, and view the same movies. It became possible for women to be taken seriously in a professional and career capacity, rather than sequestered off in suburban homes in stereotypical housewife roles. It became possible to become openly gay or even a communist. Thanks to the 1960s, virtually all things became possible, if not desirable.

When I started college in the fall of 1972, many of the previously tried-and-true rigid rules, traditions, and codes had simply vaporized. For example, young men and women were not only allowed to spend the night together; it was not uncommon for them to live together in college dorms. Only a few years earlier, visitation by the opposite sex had been highly regulated and restricted to specific supervised hours. Rules like "four on the floor" (meaning people's feet) had been widespread and strictly adhered to. But within a span of just a few years, such rules and regulations were gone. Almost anything went, not just on campus, but throughout society. There was a feeling that the older generation, the *establishment*, as it was known and called itself, had acknowledged defeat. The establishment had been proven wrong on too many issues, too many times. And not just minor issues, either. This was the generation that had been wrong about civil rights. As time went on, it became increasingly difficult to find anyone of that generation who defended segregation and forcing African Americans to be separated. But the writing was already on the wall at the end of the 1960s. And this was the generation that had been wrong about the Vietnam War as well. By the early 1970s, the middle class—what President Richard Nixon and Vice-President Spiro Agnew called the *silent majority*—had abandoned their support for the lost cause. Don't forget, it was President Nixon who ultimately delivered on democratic candidate George McGovern's promise in the 1972 presidential election: to get America out of Vietnam. Whether McGovern could have actually withdrawn American troops from Vietnam before Nixon did will remain a hypothetical and counterfactual question. The "greatest generation" was in the throes of self-doubt and self-retribution by the early 1970s. The last president who was totally committed to the managed economy and who seemed to embody the essential qualities and virtues of that era was Richard M. Nixon. Seeing him forced to resign over the Watergate burglary was perhaps the final blow to any convictions that the 1950s values were superior. This was far from the greatest moment of the "greatest generation."

Thus, when I got to campus in the fall of 1972, the palpable awareness was "Anything goes."[21] At least, almost anything. Cohabitation, fine! Alcohol and drugs, as long as they were not the lethal kind, fine! Abolishment of traditional course requirements and procedures, fine! The establishment, which included college administrators, had simply backed down, after being proven wrong on so many fundamental issues, ranging from civil rights to women's liberation to the Vietnam War. It certainly was a heady and exhilarating time to be on campus.

Whether they are viewed positively or negatively, these changes— the breaking down of rules, restrictions, and regulations, as well as the opening up of possibilities—had not come easily. Rather, they had been won at a high cost to the generation ahead of me, the 1960s generation.[22] A documentary portraying the university town of Madison, Wisconsin, during the Vietnam War, entitled *The War at Home*, starts out with an actual film clip taken from the early 1960s. The scene captures a handful of neatly groomed students, wearing ties and jackets, walking around the university mall in a tight circle carrying signs with slogans along the lines of "Stop the War in Vietnam" and "End the War." The masses of students at the University of Wisconsin are shown simply passing by this small group of tidy protestors, paying them scant attention. The next scene fast-forwards just a few years into the future. It is the same location, the mall, but the scene has dramatically changed. Now there are more than a hundred thousand unruly and unkempt freaks and hippies, vocal and belligerent, demanding relentlessly "Out of 'Nam— NOW!" among other unprintable chants. Within the span of just a few years, America had changed, and changed radically. The dam had broken, and there was no holding back the flood of change.

One of my most beloved mentors, Bob Clodius, served as acting president of the University of Wisconsin during this time. Bob told his students a story about the day the Vietnam protestors took over the main administration building, Bascom Hall. They burst into his office and demanded that he end the war. Bob would tell the story in his disarming way to lecture halls of students years later: "Hell, I couldn't end the war in Vietnam, even if I had wanted to. I couldn't even get faculty to teach what I wanted or get what I wanted for dinner at home. How was I supposed to end the Vietnam War?"[23] I am sure that at the time, being held hostage by an office full of angry, disgruntled students was not so charming.

In fact, history has been harsh to those young students of the 1960s. Raised in the harness of the 1950s and driven by an idealism instilled by their idyllic suburban upbringing, the students first questioned, then challenged, and later tore down many of the norms, traditions, and barriers that had defined the earlier decade. The 1960s made it possible to go your own way and not feel compelled to simply follow the herd. My impression is that the casualty rate of the 1960s generation was surprisingly high. There were, of course, casualties in Vietnam. But there were also the drug overdoses and suicides, spawned by lives that had become isolated and cut off from their roots.

This generation consistently seems to have had difficulties in adjusting and adapting to everything that has happened after the 1960s. Zoltan Acs, my colleague, friend, and professor of public policy at George Mason University, once remarked to me that his generation knew what they did not want, but they had a harder time figuring out what they did want. Perhaps the main contribution of the 1960s generation was the tearing down of many institutions that were the cornerstone of the managed economy, thus freeing the way for entrepreneurs—who would ultimately save the American economy in the 1990s.

If the 1950s produced the organization man, the 1960s produced the young men and women who were the organization man's antithesis. Young people certainly did not feel compelled to conform or fit in—at least not with the norms, modes, and rules inherited from the 1950s. While it was not the end of the organization man, it was the beginning of something else, something more important. Like their older brothers and sisters, the entrepreneurs springing from the seeds sown in the 1960s knew what they did not want, which was to be a cog in an organization they did not care about. Perhaps less like their older siblings, they knew what they *did* want. And what they wanted was something different.

Young people like Steve Jobs were not content, like their older siblings of the 1960s, to simply turn on, tune in, and drop out of the establishment. They may have done some or all of that, but they also started to create something different. That is exactly what the famous Super Bowl Apple ad was—more a political and social statement than a simple presentation of a new product. It was a rebellion against the status quo. Following the 1960s, rebellion against a status quo organization like IBM was hardly unusual. What was unusual was the step that followed: the creation of a new product that would ultimately change the world. That product, the personal computer, could only be introduced by also starting a new firm, in this case Apple Computer. And it wasn't just Steven Jobs creating Apple Computer. Scores of entrepreneurs and would-be entrepreneurs followed in the subsequent decades, including but not restricted to Nike, Ben and Jerry's, Dell, and Starbucks. By knowing what they didn't want, these entrepreneurs not only created new firms but also ended up helping to keep America from going under in the sea of international competition, which would later gave rise to globalization.

But the entrepreneurs didn't do it alone. They couldn't have. It is fashionable to blame the 1960s, along with its social, political, and cultural rebellion, for America's decline in the subsequent decades. Some people think that the country has never recovered, never again attained that glowing sense of grace of the golden age of the 1950s managed economy. Perhaps not. But at least one important thing was accomplished in the 1960s: Americans were liberated and freed from the constraining rigidities that had enabled the 1950s managed economy to thrive in the first place. By tearing down a number of rules, regulations, habits, and traditions—the values and institutions of the managed economy—the 1960s opened up the possibility for the next generation to not only deviate from norms but to deviate in such a way as to create new values, create new products, and ultimately generate entire new industries, like software and biotechnology. The sameness of the managed economy—the conformity, monotony, rigidity, and homogeneity—had been replaced by nonconformity, autonomy, creativity, and self-reliance. What does the T-shirt from Austin, Texas, proclaim? "Keep Austin weird."[24]

The entrepreneurial society is rooted in entirely different values, skills, and priorities than its precursor, the managed economy. As the journalist John U. Bacon observes about the avant-garde Cirque du Soleil, it embodies the characteristics and creativity that typify the entrepreneurial society. It's all about the ability "to meld collaboration and conflict together. . . . It's the opposite of Detroit. They don't care where an idea comes from. The best just bubble to the top."[25] It is perhaps an irony of history that the 1960s generation, which opposed the idea of material gain, paved the way for subsequent generations to create a new economy—and that economy ultimately led to a decade registering the greatest creation and accumulation of material wealth the country has ever seen.

It is, course, not trivial to pinpoint the exact moment when the institutional structure that had served the managed economy so well—propelling it to an American golden age of growth, employment, prosperity, and economic security in the postwar era—began to recede and ultimately break down. Perhaps the 1970s musician Don McLean could proclaim in "American Pie" to know exactly "the day the music died," but it would probably be unrealistic to identify a single event triggering first the eclipse and ultimately the downfall of the institutions supporting the managed economy. Still, one turning point was the beginning of a massive and widespread change in American public policy that reversed the far-reaching regulations that were binding American industry.[26] Unless you lived during the peak of the managed economy, it is easy to forget that in the struggle to provide a stable and manageable external environment within which the large-scale manufacturing corporations could thrive, an increasingly large part of American industry was subjected to regulations. Consumers and small businesses needed protection. The public policy response of industry regulation was an explicit attempt to protect the corporations from what was perceived to be and openly called cutthroat competition. This implied that without such government protection, these corporations would be gigantic lemmings whose urge for profits and market share would drive them off the cliff and into the abyss of failure and bankruptcy. The same might happen with consumers and less efficient competition, like small business. Such massive and pervasive industry regulation began with the passage of the Interstate Commerce Act and establishment of the Interstate Commerce Commission in 1890. The goal was to control railroad rates, and this goal subsequently spread over the next 80 years to other industries like trucking, airlines, oil, gas, banking, and finance. In addition, a myriad of other regulations imposed by regulatory agencies like the Federal Trade Commission, the Food and Drug Administration, and the Occupational Safety and Health Administration left virtually no industry untouched and certainly not unregulated. Industry regulation was an integral part of the managed economy. It provided a key mechanism that protected and nurtured corporate interests while at the same time protecting the interests of consumers, small businesses, and other important constituents.

Thus, it was a startling reversal when Congress elected to deregulate the airline industry in 1978. Contrary to conventional wisdom, the deregulation movement did not begin with the election of Ronald Reagan in 1980. Rather, the origins of the deregulation movement are rooted in the Carter administration. In particular, a committee chaired by Senator Edward Kennedy, which became known as the Kennedy Committee, provided the initial hearings and impetus for deregulating the airline industry. Deregulation rapidly spread to other important industries, like financial services, natural gas, oil, telecommunications, trucking, and railroads.

What is particularly striking in retrospect is that, by the mid-1970s and into the 1980s, the congressional records reflect a bipartisan consensus that deregulation would help the economy. This marked the beginning of the end of the managed economy. It must not be forgotten that just a few years earlier, the Republican president Richard M. Nixon had imposed his administration's very un-Republican price and wage controls on the economy in an effort to try to halt inflation. The fact that a Republican president would actually resort to such heavy-handed government intervention, not to mention that most of the country went along with the imposed controls, is a tribute to the pervasiveness of the managed economy, even in its dying gasps. Just several years later, both Republicans and Democrats were turning on the very institutions that were the heart of the managed economy. While they might have bitterly disagreed on many issues of national interest, there was a virtual consensus that the government had to stop regulating and managing the external environment for the corporations, which, in turn, would have to begin competing in a market environment they had avoided for decades. Although nobody said it at the time, this was the beginning of the end of the managed economy.

The large corporation did not become viable or succeed in a vacuum. Rather, it required the external support of institutions and public policy that created the managed economy. The budding entrepreneurs who would revolutionize the American economy also could not have thrived, or even operated, in a vacuum. Ultimately, the abandonment of the managed economy, along with the ascendance of institutional and policy support, led to the emergence of the entrepreneurial society that created the unprecedented economic growth and job explosion of the 1990s that caught most experts by surprise. Even while experts were looking anxiously over their shoulders to benchmark how America's once great industries and corporations were holding up against competitors from Japan and Germany, the entrepreneurial society was already taking root. For all of their jubilance and celebration of the American economic renaissance during the century's last decade, not many leaders and pundits recognized that this remarkable economic rejuvenation was attributable to a fundamental revolution that had taken place. All they knew was "We're back!" Perhaps how and why did not matter as much. But the revolution that made it all possible involved tearing down and shifting away from one approach, a virtual way of life and set of values, and moving toward a very different way of life and set of values. The entrepreneurial society had replaced the managed economy.

Which of these two dialectic approaches—the managed economy or the entrepreneurial society—is more consistent with inherently American values? One view sides with the managed economy, with its apex during the postwar era. These values seem squarely American— a clear sense of authority, and a respect for status quo institutions and organizations. Living in the Midwest, I believe that we have combined the values of the managed economy and what are widely held to be America's inherent values in America's heartland.

By contrast, a very different view holds that there is a deeper and longer tradition, dating back to the founding of the country, that is more reflective of the entrepreneurial society. The independent, self-reliant pioneer and frontiersman forged his way west, traveling into the unknown. He created rules as they were needed and abandoned them if they were not. This pioneer represents the values of the entrepre- neurial society more than those of the managed economy. Certainly, the Jeffersonian ideal celebrated the independent and self-reliant crafts- man who could control his destiny, by owning the means of production. The famous French observer and commentator Alexis de Tocqueville had a knack for capturing the essence of America, and pointed out nearly two centuries ago: "what most astonishes me in the United States, is not so much the marvelous grandeur of some undertakings, as the innumerable multitude of small ones."[27] The America described by de Tocqueville and idealized by Jefferson seems to reflect the free-spirited and individually driven entrepreneurial society more than the collectivist, controlled, and rigid managed economy.

It is tempting to contemplate which political party is more closely aligned with the managed economy and which with the entrepreneurial society. Although the question is seductive, it is misleading. In fact, both parties supported and fostered the managed economy during its zenith. The Republican Party might have been viewed as sympathetic to the large corporations, but the Democratic Party was no doubt the party of big labor, the unions. Until the mid-1970s, both parties supported regulation and massive government intervention in industry. All of these were core institutions of the managed economy. They may have been on opposite sides of the table, but both political parties were inevitably shaped by and responded to the view that the capital-driven economy needed to be managed.

Since the decline of the managed economy, both parties have engaged in policies that at times support the entrepreneurial society and at times work against it. For example, when he was confronted not just by economic stagnation but also by the worst job creation performance of any modern American president, George W. Bush responded with a policy that focused on entrepreneurship and small business, in order to promote economic growth:

> 70 percent of the new jobs in America are created by small
> businesses. I understand that. And I have promoted during
> the course of the last four years one of the most aggressive,
> pro-entrepreneur, small business policies. . . . And so in a
> new term, we will make sure the tax relief continues to be
> robust for our small businesses. We'll push legal reform and
> regulatory reform because I understand the engine of growth
> is through the small business sector.[28]

This echoed the 1993 State of the Union Address by his predecessor President Bill Clinton: "because small business has created such a high percentage of all the new jobs in our nation over the last 10 or 15 years, our plan includes the boldest targeted incentives for small business in history. We propose a permanent investment tax credit for the small firms in this country."[29] The Republican response to Clinton was "we agree with the President that we have to put more people to work, but remember this: 80 to 85 percent of the new jobs in this country are created by small business. So the climate for starting and expanding businesses must be enhanced with tax incentives and deregulation, rather than imposing higher taxes and more governmental mandates."[30]

However, each party has also formulated, proposed, and in some cases implemented policies that seem to support the largely defunct managed economy, which suggests that both main political parties may be oblivious to the seismic shift that has created the entrepreneurial society. For example, both main political parties remain committed to linking health coverage to the worker's employer. Such a policy may have been fundamentally sound during the managed economy when most workers were employed by large corporations, because this offered both a stable and long-term mechanism for delivering health care coverage. In the entrepreneurial society, where workers may rapidly change jobs and employers come and go, relying on the corporation-employee relationship to deliver health care coverage is not only fraught with ambiguities but can actually hinder entrepreneurship. More than a few workers have been deterred from changing jobs or starting their own business in order to hang on to coveted health coverage provided by a status quo employer.

The point is, formulating and implementing policies that would have been appropriate for the managed economy can actually have a counterproductive effect when applied to the entrepreneurial society. The very institutions and public policies that helped the managed economy thrive may actually pose a barrier to entrepreneurship. Conversely, institutions and policies that might have been detrimental to the managed economy may be necessary for entrepreneurship. Steve Beck, president of the Indiana Venture Center, a nonprofit organization funded through philanthropy to promote entrepreneurship and economic development in Indiana, has developed a unique instrument to inject entrepreneurship into Indiana. Beck targets Hoosiers who have become entrepreneurs in some other state, typically in California, and tries to persuade them to return to the Hoosier state. In the managed economy, the economic development community targeted large corporations and tried to lure them to locating in the state. Beck's focus on recruiting committed entrepreneurs to return to their home state with their entrepreneurial talents and experience is certainly consistent with creating an entrepreneurial Indiana.

Does it still make sense for regions or cities or communities to chase after the same manufacturing jobs that were coveted during the era of the managed economy? Does it make sense to regard education at all levels, from primary to college, as an add-on to already burdened community budgets? Many communities, like mine in Bloomington, Indiana, pay a lot of lip service to education. But when it's time to vote for new funding, in the form of additional taxes that would actually support education, the voters don't seem to be the same people as the education enthusiasts. Many communities seem to have an easier time funding extracurricular sports programs than educational programs. This might have been fine or even preferable at the high point of the managed economy, but surely not for the entrepreneurial society. Similarly, it's great to have a president who proclaims his main priority by self-designating himself the "Education President," pushing through the ambitiously named "No Child Left Behind Act." But when it comes time to fund education programs, all the way from kindergarten to the most advanced Ph.D. programs, where's the funding?

Shortly after the Berlin Wall fell in 1989, I had an opportunity to consult with the government of what would become the Slovak Republic. Upon hearing their admiration for the strong economy, job creation, and standard of living generated by the entrepreneurial economy of Silicon Valley, I reminded them that this was a radically different economy from what they had been accustomed to behind the Iron Curtain—which included not just a high startup rate but also a high failure rate. "We don't want any failures here!" was the conclusion of my still admiring but somewhat puzzled eastern European hosts.

Many, if not all, of the status quo institutions were actually created to enhance the managed economy. Rather than contributing to solutions, these institutions may actually cause problems in the entrepreneurial society. Several years ago, a German "Green Card" was introduced to lure foreign-born information technology workers into Germany. Given the obvious shortage of high-technology workers, this policy made sense. But there was an explicit clause on the Green Card that prohibited them from starting their own businesses. This might not have mattered much at the zenith of the managed economy, but prohibiting entrepreneurship on the part of highly skilled knowledge workers in an entrepreneurial society does not make much sense. As Bob Dylan also wrote and sang, "Come mothers and fathers / Throughout the land / And don't criticize / What you can't understand."

It is not only politicians and policy-makers who are confused by the shift from the managed to the entrepreneurial economy. Everyone is vulnerable to confusion concerning how we should move into the future. The old lessons and values designed to support success and a middle-class life in the managed economy might be a liability in the entrepreneurial society. One example is the value of unmitigated loyalty to your first employer. Today, who knows how long any employer, even the largest and most prominent, will value any particular employee, let alone maintain production and employment in any particular location? Similarly, in many towns young people learned that it was acceptable, in fact downright viable, to drop out of high school, or at least finish high school and then settle in for a lifetime job at the local plant. Once you learn how to cope with the mind-numbing work each day, the evening belongs to you—for your entire life. While this course generated a comfortable, middle-class life at the apex of the managed economy, it is clearly a liability in the entrepreneurial society.

Being burdened by the policies, institutions, values, and dictates of the managed economy in a global era in which they no longer ensure a path to a successful future is by no means an exclusively, or even mainly, an American problem. For example, in a front-page article, "Higher Learning in France Clings to Its Old Ways," the *New York Times* points out that "flexibility is not at all the tradition in France, where students are put on fixed career tracks at an early age."[31] The article quotes a recent graduate of the University of Paris, Claire de la Vigne: "We are never taught the idea of the American dream, where everything is possible. Our guide is fear."[32] To accept one's limitations may have been commensurate, if not particularly pleasant, in the managed economy. In the entrepreneurial society, it is a recipe for disappointment and disillusionment. As Bob Dylan sang, "Come senators, congressmen / Please heed the call, / Don't stand in the doorway, / Don't block up the hall. / For he that gets hurt / Will be he who has stalled / There's a battle outside / And it is ragin'." Simply following what worked in the managed economy may lead to disappointment and frustration in the entrepreneurial society. What worked only a few years earlier might not be so effective today.

Thus, a main purpose of writing this book is to make it clear that, along with the shift from the managed economy to the entrepreneurial society, there must come a reassessment of not just institutions and government policies but also the paths that individuals consider and take to attain a successful life. As Bob Dylan wrote and sang, "Come gather 'round people wherever you roam / And admit that the waters / Around you have grown, / And accept it that soon / You'll be drenched to the bone. / If your time to you / Is worth savin' / Then you better start swimmin' or you'll sink like a stone."

Let me emphasize that this book in no way suggests or argues that the entrepreneurial society is without problems or liabilities. In fact, problems and challenges awaiting new solutions abound in the entrepreneurial society, just as there were certainly problems in the managed economy. This is not to trivialize some of the most pressing problems society has faced—for example, a wildly diverging distribution of income and wealth among the participants and the outsiders has created an unprecedented gulf in society. Karl Marx focused on the division between capital and labor, Adam Smith on that between workers and consumers. In the entrepreneurial society, a great gap has erupted separating people who can work with knowledge and ideas and act on them and those who cannot. This book poses no solution to this problem but certainly acknowledges it is a problem that must be dealt with. Rather, what this book will provide is a framework for understanding how and why the driving force underlying the economy has fundamentally changed. Such a framework is useful in understanding why certain problems have arisen in our society, and why we need new approaches to creatively solve them. Trying to analyze and solve problems through an outdated framework of the managed economy would misguide us in understanding both the sources of the problem as well as finding possible solutions.

In the end, it is probably a mistake—and certainly an illusion—to look for the essence of America in either the managed economy or the entrepreneurial society. Rather, America is, above and beyond all, a country rooted in pragmatism. Perhaps the success and vibrancy of the country is grounded in pragmatism rather than with either the managed economy or the entrepreneurial society. After all, the country is bigger than any system.

Both the managed economy and the entrepreneurial society have generated two of the more remarkable decades of American history. Both decades are considered to be golden ages in terms of the American prosperity, standard of living, employment prospects, and security, as well as in propelling the country to world leadership. Each of these two decades generated such a golden age for America in ways that were decidedly different and, in many respects, diametrically opposed. But the starting point was essentially the same, and perhaps quintessentially American: the quest for creating a future with enhanced prospects for prosperity and a high standard of living—that is, for a better life. It is the path to attaining that goal that has fundamentally changed as the managed economy has given way to the entrepreneurial society. As Bob Dylan sang some decades ago, "The Times They Are A-Changin'."

2

It Don't Mean a Thing, If It Ain't Got That . . .

. . . Growth, if you're talking about an economy, and for sure if you are talking about the American economy. Six years into the twenty-first century, most developed countries, and certainly all Western countries, have grown accustomed to worrying about where future economic growth is going to originate. Ask any politician in the West about his or her number one concern, and the answer is universal: jobs, jobs, and more jobs. As presidential candidate Bill Clinton noted, "It's the economy, stupid!" How did Tony Blair manage to remain prime minister in a war-weary Britain in 2005? Certainly his allegiance to the Iraq war and President George W. Bush did not aid his cause. Countless polls documented voter discontent with Blair's actions in Iraq. However, standing in the voting booth, Brits were swayed by Blair's enviable performance in providing jobs and economic prosperity.

Conversely, the vast majority of Germans strongly approved of Chancellor Gerhard Schroeder's decision to reject joining the United States and its "Coalition of the Willing" in Iraq. His 2002 reelection was largely the result of standing up to President George Bush and the United States by objecting to the Iraq war. This was generally considered to be the first time since World War II that a German chancellor did not acquiesce, at least publicly, to American interests. So did his October 2005 defeat by Angela Merkel, an advocate of the traditional pro-American stance, mean that the Germans had somehow changed their mind and instead decided to support the Iraq War and the United States? Not at all: public opinion polls consistently demonstrated that Germans were decidedly opposed to American foreign policy toward Iraq. However, this did not sway Germans from voting with their pocketbooks. After years of increasing unemployment rates, ultimately reaching double digits, and stagnant economic growth, Germans looked for a change by voting against the incumbent Social Democratic Party of Schroeder and for Merkel's Christian Democrats.

Similarly, in Italy's spring 2006 elections, Romano Prodi became prime minister, prevailing over the incumbent, Silvio Berlusconi, largely because of the country's inability to create jobs, reduce unemployment, and grow economically. Berlusconi learned what political leaders throughout the West have been learning: it don't mean a thing if it ain't got that . . . growth!

The French have also learned it: In the spring of 2006, fears about jobs, living standards, and an unprosperous future drove thousands of young French students into the streets of Paris to protest proposed reforms reducing their traditional lifetime job protections. According to Robert J. Samuelson, writing in *Newsweek*,

> to anyone who cares about Europe's future, the French
> demonstrations and street riots protesting the government's
> new labor law must be profoundly disturbing. It's the French
> against France—a familiar ritual that mirrors Europe's larger
> predicament. Hardly anyone wants to surrender the benefits
> and protections of today's generous welfare state.[1]

The problems in France emanated from the lack of economic growth. According to the Organization for Economic Cooperation and Development (OECD), between 2001 and 2005, France's annual growth rate was a lackluster 1.6 percent. Between 1994 and 2003 unemployment among prime-age adults, including those between ages 25 and 54, was almost one in ten, officially averaging 9.9 percent. For youth between ages 15 and 25, the mean unemployment rate was nearly one in four, at 24 percent. At the same time, only one in six mature adults were actually employed. By contrast, one out of every two seniors in the United States is employed.[2]

Ask governors and mayors what their biggest concern is, and the answer is the same: jobs—preferably, high-earning and sustainable jobs. The fat years of the early post–World War II era have become a distant memory. It was a great time, at least in terms of jobs and growth. The 1950s and 1960s were a time when jobs were available, simply there, for everyone. Unemployment barely existed. As figure 2.1 shows, in the early 1960s unemployment was virtually nonexistent in western Europe and North America, with unemployment rates below 2 percent in West Germany and France and below 5 percent in the United States.

There seems to be a clear and positive relationship between job security and opportunities on the one hand and how positive people feel about where they live. This is true not just in America, a country with one of the weakest social safety nets in the developed world, but also in Europe, with its rich and generous layers of social safety protection. For example, in Germany, citizens report being the happiest and most well off in places such as Stuttgart, Munich, and Bonn.[3] What do these places have in common? They rank among the regions with the most optimistic prognoses for economic growth and employment, with Munich being at the top and Stuttgart right behind it, followed closely by Bonn. In contrast, the places where people feel the least happy also rank among the worst in terms of growth and employment prospects, such as Halle, Dassau, and Altmark. Just as it is in America, in Europe it don't mean a thing if it ain't got that . . . growth.

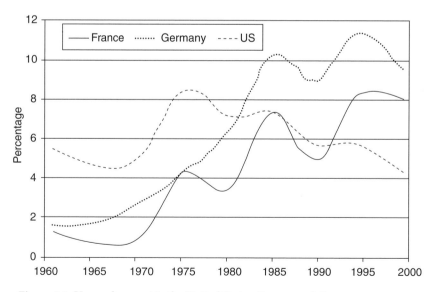

Figure 2.1 Unemployment in the United States, France, and Germany.

No wonder nostalgia abounds for the America of the 1950s. Perhaps it was the prevalence of good old-fashioned values, celebrated in the newly popular television programs of the day, such as *Leave It to Beaver*, *Ozzie and Harriet*, and *Father Knows Best*. Whether or not you graduated from college did not greatly increase your likelihood of being employed; rather, your college degree influenced what type of work you would be doing. A blue-collar job was there for high school dropouts and graduates, while white-collar jobs awaited the college educated. Not only did you have a job but, when compared to today, the wage differentials and earnings expectations were not nearly as great. For example, when one compares the mean annual income of Americans with no high school degree, a college degree, and an advanced degree, educated Americans have always earned more than high school dropouts. However, while the real earnings of high school dropouts and those who do not finish college have decreased, real earnings for Americans with an advanced degree have increased. That is, the income gap between the educated and uneducated has widened over time, especially during the 1990s.

Certainly when I was in college, in the early 1970s, nobody worried about employment. At least on campus, there was little concern about future jobs and careers. The jobs were simply there, as they had been for our older brothers and fathers in the 1950s, or at least so we thought. It seemed that Keynesian economics, which provided the intellectual framework for guiding macroeconomic growth policy, had delivered job entitlements and the resulting middle-class way of life. Starting first in America, these entitlements spread to Europe as well. The memory of a real crisis of unemployment and economic stagnation—the Great Depression, when real output fell by a third and unemployment rose to nearly a quarter of the workforce in the United States—seemed to be quietly fading. After a childhood of parental austerity—eating all of the food on one's plate, and saving pennies for a rainy day—the baby boom generation winked at their parents and grandparents, because under the sure hand of what David Halberstam termed "the best and the brightest," the well-educated policy experts in the John F. Kennedy and Lyndon Johnson administrations, economic disaster could not occur again.[4] At the heart of such optimism was an almost universal acceptance that Keynesian economics, with its reliance on the fiscal policies of taxation and government spending on the one hand and the monetary policies of interest rates and money supply implemented by the Federal Reserve on the other hand would not just correct minor turbulence caused by the business cycle but ultimately would make longer term unemployment and economic stagnation a thing of the past. If it is hard to recall the optimism accompanying Keynesian economic policy, one merely needs to recall President Richard Nixon's proclamation "We're all Keynesians now." And so it was.[5]

In yet another of history's ironies, even as Nixon convinced nearly everyone to accept the Keynesian approach to economic policy, forces were undermining its effectiveness. Although nobody called it that at the time, those forces were what we now call globalization.

The logical and strategic response of many established and reputable firms to globalization has been to try and maintain or enhance competitiveness by increasing productivity and reducing costs. As Thomas Friedman observes in *The World Is Flat*,[6] the strategic response to a globalized market often involves outsourcing and offshoring. The outsourcing occurs when the firm starts purchasing goods from a supplier that it used to produce itself. Outsourcing involves changing the organizational relationship in obtaining inputs. By itself, outsourcing will not have adverse affects on employment. But combined with offshoring it will. Offshoring refers to a change in the geographic sources of inputs. Both outsourcing and offshoring have emerged as a strategic response to global competition, helping businesses maintain and, sometimes, enhance profitability.

In Germany, this phenomenon brought on a seemingly schizophrenic euphoria in 2006. On the one hand, corporate executives celebrated a "champagne mood"[7] as profits were rising to record levels, sales were increasing, and the overall prospects for German corporations were better than they had been in years. On the other hand, at the same time, unemployment shot skyward, with five million unemployed workers. One of the most important German newspapers announced "Fear of Recovery without Jobs," or what Thomas Straubhaar, president of the Hamburg Institute of World Economics, termed "jobless growth."[8] The message to politicians was clear. As one of the most influential daily German newspapers, *Die Welt*, warned Germany's newly elected chancellor, Angela Merkel, "What use is the new strength and optimism of German companies if nothing is changed in the labor market?"[9]

The concept of "jobless growth" may seem like a vague, distant economic classification. However, it hit home when Volkswagen announced in February 2006 that it was laying off 20,000 employees, even as it celebrated strong earnings, leaving many Germans to shake their heads and wonder why, if their flagship companies are doing so well, their employment situation seemed so desperate. After all, as we will see in the next chapter, one of the great lessons from the job and growth machine that generated unprecedented prosperity in the postwar economy had been that what was good for the companies was good for the country.

3

When Father Knew Best

Why do the fifties loom so large as a benchmark of a gentler time, rendering today's world in a much harsher and more brutal light? As we saw in the last chapter, certainly the economy seemed to perform better back then than it has in the new century. Steady and vigorous economic growth made the unemployment disaster of the Great Depression seem like a distant nightmare. Flush from defeating Germany's Hitler, Japan's Hirohito, and Italy's Mussolini, America settled into a period of confident prosperity.

The newly found American prosperity was built on manufacturing. America's soldiers returned home from the battlefields of Europe and Asia with a hunger for the good life. And that good life consisted of manufactured goods. Soldiers sought new cars and homes—cars because you had to be mobile in the dynamic postwar America, and homes, usually newly constructed, in which to put their brides and growing young families. The homes, of course, were just itching to be filled up with washing machines, stoves, and other household amenities. All of these goods had to be manufactured.

If America knew how to do anything, it was how to manufacture goods. The Industrial Revolution took off following the Civil War. Prior to the middle of the nineteenth century, production was typically on a small scale.[1] Maximum efficiency in production, say, at a blacksmith, could be attained with a handful of employees. Production was undertaken in small-scale craft establishments and was centered on family-owned businesses. Scholars have determined that prior to the mid-1800s, a flat average cost curve was not a bad approximation for most firms in most industries.[2] That is, there was no advantage for large-scale production and no disadvantage for small producers. Quite the opposite—because of difficulties in transporting goods over a long distance, large-scale production might actually have been a disadvantage before the Civil War in America.

But the American idyll, the Jeffersonian dream of the small independent producer, was blown away by the dual hammer of the technological and managerial revolution that emerged following the Civil War. To win the war, the federal government invested in a massive railroad system that greatly enhanced the feasibility of shipping goods over a long distance. The fundamental cost structure changed dramatically with the advent of the corporation and the accompanying managerial revolution. The corporation emerged as the most efficient instrument of resource management during the American industrial revolution. If the application of British inventions had served as the catalyst underlying U.S. industrialization, the revolution in management techniques—the modern corporate structure—enabled its implementation. Robert Reich, who served as secretary of labor in the Clinton administration, observed:

> managerialism offered America a set of organizing principles at precisely the time when many Americans sensed a need for greater organization and these principles soon shaped every dominant American institution precisely as they helped those institutions became dominant. The logic of routine, large-scale manufacturing first shaped its original business environment and then permeated the larger social environment.[3]

Through the modern corporation's organizational structure, the new managerialism that emerged after the Civil War excelled at amassing large quantities of raw materials, labor, and capital inputs, as well as applying particular manufacturing processes, thereby achieving a very specific use of these resources. The leaps in U.S. manufacturing productivity during the late 1800s were the product of increased specialization.

The essence of the new managerialism was "command and control of effort." Labor was considered to be indistinguishable from all other inputs, as long as scientific management was able to "extract a full day's worth of energy for a full day's pay."[4] As tasks became increasingly specialized, worker skill became progressively less important. What mattered most was the consistency and reliability of each cog in the production wheel, whether mechanical or human; what mattered least was the decision-making capability of each unit. This meant that what mattered for people working in the new mass-production factories was the capacity of the workers to regularly and reliably show up to work, follow instructions, do what they were told. In the pre–Civil war Jeffersonian economy of small-scale shops, farms, and businesses, almost everyone had to use their heads to some degree. These were the self-reliant, independent Americans whom Jefferson viewed as the bedrock of the newly founded democratic experiment. As these once independent and self-reliant workers joined the meatpacking plants of Chicago, the "Hog-Butcher of the World," or the oil refineries of Cleveland, using their heads didn't matter anymore.

In Winslow Taylor's groundbreaking book *The Principles of Scientific Management*, he described how labor could be transformed into an unthinking commodity and, when combined with precious capital—machinery and factories—could generate output at an unprecedented level of efficiency and productivity. In laying out the principles underlying his new form of scientific management, Taylor made clear that a sharp division of labor was appropriate between those doing the thinking and those doing the heavy lifting:

> the science of handling pig iron is so great and amounts to
> so much that it is impossible for the man who is best suited to
> this type of work to understand the principles of the science,
> or even to work in accordance with those principles without
> the aid of a man better educated than he is.[5]

The emergence of mass production, made feasible by the organization of the corporation combined with the managerial revolution, triggered a dramatic shift in the underlying cost structure of firms and industry. Economies of scale increased dramatically in many manufacturing industries, resulting in a shift in the long-run average cost curve from essentially flat to downward sloping: big became beautiful or, at least, efficient.

According to David Halberstam,

> driven by the revolutionary vision of Henry Ford, the United States had been the leader in mass production before the war; ordinary Americans could afford the Model-T, while in Europe where class lines were sharply drawn, the rather old-fashioned manufacturers preferred building expensive cars for the rich.[6]

As Halberstam observes, "people worked at Ford or GM plants, where they mass-produced machines whose price was so low they could be bought by the very people who made them."[7]

The response to the emergence of the large corporation came in three ways. First, for the first time in American history, small-scale production was threatened. Family businesses confronted by a cost disadvantage vis-à-vis the large-scale corporations faced failure and liquidation.

Second, massive increases in output resulted from the unprecedented productivity increases generated by large-scale production. This led to chronic downward pressure on prices of manufactured goods.

Third, as large corporations emerged, they generally did not prove capable of mastering the business environment sufficiently to ensure the viability of mass production. While scientific management provided the means for controlling and assembling resources into specialized production processes, it had little to offer for controlling the external business environment. The stability, continuity, and reliability that constituted the core of successful mass production failed to materialize at the market level. The large American corporation was threatened by market volatility.[8]

Market volatility emanated from the relatively capital-intensive production processes required for large-scale mass production. Attaining enough output to exhaust economies of scale through specialization required historically unprecedented amounts of capital investment. Such investment was rendered particularly risky and vulnerable by two factors. First, profitability and survival depended on high levels of capacity utilization. Faced with excess capacity, firms resorted to *cutthroat pricing*—dropping price below average total cost but above marginal cost—in an effort to maintain capacity utilization.

Of course, such a policy pursued independently by each firm resulted in disaster for entire industries. Scientific management, which could methodically squeeze out high levels of efficiency based on large-scale production, was impotent in the face of such market volatility.[9]

Utilization of capacity also dictated an unprecedented dependence on the reliability of labor. The workforce had to show up at the prescribed hour and do what they were supposed to do; otherwise, the assembly line would stop. Stopping would cost the company thousands of dollars in wasted precious time. Here the unionization of labor played a key role. As David Halberstam observes,

> the only thing standing between the corporation and
> virtually limitless profits was the possibility of labor unrest.
> During 1945–46, there was a bitter strike over wages at
> General Motors that lasted some one hundred days. The issue
> came down to a one-cent per hour difference, which GM
> could easily have afforded.[10]

In the end, GM settled with the union, in what *Fortune* magazine called "the treaty of Detroit,"[11] observing that "General Motors may have paid a billion for peace, but it got a bargain."[12]

The second risk associated with large-scale investment was its vulnerability to technological obsolescence. The viability of any one firm investing in mass production depended on none of the other firms in the market making quantum-level technological advances. Thus, the corporation was rendered unstable by its inability to control prices and by the possibility of rivals technologically surpassing it.[13]

Just as the corporation sought to control production within the firm, it sought to control its external environment. The condemnation of business policies threatening stability—such as cutthroat pricing—was reflected at the start of Arthur Jerome Eddy's book *The New Competition*, published in 1912, which boldly noted that "Competition is War and War is Hell."

Gabriel Kolko quotes an early American Tobacco Company executive lamenting that

> unrestricted competition had been tried out to a conclusion,
> with the result that the industrial fabric of the nation was
> confronted with an almost tragic condition of impending

bankruptcy. Unrestricted competition had proven a deceptive mirage, and its victims were struggling on every hand to find some means of escape from the perils of their environment. In this trying situation, it was perfectly natural that the idea of rational cooperation in lieu of cutthroat competition should suggest itself.[14]

The first attempts by the corporations to achieve industry stabilization and offset the chronically excess output precipitating cutthroat pricing consisted of outright collusion—agreements either to fix price or to restrict output or both, enabling prices to be raised. Such agreements were typically implemented under the direction of trade associations. For example, the Bessemer Pig Iron and the Bessemer Steel associations were formed in the mid-1880s to restrict output and stabilize prices among over seven hundred companies in the blast furnace, steel work, and rolling mill industries. However, as the declining price of steel goods during 1894 and 1895 indicates, such stabilization attempts proved ineffective.

Having failed at price-fixing, the corporations attempted to attain market stability through consolidation. The drive for stabilization through mergers prevailed throughout the economy, culminating in the merger movement at the turn of the twentieth century. In 1895 only forty-three firms disappeared as a result of acquisition, representing a $41 million merger capitalization.[15] Just three years later, mergers resulted in 303 firm disappearances, for a $651 million capitalization. US Steel became a gigantic corporation largely through consolidation and acquisition. The company was created by combining twelve firms, which in turn had been created from merging some 180 independent companies, with more than 300 plants. However, such massive consolidations still fell short of achieving the desired goal of controlling or at least limiting output and halting the price reductions. According to Kolko, "the new mergers, with their size, efficiency, and capitalization were unable to stem the tide of competitive growth. Quite the contrary. They were more likely than not unable to compete successfully or hold on to their share of the market."[16] Although consolidation had succeeded in assembling large corporations, it had not succeeded in providing long-term industry stability. Kolko's conclusion is certainly consistent with the 1919 Supreme Court ruling in *U.S. v. US Steel*

Corporation[17] that "size alone is not an offence." Despite its massive size and market share of 90 percent in 1901, US Steel was unable to stem the tide of excess capacity and cutthroat pricing.

Thus, as more and more government regulation, ownership, and intervention suggested, an economy driven by large corporations was not necessarily stable and viable on its own but needed to be managed with appropriate policies and institutions. Not only did the corporation require a new organization for managing its internal functions, it also needed public policies and institutions to control, or at least attempt to influence, the external environment. Hence, the ascendance of the large corporation led to a simultaneous emergence of the managed economy.

The era of decreasing costs, ushered in by the advent of the large corporation and the managerial revolution, was therefore characterized by what seemed to be a dismal trade-off confronting economic policy—efficiency and low costs generated by large-scale production came at the cost of increased economic centralization and loss of independent decision-making. Karl Marx viewed this trade-off in a larger dimension, where capitalism itself was incompatible with democracy. According to Karl Marx, the advantages of large-scale production in the competitive process would lead to small firms inevitably being driven out of business by larger corporations in a never-ending race toward increased concentration and centralization: "the battle of competition is fought by the cheapening of commodities. The cheapness of commodities depends, *ceteris paribus*, on the productiveness of labour, and this again on the scale of production. Therefore, the large capitals beat the smaller."[18]

Thus, between the Civil War and World War II, America struggled mightily with the transformation from an agrarian society based largely on small-scale production and shops to an unstable yet efficient one based on the newly emerging large corporations. It was a volatile struggle, with many ups and downs. Out of this struggle emerged the managed economy. To bring out the best of the large corporations for society, the external environment needed to be managed. The managed economy consisted of institutions, public policy, corporations, and people designed to facilitate, accommodate, and promote the large corporations. But, as Marx warned, there was no turning back. America became a society where growth was no longer driven by the small farmer and craftsman Jefferson envisioned, but rather the giant corporation that amassed enormous capital investments in factories and plants together with labor to generate unprecedented productivity. As the great swings in the business cycle suggested, long-term prosperity proved somewhat more elusive.

A century of turbulence and volatility showed that just having capital, even if it was organized and deployed using scientific management, was not sufficient. The large corporation by itself could not stave off the severe fluctuations in demand, uncertainties regarding labor, and other sources of volatility inherent in the market.

The response by the main economic actors of the time was political. The political response was what we now call the Grange movement, followed by the Populist movement, which consisted of a coalition among small business and Midwest farms as a counterforce to the growing economic power of the railroads. At first, these movements sought a mandate to restrict the power of big business in general and the freedom of firms to contract more specifically. In responding to the demands of the Populist movement, which voiced the disgruntled concerns of affected small businesses, government was ultimately given the mandate to constrain the power of big business.

The particular concern of these political movements focused on the railroad and grain elevator trusts. The Populists managed to pressure a number of Midwest states into enacting laws that regulated interstate railroads and grain elevators. One grain elevator owner, Munn, brought a lawsuit against the state of Illinois for enacting a law that enabled the state to control the rates charged by grain elevators and warehouses. When the Supreme Court agreed to hear the case, Munn charged that the statute violated the Fourteenth Amendment of the Constitution by effectively claiming a portion of his private property in the form of forgone profits, or what is legally known as "takings." In the 1877 Supreme Court decision in *Munn v. Illinois*,[19] the Court ruled that because the product was affected by the public interest, governmental business regulation was constitutional.

The first twenty years of the post–World War II era were characterized by continued concern and vigilance against the threat to democracy posed by increasing economic concentration. This concern was expressed through a broad range of congressional hearings and the enforcement record of the antitrust agencies, as well as decisions handed down by the US Supreme Court. For example, the Committee on the Judiciary of the House of Representatives published its influential *Study of Monopoly Power* in 1950. Similarly, the Senate held hearings and published *Economic Concentration* in 1964. Jesse Markham, a scholar at Vanderbilt University, concluded from his reading of the congressional testimony leading up to the passage of the Celler-Kefauver Amendment to the Clayton Act in 1950 that "whatever else Congress may have had in mind when it amended that statute, it is clear from the Senate and House reports on the bill that one of its purposes was to check the rise of market concentration."[20]

In the high-water mark against the possession of market power in 1948, the Court ruled that "Congress . . . did not condone good trusts and condemn bad ones; it forbade all."[21] Unless a firm could demonstrate that market power was not "thrust upon it" due to "superior skill, foresight and industry," the Court would assume intent to monopolize and find a violation of the Sherman Act (the antitrust act of 1890). Similarly, the strictest ruling against mergers was made by the Supreme Court in 1962;[22] this ruling branded horizontal mergers as being virtually illegal and lasted until the Court loosened its interpretation in 1974.[23] The Court justified its strict prohibition of horizontal mergers and similar strict measures against vertical mergers by noting: "we cannot avoid the mandate of Congress that tendencies toward concentration in industry are to be curbed in their incipiency."[24] This ruling established the strict precedent that the monopoly power—in its incipiency—that could result from a merger was sufficient to disallow the acquisition. The Court also made rulings issuing the tightest restraints on product- and geographic-extension mergers.[25] This was also the same period that saw the Federal Trade Commission undertake its most aggressive cases against tacit collusion, or what was euphemistically termed *shared monopoly*, in a 1972 case against the cereal companies.[26] Similarly, with the *Schwinn* case in 1967, the Court ruled that vertical restrictions imposed by manufacturers on retailers constituted per se violations of the antitrust laws.[27] A decade later this decision, too, was significantly weakened.[28]

The strongest government intervention in terms of antitrust against big business came during a relatively small window of time during the late 1950s and early 1960s. In the managed economy characterizing America in the postwar era, the institutions of government regulation and antitrust policy, as well as the outright government ownership of business were manifestations of an attempt on the one hand to squeeze out the most from big business in terms of productivity and growth while on the other hand ensuring that the power amassed by the giant corporations was not abused to the detriment of consumers and small businesses. America was learning to live with the beast of big business, although it was a tricky balancing act that took over a century to master.

Emerging from World War II, America found itself almost alone with a relative abundance of the most important factor for growth, jobs and prosperity: capital. The auto plants of Detroit and steel mills of Pittsburgh had already been given a massive injection of investment to build state-of-the art facilities to help the war effort. In contrast, the factories of Germany and Japan had been blasted to pieces by relentless Allied bombing. What little remained, at least in Germany, had been carted away by the Soviets. Thus, at the close of World War II,

> The United States found itself an economic lord set far above the destroyed powers, its once and future competitors among both Allies and Axis powers. . . . While European and Japanese factories were being pulverized, new American factories were being built and old ones were back at work, shrinking unemployment to relatively negligible proportions.[29]

The unanticipated ascendancy of American manufacturing triggered a postwar windfall in prosperity. As one observer pointed out,

> the boom was on, and the cornucopia seemed all the more impressive because the miseries of Depression and war were near enough to suffuse the present with a sense of relief. . . . The idea of America had long been shaped by the promise of opportunity in a land of plenty, but at long last the dream seemed to be coming true. The world seemed newly spacious, full of possibilities. Americans were acquiring consumer goods at an unprecedented pace.[30]

Several years after World War II, Robert Payne, the renowned British historian, reflected:

> There never was a country more fabulous than America. She sits bestride the world like a Colossus; no other power at any

time in the world's history has possessed so varied or so great an influence on other nations. . . . Half of the wealth of the world, more than half of the productivity, nearly two-thirds of the world machines are concentrated in American hands; the rest of the world lies in the shadow of American industry.[31]

As a result of the unprecedented prosperity fueled by the capital-driven managed economy, *Fortune* magazine reported, a vast rush of families were moving up into the middle class—at the astonishing rate of 1.1 million per year.[32] In 1956, there were 16.6 million middle-class families, and by 1959, 20 million.[33]

Life magazine, the popular magazine of the post–World War II era, declared, "never before so much for so many."[34] David Halberstam reflects in *The Fifties*, "it was to be a new, even easier age, the good life without sweat."[35] Poppy Canon, a popular writer during that time, gushed in 1953, "never before has so much been available to so many of us now . . . that open sesame to wealth and freedom . . . freedom from tedium, space, work and your own inexperience."[36] She was actually referring to the invention of, or at least the widespread diffusion of, the can opener!

Fortune magazine similarly celebrated the state of the union in an October 1956 article entitled "What a Country!"[37] As David Halberstam observes in *The Fifties*,

> life in America, it appeared, was in all ways going to get better. A new car could replace an old one, and a large, more modern refrigerator would take the place of one bought three years, earlier, just as a new car had replaced an old one. . . . The market was saturated, but people kept on buying—newer, improved products that were easier to handle, that produced cleaner laundry, washed more dishes and glasses, and housed more frozen steaks.[38]

The MIT economist Robert Solow was awarded a Nobel Prize for his research in the late 1950s and early 1960s identifying what mattered for economic prosperity and growth.[39] What mattered was what America had and the rest of the world didn't have—factories, machinery, mechanization, large-scale production; in short, capital. It was surely no coincidence Karl Marx had titled his book *Kapital*.

In the capital-driven managed economy, the main goal and orientation of public policy was centered on investments into large plants, factories, in short (physical) capital. There was, however, one complication burdening the policy debates. The capital-driven managed economy predated globalization, but, ironically, it was international forces that injected the complication into what otherwise would have been straightforward.

When the premier of the Soviet Union, Nikita Khrushchev, took off his shoe and banged it on the negotiating table of the United Nations and said, threatening then president John F. Kennedy, "We will bury you," the West was scared. After all, the Soviets just beaten the Americans in the space race with the launch of *Sputnik*, and the growth in Soviet productivity was disconcerting—it appeared to greatly exceed that in the West during the 1950s. John Moore has provided compelling documentation of the "view held widely at the time that Soviet central planning would produce persistently high growth rates into the foreseeable future."[40] Even as late as 1966, the Joint Economic Committee of the U.S. Congress warned of a "planned average annual increase in industrial output of 8.0–8.4 percent during 1966–70" in the Soviet Union.[41] Thus, by the 1960s there was little doubt among politicians, intellectuals, and economists about the credibility of the Soviet threat.[42]

My father, like many Americans, responded by building a nuclear fallout shelter in our home. (I was the one who had to disassemble it a quarter of a century later.) As David Halberstam recalls,

> Khrushchev was something new for Americans to contemplate. . . . There was something chilly about Khrushchev, pounding his shoe and threatening to bury capitalism at the U.N. Contrasting his own poverty with the affluent backgrounds of those Western figures he dealt with, he seemed to imply their good manners were a weakness. "You all went to great schools, to famous universities—to Harvard, Oxford, the Sorbonne," he once boasted to Western diplomats. "I never had any proper schooling. I went about barefoot and in rags. When you were in the nursery, I was herding cows for two kopeks. . . . And yet here we are, and I can run rings around you all. . . . Tell me, gentlemen, why?[43]

However, the fear triggered by the Cold War in general and the Khrushchev-led Soviet Union was not restricted to the military threat; it included an economic threat as well. Seen through the lens of what we call the managed economy, the Soviet Union and its eastern European satellites had an advantage. They enjoyed the complete centralization and concentration of economic activity to within just a single firm in each industry, or what they called combines. Such focus, centralization, and size were expected to yield scale economies and therefore efficiency that would ultimately translate into economic growth. Western economists and policy-makers during the managed economy were nearly unanimous in their acclaim for large-scale enterprises. It is no doubt an irony of history that this consensus mirrored a remarkably similar gigantism embedded in Soviet doctrine, fueled by the writings of Marx and ultimately implemented by the iron fist of Stalin. This was the era of mass production when economies of scale seemed to be the decisive factor in determining efficiency. This was the world John Kenneth Galbraith described so colorfully in 1956 with his theory of countervailing power, in which big business was held in check by big labor and big government. After all, when David Halberstam concludes that the essence of post–World War II America was "Bigger is Better," the Soviet's industrial structure certainly consisted of bigger production facilities and therefore presumably might actually become better. Competing against the awesome Soviet industrial structure seemed to pose a daunting challenge to the West. A fundamental commitment to decentralization and democratic traditions in the West precluded allowing such massive centralization and concentration, even in the name of efficiency, productivity, and growth.

After all, in arguing for the passage of the 1890 Sherman Act, Senator Sherman argued:

> if we will not endure a King as a political power we should not endure a King over the production, transportation, and sale of the necessaries of life. If we would not submit to an emperor we should not submit to an autocrat of trade with power to prevent competition and to fix the price of any commodity.[44]

The Soviets thought they had the West over a barrel, with the inherent compatibility between ideology and economics on their side, while the

United States and her western European allies were stuck with a seemingly inherent contradiction between ideology and economics.

Even small business advocates agreed that small firms were less efficient than big companies. These advocates were willing to sacrifice a modicum of efficiency, however, because of other contributions—social, political, and otherwise—small business made to society. Small business policy was thus "preservationist" in character. For example, the passage of the Robinson-Patman Act in 1936, along with its widespread enforcement in the postwar era, was widely interpreted as one effort to protect small firms, like independent retailers, that would otherwise have been too inefficient to survive in open competition with large corporations.[45] According to Richard Posner, a leading legal scholar at the University of Chicago as well as a district court judge, "the Robinson-Patman Act . . . is almost uniformly condemned by professional and academic opinion, legal and economic."[46] Similarly, legal scholar Robert Bork observed: "one often hears of the baseball player who, although a weak hitter, was also a poor fielder. Robinson-Patman is a little like that. Although it does not prevent much price discrimination, at least it has stifled a great deal of competition."[47]

Preservationist policies were clearly at work when, in the Small Business Act of July 10, 1953, Congress authorized the creation of the Small Business Administration, with an explicit mandate to "aid, counsel, assist and protect . . . the interests of small business concerns."[48] This Act was clearly an attempt by the Congress to halt the continued disappearance of small businesses and to preserve their role in the U.S. economy.

Thus, it became the task of the scholars toiling in the field of industrial organization within the discipline of economics to explicitly identify what exactly was gained and lost as a result of large-scale production and a concentration of economic ownership and decision-making. During the postwar period a generation of scholars galvanized the field of industrial organization by developing a research agenda dedicated to identifying the issues involving this perceived trade-off between economic efficiency on the one hand and political and economic decentralization on the other.[49] Scholarship in industrial organization generated a massive literature focusing on essentially three issues: (1) What are the gains to size and large-scale production?

(2) What are the economic welfare implications of having an oligopolistic or concentrated market structure, that is, is economic performance promoted or reduced in an industry with just a handful of large-scale firms? (3) Given the overwhelming evidence that large-scale production resulting in economic concentration is associated with increased efficiency, what are the public policy implications? The classic 1968 treatise by the economist Oliver Williamson of the University of California at Berkeley, "Economies as an Antitrust Defense: The Welfare Tradeoffs," published in the *American Economic Review*, became something of a final statement demonstrating what appeared to be an inevitable trade-off between the gains in productive efficiency that could be obtained through increased concentration and gains in terms of competition, and implicitly democracy, that could be achieved through decentralizing policies. But it did not seem possible to have both, certainly not in Williamson's completely static model.[50]

Thus, one of the most fundamental policy issues confronting western Europe and North America during the postwar era was how to live with this apparent trade-off between economic concentration and efficient production versus decentralization and democracy. The public policy question of the day centered on: *How can society reap the benefits of the large corporation in an oligopolistic setting while avoiding or at least minimizing the costs imposed by a concentration of economic power?* The policy response was to constrain the freedom of firms to contract. Such policy restraints typically took the form of public ownership, regulation and competition policy, or antitrust. At the time, considerable attention was devoted to what seemed like different countries' glaring differences in policy approaches to this apparent trade-off. France and Sweden resorted to government ownership of private businesses. Other countries, such as the Netherlands and Germany, tended to emphasize regulation. Still other countries, such as the Untied States, had a greater emphasis on antitrust regulation. In fact, most countries relied on elements of all three policy instruments. While the particular instrument may have varied across countries, all the measures were, in fact, manifestations of a singular policy approach—how to restrict and restrain the power of the large corporation. What may have been perceived as a disparate set of policies at the time appears in retrospect to constitute a remarkably singular policy approach during the era of the managed economy.

Thus, while a heated debate emerged about which approach best promoted large-scale production while simultaneously constraining the ability of large corporations to exert market power, there was much less debate about public policy toward small business and entrepreneurship. The only issue was whether public policy-makers should simply allow small firms to disappear as a result of their inefficiency or to intervene and preserve them on social and political grounds. Those who perceived small firms as contributing significantly to growth, employment generation, and competitiveness were few and far between.

In the postwar era, small firms and entrepreneurship were viewed as a luxury, perhaps needed by the West to ensure decentralized decision-making, inefficiently obtained. Certainly the systematic empirical evidence, gathered from both Europe and North America, documented a sharp trend toward a decreased role of small firms during the postwar period.[51]

Public policy toward small firms generally reflected the view of economists and other scholars that they were a drag on economic efficiency and growth, generated lower quality jobs in terms of direct and indirect compensation, and were generally on the way to becoming less important to the economy, if not threatened by long-term extinction. Some countries, including the Soviet Union, but also Sweden and France, adapted the policy stance of allowing small firms to gradually disappear and account for a smaller share of economic activity. Rather, it was large-scale production amassed and managed by large corporations utilizing the principles of "scientific management" that was expected to not only serve as the engine of growth, jobs, and prosperity for the West but also deliver economic protection from the very real threat posed by the Soviet Union and its Eastern Bloc satellites.

The major industrial engines of American economic success—automobiles, steel, tires, chemicals, aluminum, and later computers—were all characterized by an oligopolistic market structure consisting of a few dominant firms, resulting in high and increasing rates of concentration. The long-term trend toward increased concentration in economic activity at both the aggregate and individual levels was identified early on. For example, the percentage of total U.S. manufacturing assets accounted for by the largest one hundred corporations increased from about 36 percent in 1924, to 39 percent at World War II, and to over

50 percent by the end of the 1960s, leading the Harvard economist F. M. Scherer to conclude: "despite the (statistical) uncertainties, one thing is clear. The increasing domestic dominance of the 100 largest manufacturing firms since 1946 is not a statistical illusion."[52]

Consistent with the trend toward increased concentration was the shift in employment away from small firms and toward large ones. The share of employment accounted for by small firms decreased substantially in every major sector of the economy during the postwar period. Perhaps most striking was the nearly one-quarter decrease in the share of employment accounted for by small firms in manufacturing between 1958 and 1977.[53]

Thus, there was little doubt that the driving force of the American postwar success was the nation's preeminence not just in its abundance of factories, establishments, and plants but the extent to which this physical capital was highly concentrated within just a few large corporations in the most important and key industries.

Both Karl Marx and Robert Solow were in agreement that it took more than just machines to produce goods. It also took people, or what economists call labor. What kind of people and what kind of labor? I probably learned this lesson in my 1972 freshman economics class, but the practical reality hit home as I was working my way through college in the 1970s. My summer job consisted of working on an assembly line at a now defunct printing plant. Off the assembly line rolled Betty Crocker cookbooks, Dell paperbacks, and all kinds of bestsellers. My task was to stand at the end of an assembly line, pick up each individual book as it rolled off the line and place it on a wooden pallet. I would repeat this task every few seconds, until, after about thirteen minutes, the pallet was full, at which point came the excitement: I pressed a red button, sounding an alarm bell, which summoned a forklift driver to come by, lift up the book-laden pallet and drive it somewhere, presumably to a warehouse for delivery. In the meantime, I picked up a new pallet and started the process all over.

As an ambitious college student, I had one of the more intellectual jobs on the assembly line. What mattered was consistency and reliability. Coworkers, typically other college students working during the summers, who aimlessly wandered away from the assembly line didn't last long. Because more than anything, negligence on the assembly line meant having to shut it down. If I had neglected the books coming off of my line, they would have piled up into a mountain of literature, which would have surely required shutting down the line in order to clean up the mess and restore order. My great qualification was reliability and consistency. A recent study found that one minute of downtime in a production line costs the average manufacturer $22,000.[54] And that is just sixty seconds; most production line downtime takes longer than a minute to fix!

And so it was with most assembly line workers in the book plant where I worked, the printers and machine operators. And so it was in manufacturing plants, ranging from steel to autos to rubber all across America. Perhaps the company that made the greatest investment in factories and plants, in *capital*, was General Motors. And just as the Solow model predicted, GM reaped a rich reward for its massive investment, for doing the right thing:

> No one at GM could ever have dared forecast so much prosperity over such a long period of time. It was a brilliant moment, unparalleled in American corporate history. Success begat success; each year the profit expectations went higher and higher. The postwar economic boom may have benefited many Americans, but no one benefited more than General Motors. By rough estimates, 49.3 million motor vehicles were registered when the decade began, 73.8 when it ended.[55]

Not everyone, of course, wore a blue collar and worked with dirty hands. White-collar workers were indispensable to large-scale production. Information and decisions had to be handed up and down, from the factory floor up through supervisors, ever upward through the ranks of middle management, and, if merited, reaching top management. And then back down again. What kind of labor, or men, was needed to manage the successful and ever larger American corporations? In his bestselling book *The Corporation Man*, William H. Whyte asked this very question. The answer he gave America was at once disturbing and controversial. According to Whyte, gone were the proudly independent, freethinking, American men who had once pushed west in order to tame the frontier. What had replaced the fierce and independent mavericks were corporation men, who, beyond all, were obedient to their bosses, conformed to society's rules and regulations, did what they were told, obeyed social norms, and valued reliability, regularity, predictability, and loyalty to the corporation above everything. Conformity bought "contentment."[56] Certainly this kind of absolute loyalty and conformity was a prerequisite for employment at General Motors.

> There was in all of this success for General Motors a certain arrogance of power. This was not only an institution apart; it was so big, so rich, and so powerful, that it was regarded in the collective psyche of the nation as something more than a mere corporation: It was like a nation unto itself, a separate entity, with laws and a culture all its own: Loyalty among employees was more important than individual brilliance. Team players were valued more highly than mavericks. It was the duty of the rare exceptional GM employee to accept the limits on his individual fame. . . . The individual was always subordinated to the greater good of the company.[57]

According to Whyte, the basic rule was "be loyal to the company and the company will be loyal to you. After all, if you do a good job for the organization, it is only good sense for the organization to be good to you."[58] One observer of the 1950s observed that "painting by the numbers was one fad that all by itself contained the contradictory aspirations of the middle-class aspirations of the middle-class Fifties: creativity and security at the same time."[59] David Halberstam describes the result as "blandness, conformity, and lack of serious social and cultural purpose in middle-class life in America."[60]

Whether Whyte's scathing portrayal of the corporation man was anything more than a parody was contentiously debated. The fear of deviating from social norms, the pressure to conform and be like everyone else is evident in the portrayal of Senator Joe McCarthy's Red scare of the 1950s in the 2006 film *Good Night and Good Luck*. While the film shows a side of America that most would prefer to forget, an era when the mere mention of communist associations could end a person's career or worse, a kinder, gentler side of the corporation man is portrayed in the popular sitcoms of the 1950s and 1960s *Father Knows Best*, *The Donna Reed Show*, and *Ozzie and Harriet*—shows that are often held up as paradigms of what television, and ultimately society, should be like today.

However, some critics expressed dismay over a society centered on conformity and homogeneity. David Riesman, in his bestselling book

The Lonely Crowd, C. Wright Mills, in *White Collar*, published in 1951, and Sloan Wilson, in *The Man in the Gray Flannel Suit*, concurred with Whyte that the type of man, or labor, as the economists termed it, who was best suited to manage the capital-driven large corporation was doomed to alienation and loneliness. *The Lonely Crowd*, in particular, depicted a shift in American values from being essentially inner-directed to outer-directed, resulting in a new type of societal alienation. Corporate conformation was costing America its soul.

What about the women? Betty Friedan, in her bestselling and hotly controversial *The Feminine Mystique*, observed that there were no women; the American woman typically stayed home. Her job, as housewife, was to create a home, attend to the family's needs, and make sure that her husband was sent off to work with a sound breakfast and in the state of mind required to meet the demands of running the large corporation:

> The ideal fifties women were to strive for what was
> articulated in *McCall's* in 1954: *togetherness*. A family was
> as one, its ambitions were twined. The husband was
> designated leader and hero, out there every day braving
> the treacherous corporate world to win a better life for his
> family, the wife was his mainstay on the domestic side, duly
> appreciative of the immense sacrifices being made for her
> and her children.[61]

Even the television shows of this period, such as *The Jetsons, The Flintstones*, and *Lost in Space*, reflected these now stereotypical roles for husbands and wives. Who could ever forget Fred Flintstone coming home from a hard day's work under his insufferable boss and yelling for "Wiiiiilma!"?

This is not to say that women were happy with their role in the postwar managed economy. As Betty Friedan wrote:

> It was a strange stirring, a sense of dissatisfaction, a yearning
> that women suffered in the middle of the twentieth century in
> the United States. Each suburban wife struggled with it
> alone. As she made the beds, shopped for groceries, matched
> slipcover material, ate peanut butter sandwiches with her
> children, chauffeured Cub Scouts and Brownies, lay beside
> her husband at night—she was afraid to ask even of herself
> the silent question—"Is this all?"[62]

Peggy Lee would later put that phrase to music, immortalizing it in her famous song "Is That All There Is?" Friedan went on to observe:

> Experts told them how to catch a man and keep him, how
> to breastfeed children and handle their toilet training, how to
> cope with sibling rivalry and adolescent rebellion; how to
> buy a dishwasher, bake bread, cook gourmet snails, and build
> a swimming pool with their own hands; how to dress, look,
> and act more feminine and make marriage more exciting. . . .
> They were taught to pity the neurotic, unfeminine, unhappy
> women who wanted to be poets or physicists or presidents.
> They learned that truly feminine women do not want careers,
> higher education, political rights.[63]

Friedan's description evokes the scenes from the popular movie *The Stepford Wives*.

Similarly, David Halberstam observes: "the move to the suburbs also temporarily interrupted the progress women had been making before in the workplace; for the new suburbs separated women physically from the workplace, leaving them, at least for a while, isolated in a world of other mothers, children, and station wagons."[64] Certainly it was this isolation in the suburbs that got Tom Ewell into (humorous) trouble with a young Marilyn Monroe left behind in New York City in the celebrated film *The Seven-Year Itch*. Thus, there was

> Mom, who would spend the bulk of her life supervising her
> conveniences, and the kids, who would grow up knowing how
> good the things of life could be. Dad's wage underwrote the
> whole family's division of labor and pleasures; after the jarring
> wartime years, when vast numbers of women were mobilized
> into jobs, women were now expected—and expected
> themselves—to secure the home front. This delicate bargain
> was secured by an unwritten contract, a division of labor, that
> was trumpeted through all the linkage networks of the modern
> mass media. Against the centrifugal pressures inherent in Mom
> and Dad's division of labor, the nuclear family was bound
> together through the cementing idea of "togetherness."[65]

Friedan recalls the main speaker at a meeting of magazine writers in the 1950s. He was a leader of the desegregation battle, and he outlined the market for women's magazines:

> Our readers are housewives, full time. They're not interested in the broad public issues of the day. They are not interested in national or international affairs. They aren't interested in politics, unless it's related to an immediate need in the home, like the price of coffee. Humor? Has to be gentle, they don't get satire. Travel? We have almost completely dropped it. Education? That's a problem. Their own education level is going up. They've generally all had a high-school education and many, college. They're tremendously interested in education for their children—fourth-grade arithmetic. You just can't write about ideas or broad issues of the day for women.[66]

Listening to the speech that evening, Friedan recalls the chilling German slogan during the Nazi regime, "Kinder, Küche, Kirche."[67]

Two years before Betty Friedan's *Feminine Mystique* was published, Nora Johnson lamented: "probably every educated wife has found herself staring at a mountain of dirty diapers and asking herself desperately, 'Is this all there is?' "[68]

David Halberstam, reflecting on the image painted by the sitcoms of the managed economy, observes:

> In this world the moms never worked. These were most decidedly one-income homes. . . . These families were living the new social contract as created by Bill Levitt and other suburban developers like him and were surrounded by new neighbors who were just like them. . . . In the Cleaver family of *Leave It to Beaver*, the family always seemed to eat together and the pies were homemade. June Cleaver, it was noted, prepared two hot meals a day. The Cleavers were not that different from the Nelsons, who preceded them into the television suburbia. . . . As Beaver Cleaver once told June Cleaver (who was almost always well turned out in sweater and skirts), "You know, Mom, when we're in a mess, you kind of make things seem not so messy." "Well," answered June, "isn't that sort of what mothers are for?"[69]

Whatever one's views were, or still are, about the relative merits, virtues, or liabilities of the roles of men and women and how they were shaped by working in the large corporation, one thing is indisputable. It was the most efficient type of production, at least in the postwar era at the zenith of the managed economy, that the world had ever seen.

No small wonder that the goal of most men in postwar America was to work in a large corporation. If you had a college education, you would take a managerial position. If you had only a high school education, you sought a blue-collar job with one of the same large corporations, such as General Motors, Ford, or US Steel. And if you were a young woman coming of age in the 1950s or early 1960s, you dreamed of marrying one of those men.

Of course, there were countless young men and women who did not share this common vision, entertaining a different one—thousands started firms and worked for small businesses; but this is not where the action was thought to be. Rather, as first Karl Marx feared, and later Robert Solow analyzed with razor precision sufficient to win a Nobel Prize, the action was where the capital was, and the capital was with the large American corporation.

What did all this conformity produce? According to David Halberstam, in his keen and insightful analysis, "if there was a symbol of America's industrial might in those years, it was General Motors, a company so powerful that to call it merely a corporation seemed inadequate. It was the largest, richest corporation in the world and would, in the coming decade, become the first corporation in the history of mankind to gross a billion dollars."[70]

What about those nonconformists, the deviants, those who did not buy into the postwar American Dream? America, like every society, has always had its share of nonconformists and people going in their own direction. This was no less true in postwar America. Such nonconformists found their way to the beatniks. Allen Ginsberg, Jack Kerouac, William Burroughs, and Neal Cassady were beatnik stalwarts who, first and foremost, refused to become corporation men:

> If other young people of their generation gloried in getting
> married, having children, owning property and cars, and
> socializing with neighbors much like themselves, these
> young men and women saw suburbia as a prison. They
> wanted no future of guaranteed pensions but instead sought
> freedom—freedom to pick up and go across the country at a

moment's notice, if they so chose. They saw themselves as poets in a land of philistines, men seeking spiritual destinies rather than material ones.[71]

The popular musicians Pete Seeger and Woody Guthrie provided a musical voice to the urge to shake off the shackles of the conformity of the managed economy and instead embrace the freedom of the road. They sang of the vast and unbounded freedom of America, as viewed from the road and from the rails. "This Land Is Your Land" was not land that could be purchased or even earned and hoarded, but only experienced. Rejection of the tyranny of the irons of the conformity ruling the *Zeitgeist* was the prerequisite for the claim that "this land was made for you and me." Woody Guthrie's son Arlo sang, in "The City of New Orleans," "Good morning America how are you? / Don't you know me I'm your native son, / I'm the train they call The City of New Orleans, / I'll be gone five hundred miles when the day is done."[72] As David Halberstam relates, "one night during the mid-fifties, the writer Jack Kerouac and a friend got drunk and drafted a message to the President: Dear Eisenhower, We love you—You're the great white father. We'd like to f____ you."[73]

The beatniks, as described by Jack Kerouac in *On the Road*, refused to conform to the prevalent norms ruling the managed economy:

> The Beats, as they came to be known, revered those who were different, who lived outside the system, and particularly those who lived outside the law. . . . They were fascinated also by urban black culture, and they appropriated phrases from it: *dig* and *cool* and *man* and *split*. They saw themselves as white bopsters. They believed that blacks were somehow freer, less burdened by the restraints of straight America and they sought to emulate this aspect of the black condition.[74]

As the songwriter and later actor Kris Kristofferson wrote in the song later made famous by Janis Joplin, "Freedom's just another word for nothing left to lose."[75]

As we shall see in chapter 7, there is a huge contrast between the beatnik generation of rebels and their counterparts, such as Steve Jobs, just a few years later. These later rebels who dropped out of the expected corporate employment paths, turned to entrepreneurship by starting new businesses in their garages, and in some cases, ended up creating the most successful firms in the world. But the dropouts in the relatively safe and constrained postwar America did only that—drop out. While their social protest, and perhaps what some might consider cultural protest, or cultural contribution,[76] caught some attention, few would claim it had a significant economic impact. Rather, it was first and foremost capital that mattered, and everything that helped it—machines, factories, and men who would tirelessly work it and organize it. With the dazzling unprecedented postwar prosperity pouring out of America's factories and plants, there seemed to be plenty to go around for every American. That is, until the world changed.

4

The Deluge

"It'll soon shake your windows and rattle your walls . . . " That's what Bob Dylan warned when he sang that "the times they are a-changin'." Dylan was referring to the eruption of widespread social and political change, as a new generation of Americans latched on to a new identity and rebelled against the order, values, and rigidities inherent in the managed economy.[1] In fact, every generation seems to have its own unique mission. For the generation Tom Brokaw called "the greatest generation," this meant saving the world from fascism and making it safe for democracy.[2] But this was surely not the only generation to have a mission, great or not. An earlier generation had been shaped by the horrors of the Great Depression. How many of us had grandparents from that era who proved unable to throw away any leftover food, let alone part with any of the "treasures" stuffed away in closets that might conceivably come in handy on a rainy day? In his moving documentation of the Great Depression, *Hard Times*, Studs Terkel lets those living through the hardships of the 1930s tell their stories in their own voices.[3] Yet an earlier generation had clearly been shaped by the Roaring Twenties, and that was the "lost generation" of the World War I veterans.

More recently, the generation shaped by the 1960s and the Vietnam War, the baby boomers, weaned on television series like *The Donna Reed Show*, *Father Knows Best*, and *Ozzie and Harriet*, were raised to go to the prom, play high school sports, and assume their rightful place as their parents' successors. It didn't work out that way. Karl Marx's warning that "capitalism bears the seeds of its own self-destruction" might not have been accurate, but the early identity of the baby boom generation did seem to bear the seeds of its own destruction: despite their early upbringing, when confronted with racial segregation, unequal opportunities between the genders, and an ever escalating, unpopular war in Vietnam, they balked. The 1960s may have been about rebellion, squalor, good or bad music, however you view it or heard it, but it was also about the rejection of parental values.

If earlier generations were rooted in World War I, the Great Depression, World War II, and Vietnam, it may be globalization that is shaping the current young generation. The challenge of this generation is not so much to win a war as to rise to the challenge and opportunities of globalization. Just as the baby boom generation had educational opportunities beyond anything imagined by their Great Depression and World War II parents, the global generation has grown up with freedom to travel far beyond anything imagined by their baby boom–generation parents. Travel, communication, and, more than anything, the internet have blurred the inevitability of place.

As a young teaching assistant at the University of Wisconsin in Madison in the 1970s, I was struck by the number of students for whom going to college was their first journey from their small and secluded hometown. A not insubstantial part of the value of their education in Madison, which was undoubtedly mirrored on hundreds of campuses throughout the United States, consisted of these homegrown young people being exposed, for the first time, to times and places beyond their hometowns. Exposure to the great thinkers of all time, the great events of history, and the great movers of the world opened such young people's eyes, making a return to where they come from not only undesirable but also impossible. As Thomas Wolfe observed, "you can't go home again."

Today's college students are quite different: few have experienced geographic and social isolation. This is the first generation that has grown up connected, logged on, and networked. What is important is not just the breadth and diversity of their experience and exposure, but the fact that it also spans national borders. Internationalization has seen country after country, and society after society, realize that they are small vis-à-vis both larger and a large number of trading partners and global neighbors. Some countries, such as the Netherlands and Sweden, have thrived for years with a small-country mentality. It might be harder to meet a person who does not speak English in Amsterdam than in New York or Miami. Part of being a small country in a big world is not just speaking foreign languages and respecting foreign cultures but also a certain openness, versatility, and flexibility, both accepting differences while at the same time finding common ground.

America's new global generation provides a stark contrast to the Americans manning the assembly lines to pump out mass-produced manufactured cars and steel or their white-collar counterparts keeping track of the monthly output and anticipating future production adjustments in the corporate hierarchy during the capital-driven managed economy. As David Halberstam points out, America longed for isolation from the rest of the world:

> The Midwesterners were supremely confident that theirs was
> the more American culture, one less imitative of the English
> and less sullied by foreign entanglements and obligations
> than those in the East. . . . The leading voice of Midwestern
> isolationism was Colonel Robert McCormick, publisher of the
> *Chicago Tribune*, a paper that modestly referred to itself as
> "The World's Greatest Newspaper." The *Chicago Tribune*
> shared and orchestrated those same isolationist feelings, even
> as technological change ended any remaining possibility of
> isolation.[4]

More recently, countries like Germany, France, and Japan have struggled with the evolution from being a large country in the postwar West to being a small country in the global economy. National futures depend on this transition. It is no longer sufficient to lord it over neighbors with one's large, rich, domestic market backed by a rich history and strong cultural tradition. These countries have learned only too painfully that unless their citizens are proficient at foreign lan-guages, linking and integrating themselves with people from other countries and cultures, both near and far, there is a cost to be paid in terms of stagnant economic growth and rising unemployment.

There are compelling reasons to think that these countries, too, are currently producing a global generation. It used to be that Europeans shook their heads in bewilderment, if not pity, at the poor Americans, who seemed to be either rootless or doomed to constantly move from one place to the next. In contrast, the postwar European typically grew up where he or she was born, went to the local university, and ultimately got a job and lived in that same place. In my travels around Europe, and indeed much of the world, I have met many people who not only grew up in their hometown but also attended college at a nearby university, never moving more than fifty miles from their birthplace. This describes not just businesspeople and blue-collar workers but also academics. In recent years I have witnessed the "global generation" of Europeans breaking this traditional bond with their birthplaces—something they used to see only in Americans, often wondering how Americans could cope with so much change and rootlessness.

Globalization is changing this. One of the premier German weekly magazines, *Der Spiegel*, identifies the emergence of "the global generation."[5] According to *Der Spiegel*, "today's young Germans are scouring the world in search of self-fulfillment and job qualifications. But these new global citizens still long for old values: friendship and stability."[6] *Der Spiegel* highlights Felix Fischer as typical of the new European global generation: "within his 28-year lifespan to date, Fischer has lived in more countries than many experienced executives do in 40 full years on the job. Fischer does not consider himself particularly unusual in this regard; 'Acquiring experience abroad is simply par for the course.'"[7] Europe's global generation may be ahead of America's in mastering the skills required to participate in the global society; its members typically command at least one and often several foreign language, can list numerous countries where they have lived and even more where they have visited, and have a broad and rich social network spanning the globe. Heiner Keupp, a social psychologist at the Ludwig Maximilian University in Munich, observes that "nowadays we are citizens in a multi-option society. The new generation is tapping into the many opportunities as well."[8] They had better tap into these opportunities if they want to succeed. Harro Honolka from the Students and Job Market Institute at the University of Munich reports that "students who haven't spent enough time abroad no longer seem flexible enough for today's requirements."[9] As *Der Spiegel* observes, an excellent command of English has become obligatory, and personnel managers demand above-average grades anyway. Moreover, anyone who has never spent time abroad, speaks no foreign languages and cannot score with social activities need not waste their time. Such (job) applications go straight into the shredder at global players like the management consulting firm McKinsey.[10]

The emergence of the European global generation first struck me a few years ago, when, as part of an international exchange program between Erasmus University in the Netherlands and Indiana University, a large group of Dutch students spent a week in Bloomington to work with their American counterparts on a common project. At the kickoff reception, having just arrived, with suitcases unpacked or at least deposited in their rooms, the Dutch partner students were remarkably relaxed, at ease, and quick to engage their American hosts in conversation and discussion. Remembering my own angst and disorientation during my first trip abroad, I assumed that somehow most of these students had previous experiences visiting the United States. In fact, virtually none did. Later, when I mentioned my surprise at their ease and seeming familiarity with everything American, I was told, "We've seen it all on TV and the movies, and are so used to travel that this just seems like another trip." I could not relate.

The global generation of the United States may have not proven to be America's greatest, but they are still confronted with a formidable mission. Their parents and grandparents came of age assuming leadership of a nation that was the undisputed leader of the free world, if not the entire world. It was not just the young men dying on the beaches of Normandy who saved the world from dictatorship but also, in the postwar era, the generosity, wisdom, and leadership of America that provided a model of democracy that was actively embraced by the defeated countries of Germany and Japan, as well as the Allies of western Europe. Perhaps to the "greatest generation," globalization meant that the world was following America's example. Being global required speaking America's language (which had been appropriated from the British), being at ease with America's culture, and understanding, if not accepting, America's way of life. The "greatest generation" had not just saved the world, it had gotten used to the rest of the world accommodating itself to America, just as the eldest son typically expects his younger siblings to adjust and fit themselves around him.

But the attacks of September 11, 2001, combined with the outright refusal of traditional allies such as Canada, France, Germany, and much of western Europe to support the subsequent Iraq war, has led the younger generation to wonder what went wrong. Robert Wright exclaims, in the *New York Times Book Review*, "They Hate Us, They Really Hate Us."[11] Julia E. Sweig, a senior fellow at the Council on Foreign Relations, writes of "losing friends and making enemies," while Andrew Kohut and Bruce Stokes explain "how we are different and why we are disliked."[12] According to Wright, "only a few years ago, anti-Americanism focused on government policies; the world 'held Americans in higher esteem than America,' Kohut and Stokes note. But foreigners are 'increasingly equating the US people with the US government.' "[13]

Josef Joffe, editor of the prestigious German weekly newspaper *Die Zeit*, points out that what Joseph S. Nye Jr.—former dean of the John F. Kennedy School of Government at Harvard University—called America's "soft power," referring to the widespread acceptance of and enthusiasm toward American culture and its way of life, does not guarantee that the United States will be seen favorably: "soft power does not necessarily increase the world's love for America. It is still power, and it can still make enemies."[14] According to Joffe,

> America's soft power isn't just pop and schlock; its cultural
> clout is both high and low. It is grunge and Google, Madonna
> and MoMA, Hollywood and Harvard. If two-thirds of the
> movie marquees carry an American title in Europe (even in
> France), dominance is even greater when it comes to
> translated books. . . . There may be little or no relationship
> between America's ubiquity and its actual influence. . . .
> Great soft power does not bend hearts; it twists minds in
> resentment and rage.[15]

As Wright suggests, "by the late '90s America was becoming a more natural target for ill will, even as its national security rested increasingly on good will."[16]

The answer seems to lie in the changing the relationship of America vis-à-vis the rest of the world. I was struck by this changing relationship when I heard the aspirations of one my graduate students at Indiana University. This particular young student who shared her dream with me had been a social worker in the Chicago projects. She was committed to do similar work in Africa through an international nonprofit organization. She had been on a trip to Africa with a large group of Americans and was shocked by what she perceived to be the condescending and offensive attitude of some of the group. Her goal in life was to change the negative view toward America that seems to have exploded with worrisome pervasiveness in the aftermath of September 11, 2001. Her patriotism and love for her country had instilled in her a passion not just to change the world and its views toward America but also to change America itself. In aspiring to globalize America, she is part of America's incipient global generation. She is, if not typical of her generation, then certainly consistent with a growing trend. The global generation wants to go out in the world in the way that is typical of other young people from other nations going out into the world—not as superiors or saviors but as equal participants. As Sweig points out, historically, "Americans think of themselves as kings and queens of the world's prom."[17] No more. This means doing what all other global participants do—learn foreign languages, respect foreign cultures and customs, and become linked up to the rapidly emerging global society. And by globalizing America, this generation may make its indelible and unique contribution to the country, just as previous generations have done, albeit in a manner that is singularly their own.

Where did all this globalization come from? Perhaps it was in Europe that the contemporary brand of globalization has, if not its origins, then its most apparent manifestation and symbol. When the Berlin Wall fell on November 9, 1989, it triggered not just the end of twentieth-century communism but also the end of the postwar geopolitical rules and boundaries. The fall of the Berlin Wall ushered in contemporary globalization. Before then, it had been inconceivable for Western companies to do business in vast parts of the globe, ranging from China in eastern Asia, the Soviet Union, as well as Poland and other Eastern Bloc countries in Europe. But with the fall of the Wall, this all changed. It became possible to do business throughout the world, and this, combined with the emerging communication technologies and transportation networks, ushered in modern globalization.

What exactly did "doing business" mean? Perhaps the first impulse was to salivate at the prospects of new export markets. Millions of customers, formerly protected by what the East Germans had called the Anti-Fascistische Mauer (the anti-fascist wall), could now simply be accessed like customers everywhere else. The fall of the Berlin Wall promised booming exports for Western companies, thus meaning increased production, more and better jobs, and higher wages to workers in the victorious West.

At one of the first conferences I attended concerning globalization, back in 1990, the chairman of the board of Mercedes-Benz, now Daimler-Chrysler, threw up his hands when asked about globalization, no doubt annoyed by academics asking rather, well, academic questions. "We at Mercedes have always been a global company!" By that, of course, he meant that Mercedes had profited from lucrative export markets for a long time. And not just Mercedes-Benz: West Germany had surged forward to become the world's leader in exports by the 1980s, despite the fact that it was considerably smaller than the United States. The fall of the Berlin Wall delivered the promise of even vaster, greatly vaster, export markets, spanning consumer goods–starved eastern and central Europe, including the former Soviet Union. No wonder that European companies were excited at the prospect of a new wave of unprecedented exports and sales, to be produced by bustling factories full of happily employed and unionized workers. By bringing Europe to the world, Europe would also be making Europeans more secure and better off, with more promising prospects than were ever possible back when half the continent was locked behind the Cold War's Iron Curtain. Thus, Europe celebrated the fall of the Wall not just because it was the end of communism and the Iron Curtain but also because it would usher in a new era of prosperity powered by the very economic and social model that had built postwar European prosperity—the European managed economy, which was called the social market economy, or what in the United States is commonly referred to, typically with a sneer, as the social welfare state.

One example of this is the German version of the managed economy consists, the *Sozialmarktwirtschaft* (social market economy).[18] Ever since its famous economic miracle of the 1950s (*Wirtschaftswunder*), Germany had been associated with remarkable prosperity and stability, providing both high employment and wage rates. The

Sozialmarktwirtschaft generated a standard of living (*Wohlstand*) that not only created the kind of material wealth found in the United States but also provided the high levels of social services and security found elsewhere on the European continent. The German managed economy provided a unique policy approach to balancing economic efficiency accruing from large-scale production with political safeguards to preempt abuses of that power.

The managed economy of the *Sozialmarktwirtschaft* at the heart of the German *Wirtschaftswunder* and general *Wohlstand* of the postwar era were based on consensus. This consensus embraced three principle actors—the industry employer associations (*Arbeitgeberverbaende*), the labor unions (*Gewerkschaften*), and the government. Through a broad spectrum of institutions, such as work councils (*Betriebsrat*), industry-wide wage agreements, and an apprentice system (*Lehrstellen*), these actors provided the basis for unparalleled success in generating high wages and levels of employment. Under this consensus, labor fulfilled its obligation in the social contract by supplying highly skilled and disciplined workers. For their part, the employers' associations—the leading German industrial firms—provided stable and generous employment, including a wide array of social services. With labor and industry working together under a consensus facilitated by the government, industries such as automobiles and metalworking were more competitive in Germany than anywhere else in the world. The task of the major political parties was to shift the fruits of this enviably productive consensus more toward either labor (represented by the Social Democratic Party; or the status quo firms making up the *Arbeitgeberverbaende* (represented by the Christian Democratic Party).

Similarly, in what was called the Polder model in the Netherlands, a consensus emerged among the labor unions, large corporations, such as Phillips, and the government. By contrast, the Swedish model, as did the French model, involved a greater share of ownership by the government.

Whatever their specific brand of the managed economy, the different European countries anticipated the post–Berlin Wall future as one with unprecedented peace and prosperity. It didn't quite work out that way. The Europeans might have done well to look to the other side of the Atlantic and consider how the United States had fared with what was perhaps not globalization but was in the 1960s and 1970s called *postwar internationalization.* In his 2005 book *The World Is Flat,* Thomas Friedman proclaims that globalization has leveled the playing field, enabling virtually very corner of the globe to participate and interact in the new global society and economy.[19] Many critics of the term *globalization* object to the notion that this is anything new. After all, there has always been much cross-border connectedness. Perhaps the point is rather a quality of interdependence and interaction that is clearly different today, in an era of instant and costless email, from what it was only a few years ago, when telephone calls were prohibitively expensive, not to mention complicated, and surface mail was prohibitively slow. As Friedman points out, in order to engage in international business in the fifteenth and sixteenth centuries, the permission of the Crown had to be obtained first. By the twentieth century, international business typically required the support of the large multinational corporation. In the twenty-first century, engaging in business across borders is significantly easier: it only requires logging on and connecting to the internet.

Still, America did learn from the post-World War II internationalization what happens when trading partners catch up and are able to offer the same goods at lower costs. After all, it was the ability of the Europeans, and in particular the Germans, to master the internationalization of markets in the 1960s and 1970s that thrust them into unprecedented prosperity. Never mind that the autos and steel pouring out of their shiny new postwar factories were initially financed to no small extent out of the generous coffers of the Marshall Plan. The German exports were met by an appreciative American consumer, hungry for the new Volkswagens and other products. These German exports came with a cost: an onslaught of job reductions and plant closings in the American Midwest, an area that eventually came to be known as the Rust Belt.

Before that time, such a hollowing out of the proud manufacturing Midwest—America's center and pride—had been unimaginable. I remember learning as a college student that American manufacturing workers earned the highest wages in the world. After all, they had the best factories, plants, machines, and capital to work with. Trading partners and allies in western Europe were to be pitied, not envied, because of the limited economic prospects associated with a depleted and worn out, if not bombed out, capital stock.

But by the mid-1970s, it was clear that the era of American superiority emanating from the manufacturing heartland was over: Europe and Japan had more than caught up. Having rebuilt their factories and plants, Europe and Japan now had the newest, state-of-the-art blast oxygen furnaces in steel, assembly plants for autos, and radial tire plants in the rubber industry.

Throughout the 1980s and the 1990s, Europe, and certainly Germany, shook their heads when looking across the Atlantic. The prevailing view was that America had grown soft when confronted with the more disciplined production style of its international trading partners across both the Atlantic and the Pacific. This view suggested that it was faulty American institutions—an undisciplined approach to education, a haphazard approach to vocational training, and a generally undeveloped apprentice training system, as well as a failure to provide coherent, systematic social and economic planning—that were responsible for this American softness in manufacturing. America had simply squandered its hard-earned postwar manufacturing advantage it had gained by winning World War II.

The institutions and cultural heritage of Europe seemed better equipped to produce the characteristics in people that were needed for these countries to excel in the capital-based, managed economy. After all, northern Europe had cultural traditions and institutions that stressed discipline, conformity, reliability, and consistency: traits ideally suited for the assembly line.

I confronted these German postwar values on my first day in West Berlin. It was a Sunday in 1984. I was amazed at the lack of any graffiti in the West Berlin U-Bahn, in sharp contrast to the subways of New York and Chicago. The system ran on an honor system: you were supposed to purchase a ticket with an occasional inspector from the transit system, but mainly you were on your honor to pay. And people did, because they were supposed to. Because of the *Ladenschluss Gesätze*, or laws requiring all stores to be closed on Sundays (as well as after 6 p.m. on weekdays and 2 p.m. on Saturdays), there were very few cars on the streets. I would later learn that the options available to Germans were actually quite limited on Sunday afternoons, and centered around just a few possibilities: strolling through the park, visiting a museum, or indulging at a *Kondeterei* (bakery) in *Caffe-Kuchen* (coffee and cake), to name a few. Other activities, such as washing your car or playing with your children outside during certain afternoon hours (*Ruhezeit*, the quiet time) were actually illegal.

All this contributed to generating a remarkably homogeneous population. People had more or less the same experience at the same time, providing a common cultural basis and outlook on life, or *Weltanschauung*. On this particular Sunday afternoon, my first not just in Berlin but in all of Europe, I ventured out to get to know my new surroundings. Since traffic was light (after all, there wasn't a lot to do or places to go to), at a street corner with a red "don't walk" signal, I started to cross the street anyway. After all, there was not a car in sight, and I felt foolish just standing there, waiting for a command from a mechanical signal. Even as I set off to cross the street, a small group of pedestrians caught my eye who determinedly were fixed upon waiting for the "walk" light. What struck me the most, though, was that this small group consisted of punks, complete with the requisite spiked green and purple hair and rings through their noses and eyebrows. Germany's most rebellious citizens were obedient to the rules. At least back then, in the early 1980s, children were raised with a great respect for, perhaps even obsession with—at least as seen through American eyes—the rules, and a great reverence for obedience to them. When my eldest son was in a preschool program called a "miniclub" in Berlin (what Americans would call a *kindergarten*, in an irony of globalization), the children were expected to remove their shoes and place them in the appropriate cubbyhole in the shelves assigned to them. Children, being children, did not always put their shoes in the right place. On more than one occasion, I witnessed irate parents and teachers intervening in the activities, taking children aside, and instructing them to place their shoes in the correct cubbyhole. What might have seemed blown out of proportion to an American made sense in the German context. After all, children's futures depended on doing what they were told and obeying the rules. (Interestingly, upon moving back to the United States some years later, I witnessed, in the American context, the teacher simply letting the children play while picking up the misplaced shoes and properly storing them herself. Apparently Americans value playful activity more highly than meticulously obeying the rules.)

Germany brought itself back to its feet following the total devastation of World War II largely by a slavish adherence to the logic of the capital-based managed economy. The weekend laws were not the only policy reinforcing stability and homogeneity, reducing the number of distractions, and generating a set of common activities and experiences among the population. In the postwar era, every German ate pretty much the same thing for breakfast, or *Frühstück*: dark bread, butter, jam, and a boiled egg. Promptly at 10:30, every German enjoyed a break at work, or what was called *das zweite Frühstück*, or second breakfast, which consisted of bread and wurst or cheese. And so it went, affecting holidays, vacations, and pretty much everything else. There was a standard, prescribed way of doing things, and most Germans not only followed the rules but followed them precisely. There was even an official book telling people what they could legally name their children. This standardization, with the emphasis on obedience to the rules and reliability, was ideal for a society where everyone had their role in the factories. This was perhaps perfecting the managed economy to a new level of efficiency, one unimaginable in United States. This adherence to efficiency, reliability, consistency—in short, to the logic of the managed economy—ensured that the assembly lines kept purring, churning out shiny new Volkswagens and Mercedes-Benzes ready to be shipped to the United States and elsewhere.

Germany had succeeded in producing corporate men beyond anything America could rival, and the results showed. As the first factory layoffs were followed by plant closings, the mighty American manufacturing machine in the heartland came to a grinding halt. It has never restarted. The devastation of families and entire communities has been massive. As Bruce Springsteen translated the loss of jobs into the loss of communities in his 1985 song "My Hometown"[20]:

> Now Main Street's whitewashed windows and vacant stores
> Seems like there ain't nobody wants to come down here no more
> They're closing down the textile mill across the railroad tracks
> Foreman says these jobs are going boys and they ain't coming
>   back to your hometown

Meanwhile, in the United States, discipline, conformity, and adherence to the rules had their limits. Try crossing the street in New York, or most other American cities, and you took your life in your own hands. Thus, the European view by the 1980s was that America lacked the cultural traditions and the institutional framework to effectively compete in international markets. This view was certainly prevalent in America as well, as was reflected by the publication in 1990 of the book *Made in America*, mentioned in chapter 1, which concluded that the United States had lost its manufacturing edge to Europe and Japan, which posed a threat to future American prosperity and global leadership. The solution was to become more like Germany and Japan. Apparently, by not developing the types of industrial policies, industrial targeting, economic planning, and central coordination of postwar Germany and Japan, America had simply blown its manufacturing advantage, and therefore economic supremacy; a dismal and diminished future would result.

Thus, by developing their own—perhaps superior—versions of the managed economy, Germany and its European neighbors had benefited from postwar internationalization and were anticipating the impending new era of globalization with optimistic expectations, not just of unprecedented peace and stability but also of economic growth, plenty of jobs, and a heightened standard of living. Living in Berlin during the 1980s, I could feel the standard of living appreciably rise. Each year the country grew more prosperous, more confident, and, with unprecedented abundance, more generous. While America strug-gled with massive job downsizing and the hollowing out of its most cherished corporations and entire industries, triggering concern about jobs and prospects even among college graduates, Germans possessed an assumed self-assurance that they would continue to harvest prosperity and their high standard of living from their carefully sown seeds of economic and social growth in a managed economy.

No wonder that Europeans entered into Thomas Friedman's global era with such optimism and self-assurance. After all, all European boats had been lifted by the rising tide of postwar internationalization. If the Americans had not managed to catch this wave they had nobody to blame but themselves, as the authors of *Made in America* eloquently and compellingly pointed out.

So what went wrong for Europe? The post–Berlin Wall boom never materialized. Rather, the opposite occurred. Europe entered into what continues to be a long saga of economic stagnation burdened by low growth and inability to create jobs, resulting in an unemployment rate that is steadily ratcheting upward. How did this happen? As a result of globalization, or at least Thomas Friedman's 1989 rendition of globalization, Europe, like North America, lost competitiveness in the traditional manufacturing industries. The entire West lost the competitive advantage for economic activity that had been based and centered on capital. This loss of the competitive advantage devastated production and employment in the manufacturing industries—the traditional strength and pride of the most developed countries. Western nations felt like Samson, whose powers vanished when he lost his hair at Delilah's hands.

And who is the contemporary Delilah, shearing away the strength and power of the once proud manufacturing prowess of the West? Just as the United States learned from the postwar internationalization of the 1970s and 1980s what it was like to take on international trade with trading partners and allies who enjoyed lower costs of production for important and mainstay industries, such as autos, textiles, machine tools, steel, coal, shipbuilding, electronics, and consumer goods, Europe started learning what it was like to compete against countries that could do the same things they were doing but at lower cost, not just in central and eastern Europe but also in Asia. It wasn't that imports started pouring in but rather that companies' direct investment in their own domestic economics slowed: the building and expansion of plants and factories stopped, and new employment, especially in high-wage and high-profile industries, stopped. Instead, European companies started increasingly to invest in new plants and factories and ultimately in production outside of their own high-cost home countries.

Such a loss of competitiveness in the backbone industries of Europe and North America, such as machine tools, textiles, steel, and autos, would have been unfathomable only a few years earlier. But globalization made it first possible and then essential to locate new investments in capital (that is, in factories and plants) not only in eastern and central Europe but increasingly in Asia, especially China and India. Unless large Western firms increasingly located production outside of the high-cost western European regions, they would be unable to compete in globally linked markets.

One indicator of the increasing pervasiveness of globalization is the total measure of world trade. The share of the world gross product accounted for by exports skyrocketed from under 10 percent in 1960 to well over one-quarter by 2005 (see fig. 4.1).

Similarly, foreign direct investment as a share of gross world product exploded between 1980 and 2004 (fig. 4.2).

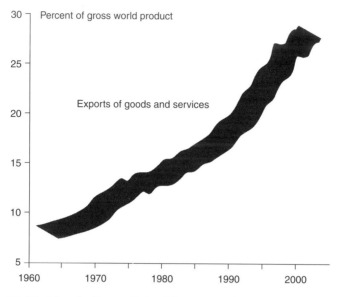

Figure 4.1 World trade. Source: Federal Reserve Bank of Dallas, 2005 Annual Report.

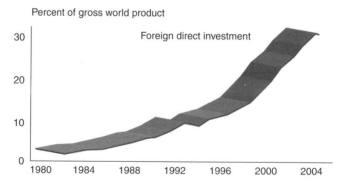

Figure 4.2 Assets abroad. Source: Federal Reserve Bank of Dallas, 2005 Annual Report.

As a result of this increased globalization, what did we see in Europe and North America? Jobs that were once safe and secure were lost or insecure—because of downsizing and outsourcing. As Thomas Friedman observes in *The World Is Flat*, Christopher Columbus was apparently wrong about the round earth: on Friedman's "flat world," economic activity can move almost costlessly across national borders to find the most favorable (cheapest and most productive) location.

Companies such as then Daimler Benz, now DaimlerChrysler, quickly discovered that the fall of the Berlin Wall and the ensuing advent of late twentieth-century globalization meant a lot more than just enjoying increased sales accruing from expanded export markets. Rather, to keep pace with global competitors, and to make the most of the new opportunities afforded by a global market, companies had to meet lower cost competition that was accessing low-cost production in previously inaccessible parts of the world. As *Business Week* observed about central Europe, "the region's population of 100 million can provide a lot of affordable labor."[21] Taking advantage of a global company once meant exporting your product to willing customers hungry for your goods in other countries. Now it also means being integrated— being forced and compelled by competitors located elsewhere around the globe to move production to new and different locations in a relentless effort to match production with the best and least costly resources, both in terms of inputs and labor.

Globalization would not have occurred to the degree that it has if the fundamental changes had been restricted to the advent of the microprocessor and telecommunications. It took a political revolution in significant parts of the world to reap the benefits of these technological changes. The political counterpart of the technological revolution was an increase in democracy and resulting stability in areas of the world that had previously been inaccessible. During the Cold War, investments in eastern Europe and much of the developing world were risky and impractical. After the end of World War II, most trade and economic investment was generally confined to Europe and North America, and later a few of the Asian countries, principally Japan. Trade with countries behind the Iron Curtain was restricted, if not prohibited. Even trade with Japan and other Asian countries was highly regulated and restricted. Similarly, investments in politically unstable countries in South America and the Middle East resulted in episodes of nationalization and confiscation in which the foreign investors lost their investments. Such political instability rendered foreign direct investment outside Europe and North America too risky and, consequently, of limited value.

The fall of the Berlin Wall and subsequent downfall of communism in eastern Europe and the Soviet Union was a catalyst for parts of the world that had been inaccessible for decades to become stable and accessible. As Lester Thurow points out in his book *Fortune Favors the Bold*, "much of the world is throwing away its communist or socialist inheritance and moving towards capitalism. Communism has been abandoned as unworkable (China), imploded (the USSR), or has been overthrown (Eastern Europe)."[22]

Within a few years it became possible not just to trade with but also to invest in countries such as Hungary, the Czech Republic, Poland, and Slovenia, as well as China, Vietnam, and Indonesia. For example, India became accessible as a trading and investment partner after opening its economy during the early 1990s. Trade and investment with the developed countries quickly blossomed; trade and investment with the United States tripled between 1996 and 1997, reflecting the rapid change in two dimensions. First, India was confronted with sudden changes in trade and investment, not to mention a paradigmatic shift in ways of doing business. Second, to the foreign partner, in this case the United States, taking advantage of opportunities in India also meant downward pressure on wages and plant closings in the home country. As Thurow concludes, "as long as communism was believed to be a viable economic system, there were limits to global capitalism whatever the technological imperatives. Capitalism could not go completely global because much of the globe was beyond its reach. Forty percent of humanity lived under communism."[23]

With the opening of some of these areas and their participation in the world economy for the first time in decades, the postwar equilibrium came to a sudden end. This created the opportunities associated with gaping disequilibria. Consider the large differentials in labor costs. As long as the Berlin Wall stood, and countries such as China and Vietnam remained closed, large discrepancies in wage rates could be maintained without eliciting responses in trade and foreign direct investment. The low wage rates in China and the Soviet Union neither invited foreign companies to build plants nor resulted in large-scale trade with the West based on access to low production costs. Investment by foreign companies was either prohibited by local governments or considered to be too risky by the companies. Similarly, firms in Communist Bloc countries were restricted or prohibited from trading with Western nations.

Thus, the gaping wage differentials that existed while the Wall stood and much of the communist world was cut off from the West were suddenly exposed in the early 1990s. There were not only unprecedented labor cost differentials but also massive and willing populations yearning to enjoy the high levels of consumption that had become the norm in western Europe and North America.[24]

The wage gap between the developed countries and developing countries has not been quick to narrow. In 2005 the hourly wage of the average factory worker was $18.80 in Germany but only $0.43 in India and $0.80 in China, in the Asian context, and $0.73 in Bulgaria and $2.81 in the Czech Republic, in the European context (see table 4.1). It is not just hourly wages that matter but also the numbers of hours worked. While Germans work an average of 1,362 hours per year, and Americans 1,777 hours per year, the mean number of hours worked in Poland is 1,984 hours. As *Business Week* points out, "what ultimately sets Central Europe apart from the rest of the continent is the ambition of the younger generation."[25]

Figure 4.3 shows the prevalence and magnitude of the job losses in the United States between 1995 and 2005 resulting from globalization. Some sectors, such as textiles and apparel have been particularly hard hit by globalization, where well over half of the jobs were lost during this period.

Table 4.1. Hourly Wages in International Comparison, 2005

Country	Factory worker	Engineer	Accountant	Middle manager
Poland	$3.07	$4.32	$4.03	$6.69
Czech Republic	2.81	5.38	4.10	6.81
Hungary	1.96	5.09	4.62	7.44
Slovakia	2.21	4.15	3.37	5.48
Romania	1.41	2.58	1.23	3.23
Bulgaria	0.73	1.43	0.83	2.80
China	0.80	3.50	3.20	4.42
India	0.43	2.40	1.93	3.13
Germany	18.80	38.90	26.40	40.40
United States	14.18	30.32	27.48	38.77

Amounts are in U.S. dollars.
Source: *Business Week*, European ed., December 12/19, 2005, p. 56.

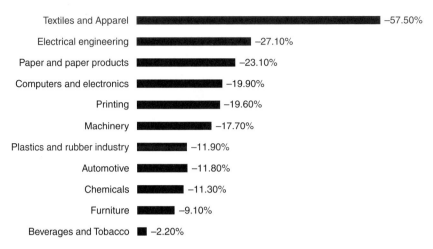

Figure 4.3 Job losses in the United States. Percent change from Jan. 1995 to Sept. 2005, by industry. Source: Bureau of Labor Statistics, in *Der Spiegel* Spec. Int. Ed. 7, 2005.

While the wage gap, the hours worked gap, and perhaps the more vague "ambition" gap between developed countries such as Germany and its eastern and central European neighbors may be enormous, the talent gap is much narrower. In 2003, central Europe, which consists of the Czech Republic, Estonia, Lithuania, Hungary, Poland, Slovakia, Slovenia, and Romania, produced 41,400 graduates in science, math, and computing. By contrast, the powerhouse of western Europe, Germany, produced only 26,600 graduates.[26] Similarly, in engineering, manufacturing, and construction, the countries of central Europe generated 96,600 graduates, while Germany graduated only 51,700.

What has been the response of not just corporate America but corporations throughout Europe and the developed world, at least in the traditional manufacturing industries? Outsource, offshore, and downsize, downsize, downsize. What production does remain is increasingly manufactured by high-technology and sophisticated machinery that requires only a minimum of (expensive) labor. The corporate response to globalization has been prevalent throughout the developed economies. For example,

> some companies have outsourced production to China and export their wares home. Siemens, for example, markets several cell-phone models in Germany that have been

produced in Shanghai. The Chinese plant could be a twin of the German counterparts: eleven state-of-the art production lines are housed in a sparking clean hall. A handful of employees in white overalls are perched at their workstations, attaching circuit boards to cases. A poster on the wall encourages workers to submit suggestions for improvement: "150,000 renminbis could be yours!" This corresponds to about 14,000 euros, a mind-boggling bonus for people who earn 300 euros a month. The quality produced in Shanghai is comparable to that in Germany. But the labor costs are not. Although employees in Bocholt or Kamp-Lintfort are now back up to full 40-hour workweek without extra pay, Siemens cannot match the cost benefits of cheap Chinese labor.[27]

As an article entitled "Germany: World Leading Exporter (of Jobs)," in the most prestigious weekly German magazine, *Der Spiegel*, reports, employment in manufacturing rose throughout the era of the managed economy, increasing from 12.5 million in 1970 to 14.1 million in 1991; then, as globalization hit Germany, manufacturing jobs crashed to 10.2 million in 2004.[28] Between 1991 and 2004, the number of jobs in the German textile industry fell by 65 percent, from 274,658 to 94,432. In the construction industry, there was a 58 percent decrease in employment in Germany, from 1.9 million jobs to 778,000. In the metalworking industries, employment decreased from 476,299 to 250,024, or 47.5 percent. And in the heart and soul of German manufacturing, the machine tool industry, the number of jobs fell from 1.6 million to 947,448, or 39.1 percent.

When the high-cost manufacturing plants of Germany are compared to the more moderate factories located not that far away in central and eastern Europe, it is hard to imagine that manufacturing will ever regain its prowess and pervasiveness in the German economy and society. Comparing two major auto plants, both operated by Opel, one finds major differences across a national border: workers in Bochum, Germany, spend 35 hours a week at work, earning €2,900 monthly, while in Gliwice, Poland, workers spend 40 hours a week, earning €700 monthly. German workers also get more vacation days: thirty-one compared to only twenty-six in Poland. It was these differences that led *Der Spiegel* to conclude: "new manufacturing jobs in Germany will not be created."[29] Experts blame globalization for Germany's devastated economy. Ulrich Beck, a sociologist at the University of Munich, said: "our jobs are being exported" as a result of globalization.[30] As *Der Spiegel* reports, "the land of machine tool engineers, mechanics and industrial laboratories is losing its industry."[31]

Such corporate downsizing, due to globalization, has been rampant in the United States. Just recently, in March 2006, General Motors announced that it was planning on reducing its workforce by 30,000 by 2008.[32] In addition, one of its main suppliers, Delphi, announced sizeable job cuts. General Motors was so desperate to shed workers that it reached an agreement with its major labor union, the United Auto Workers, to offer highly lucrative employee buyouts to 126,000 hourly employees to "cut all ties" with the company. Such buyouts ranged from an early retirement package of $35,000 to a severance agreement ranging between $70,000 and $140,000.

One could hardly claim the situation to be better on the other side of the Atlantic. The substitution of capital and technology for labor, along with the shifting of production to lower cost locations, has resulted in waves of corporate downsizing, which, albeit painful, generally preserved the viability of many of the large corporations. The *Financial Times* reports that "French and German businesses have competed well on global markets."[33]

The workers of Europe, however, have not fared as well. Statistics gathered in a careful study undertaken by Germany's Ministry of Economics and Technology (2000) show that Siemens increased its number of employees outside Germany by 50 percent from 108,000 in the mid-1980s to 162,000 in by the mid-1990s (see fig. 4.4). At the same time, Siemens eliminated thousands of jobs in Germany. Volkswagen increased its number of employees in foreign countries by 24 percent, over the same period, Volkswagen trimmed employment in Germany by 10 percent. The increase in outside jobs at Hoechst was 9 percent, while the number within Germany fell by 26 percent. As *Der Spiegel* observes, "globalization is bursting at the seams, it seems. Long-established companies are muting into supranational conglomerates. But is there anything still German about Metro, Siemens or Deutsche Bank?"[34] For example, the flagship German bank actually employs 66 percent of its workforce abroad. Similarly, by 2005, well over a half of Volkswagen's 305,695 workers were employed outside of Germany.[35]

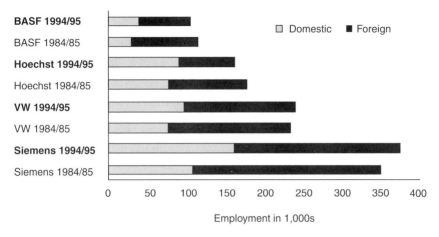

Figure 4.4 Employment in large German corporations.

Only 158,570 Volkswagen employees actually worked in Germany. The reason? According to one of the leading German business newspapers, the *Handelsblatt*, "Production in West German VW factories is much too expensive. Costs have to be reduced, primarily through downsizing and layoffs."[36] By contrast, employment has continued to increase in Volkswagen establishments outside of Germany. As of 2005, there were 23,456 Volkswagen employees in the Czech Republic, 23,240 in Spain, 21,860 in Brazil, 21,190 in China, 15,110 in Mexico, 8,150 in the Slovak Republic, and 6,940 in Poland.[37]

These examples are not isolated but are typical of the wave of German downsizing in the 1990s that resulted in levels of unemployment not seen since World War II. As *Der Spiegel* points out, "worldwide competition has its dark sides: globalization is putting more pressure on German workers. Every week companies are announcing plans to relocate operations and jobs. Organizations such as Siemens, Schering, and Deutsche Post—which are reporting strong, even record earnings—are laying off thousands of domestic employees."

The pervasiveness of job displacements resulting from job downsizing triggered by outsourcing and offshoring in German manufacturing subsequent to the fall of the Berlin Wall is evident in table 4.2. Between 1991 and 1995, manufacturing jobs decreased by 1,307,000, while they increased in foreign subsidiaries by 189,000 (see table 4.2).[38] In the chemical sector, the decrease of domestic employment was 80,000, while 14,000

Table 4.2.   Change in Employment Figures in Germany and at Foreign
Subsidiaries (1991–95, in thousands)

Employment sector	Foreign locations	Domestic locations
Manufacturing	189	−1307
Chemicals	14	−80
Electrical engineering	−17	−198
Automotive	30	−161
Mechanical engineering	16	−217
Textiles	−6	−68
Banking and insurance	21	28

Source: Bundesministerium für Wirtschaft und Technologie (German Federal Ministry of Economics and Technology), *Annual Report 2000* (Berlin: Bundesministerium für Wirtschaft und Technologie, 2000).

jobs were added by German chemical companies in plants located outside of Germany. In electrical engineering, employment in German plants decreased by 198,000. In automobiles, employment in Germany decreased by 161,000, while 30,000 jobs were added outside of Germany.[39] The reaction of the German public was to accuse German firms of not fulfilling their social contract. One of the leading newspapers, *Die Zeit*, complained: "When Profits Lead to Ruin—More Profits and More Unemployment: Where Is the Social Responsibility of the Firms?"[40]

Thus, while the postwar internationalization may have affected America and Europe differently, the post–Berlin Wall type of globalization had a similar affect on both sides of the Atlantic: between 1979 and 1995, more than 43 million jobs were lost in the United States as a result of corporate downsizing.[41] This includes 24.8 million blue-collar jobs and 18.7 million white-collar jobs. Similarly, the five hundred largest U.S. manufacturing corporations cut 4.7 million jobs between 1980 and 1993, or a quarter of their workforce. Perhaps most disconcerting, the rate of corporate downsizing has apparently increased over time in the United States, even as the unemployment rate has fallen. During most of the 1980s, about one in twenty-five workers lost a job, while in the 1990s, the proportion rose to one in twenty.

Thus, one of the most profound consequences of globalization has been to trigger a shift in the working experience of most people, away from being directly or indirectly involved with manufacturing and toward some type of nonmanufacturing activity, such as services or retailing. This shift has in no way been restricted to the United States. For example, in 1970, about 50 percent of German employment was in manufacturing. By 2005, the share of manufacturing employment had fallen to 27 percent, or just one in four workers. As *Der Spiegel* comments, "a sad record: in this land of engineers and automakers, the industrial core is melting away. With jobs being relocated to low-wage countries and processes performed by computers and robots, in the long term only a tiny, high-tech production will survive."[42]

A situation that is typical of the shift away from traditional manufacturing can be found in Franconia in southern Germany, home to the sporting goods manufacturer Adidas-Salomon. The original shoe manufacturer, Adidas, was a German company manufacturing shoes using a largely German workforce. But, as *Der Spiegel* observes, "most German companies are now tightly woven into the global economy. For many, international business now plays a much larger role than the domestic German market. Their benchmark is no longer the national economy, but the world."[43] This is certainly true for Adidas-Salomon. Its workforce spans some forty nationalities. There is not a production facility in sight. The manufacturing of shoes and other sporting goods has been outsourced since the mid-1990s. Thus, "most likely, none of them [the workers] have ever come close to performing exercises such as pulling the shaft of a sports shoe across a stretcher."[44]

According to the *Financial Times*, "globalization has intensified and accelerated shifts in comparative advantage. In France, Germany and beyond this has hardened the divisions between insiders and outsiders—between the skilled and unskilled, the securely employed and the jobless. . . . The unemployed have lacked a political voice."[45]

In a 2006 exhibition of the work of the photographer Henrik Spohler, entitled "Made in Germany," that was displayed at the Hamburg Museum of Labor,

> the photos are chilling. They depict a work environment that is frosty and barren. Busy burrows of manual labor—like the Volkswagen plant in Wolfsburg, where overall-clad workers once assembled Beetles by hand—have yielded to the sterile laboratories of postindustrial process. These places are

interchangeable. Most are highly profitable, but they remain social wastelands. Phantom atolls where the so-called human resources are confined to supervising futuristic machines that resemble aliens or disemboweled insects. The vestiges of human labor—a misplaced hammer, a sandwich, an oily cloth—would seem extraterrestrial here.[46]

Globalization involves more than simply offering inexpensive, unskilled labor to Western companies. The winner of the 2005 TopCoder Open, a global competition to crack a perplexing computational challenge, sponsored by Sun Microsystems, is not from MIT or Cal Tech, or even from the United States, but from Poland.[47] According to *Business Week*,

> [Eryk] Kopczynski's triumph in this year's TopCoder
> Open was no fluke. He was following in the footsteps of a
> slew of computing geniuses to emerge from the monolithic
> Soviet style buildings of Warsaw University. "Poles like to
> compete," says Warsaw University computer science student
> Marek Cygan, winner of this year's Google Code Jam. No
> kidding. Warsaw University is ranked Number 1 in the world
> in top coder events, ahead of the likes of Massachusetts
> Institute of Technology. Just like India's best tech schools,
> Warsaw University has confounded a scarcity of resources
> to identify and nurture bright students.[48]

A corporate survey of around seventeen thousand foreign direct investment projects undertaken by Ernst & Young International revealed that European companies expected to locate over a third of their R & D investments in central Europe.[49]

One central European magnet for R & D investments is Krakow, Poland, which offers three high-quality universities within a hundred-kilometer radius, and a significant number of the universities' fifty-five thousand annual graduates earn math, science, computing, and engineering degrees. This hub of scientific and engineering knowledge that can be accessed at comparatively low prices has generated a flow of investments from companies such as Motorola, Capgemini, and Delphi.[50] Not only have all three of these companies established R & D centers in the Krakow region but also, most striking, Delphi, which manufactures automobile parts, and in 2005 announced mass layoffs in the United States, has been rapidly adding employees to its R & D center in Krakow, which serves as its global headquarters for the design of suspension and fuel-handling systems, along with the development of electronics and safety components. Delphi expects to employ nearly one thousand highly skilled workers in Krakow. As chief engineer Jack Hackett, whose main job is to ensure that his staff meet the quality standards required by BMW, DaimlerChrysler, and other auto manufacturers, has learned, "the Poles are extremely fast learners."[51]

Similarly, Siemens employs five hundred telecom-software and systems-software engineers at its R & D center in Wroclaw. Richard Lda, the vice-president for central and eastern European operations at Motorola, has learned that "Poles have a can-do spirit."[52]

Writing from Germany, Karl Marx warned the Western world of a specter that was haunting capitalism and would ultimately pull it down—the increased consolidation and power resulting from ever greater control in the hands of fewer people, whom he called capitalists. Perhaps one day Marx will be proven right. Meanwhile, the specter now haunting the West has come from an entirely different direction— the East, and the South as well—in the form of the post–Berlin Wall globalization identified by Thomas Friedman. Unprecedented success in mastering the economics of the managed economy, particularly in terms of production, management, and distribution, resulted in unprecedented prosperity, growth, and employment in the West during the postwar era. The fall of the Berlin Wall, which was expected to extend this postwar prosperity by facilitating access to new and previously untapped markets, resulted in a shock to the system—the system focused on and organized around the factor of capital, which had thrived so long and served the West so well. But even as the Europeans were beginning to realize that their social market economies, which had been adapted and evolved to exploit the capital-based economy better than the American postwar version of the managed economy, were not immune to the very forces that had undermined the American one, a new strategy for prosperity in the era of globalization was emerging. This new strategy is the subject of the chapters that follow.

5

Brains Not Brawn

Does chapter 4 suggest that, because of globalization, the United States, along with the other developed economies, has passed its glory days and is on the way to managing its own decline? Is that the best the managed economy of the West can now do? It seems that globalization has rendered the type of production—capital, that is, factories, manufacturing establishments, and machines—that drove economic growth, jobs, and prosperity throughout most of the last century as no longer competitive in economies burdened with high costs in general, and certainly high wages. Is it inevitable, as chapter 4 might seem to suggest, that in order to keep capital located in the West, wages must keep dropping until they are so low that the low wages in developing countries are no longer sufficiently attractive to lure away capital investment?

Perhaps the iron law of globalization will inevitably force wages down in the developed countries toward the lowest common denominator found on the globe. Certainly, if you ask the textile workers or auto workers in the United States who are still lucky enough to have jobs, they will no doubt enthusiastically endorse the validity, if not virtue, of the iron law of globalization. Their wages, in real terms, have been diminishing steadily for decades now. Their counterparts in certain European countries, such as France and Germany, thanks to the preservation of strong trade unions, might contest the point. However, a quick recall of the massive loss of jobs throughout Europe, especially in

Germany, that has resulted in record levels of unemployment suggests a footnote to the iron law of globalization: if wages are not allowed to fall, jobs will disappear from high-cost regions only to reappear in low-cost regions. Perhaps the law of globalization confronting the developed countries is that you pay either through reduced wages or reduced employment prospects, or a combination of both.

The nineteenth-century British economist Thomas Malthus remains famous to this day for having discovered, or invented, his famous iron law of wages. According to this law, which was so inevitable that it was not just a law but an iron law, increases in population will always drive wages down to subsistence level. While Malthus was certainly correct about population increase continuing to occur, his prediction of subsistence-level living standards, at least for the developed countries, has been proven wildly wrong. The West has simply gotten richer and richer over time. What was the flaw in Malthus's thinking? He never considered technological change and progress. As long as technological change and progress remain ahead, both population and prosperity can increase together, as has been the case not just in the United States over centuries but also in virtually every other developed country.

Just as there was a flaw in the iron law of wages, there also is a fatal flaw in the iron law of globalization. The flaw does not involve the factor of capital. New factories in traditional industries such as textiles, clothes, shoes, steel, ships, and automobiles are being built outside of the most highly developed countries. This does not mean that consumers in the United States and elsewhere in the West are no longer interested in buying these products. The demand for manufactured goods, such as autos, for better or for worse, is higher than ever. But the *location* of their production has shifted, and will continue to shift, dramatically. As we saw in chapter 4, outsourcing and offshoring are not only more cost-effective strategies but are essential to a firm's survival in the global market. Woe is the producer who does not locate to a lower cost location when all of her competitors do. It's like playing musical chairs. Just as nobody wants to be caught as the one without a chair, no producer wants to be caught with costs higher than its rivals.

Rather, just as the flaw in the iron law of wages lay in a factor not considered by Malthus, who only focused on population and subsistence, the fatal flaw in the iron law of globalization involves something other than the two factors, capital and labor, that were the focus of the postwar economic growth miracle.

My friend and research partner Zoltan Acs first pointed out this additional factor to me back in the early 1980s. As young professors at Vermont's Middlebury College, we found the time to enjoy hiking and bicycling in the beautiful Green Mountains. It was during these hikes and bike adventures that Zoltan explained to me the focus of his research. One of the great engines of American postwar prosperity, the steel industry, had a few years earlier taken a harsh and stunning blow, as steel imports from Japan and Germany poured in to the United States, wreaking havoc on the profitability of steel mills and leading to massive layoffs, downsizing, and plant closures in the steel industry. In retrospect, we now see this as another example of globalization. However, at the time it was an unprecedented blow to a major industry in a nation that had won a great war and was now prospering in a well-deserved peacetime. But with the flood of steel imports, it became suddenly apparent to all that the Japanese and Germans, thanks to the—perhaps unprecedented—generosity of the Americans, had been restored and were more than back on their feet. In fact, the Japanese and German steel companies had learned how to copy the American steel technology.

Zoltan's 1984 doctoral dissertation documented how—even as the mighty steel giants, such as US Steel and Bethlehem Steel, along with their workers and communities, were being devastated by cheaper imports pouring in from Japan and Germany—a quiet and quite puzzling phenomenon was taking place. New steel plants, based on different and new production methods, were thriving, ultimately to become known as the minimills of American steel. How was that possible? They didn't just follow business as usual, but rather innovated by applying new and different ideas to the production of steel.

In fact, postwar internationalization, which opened up America to a flood of imports from Europe and Japan, and ultimately devastated the traditional manufacturing industries in the Midwest, also had some positive aspects. Not everyone lost or suffered: consumers were able to purchase less expensive and better foreign products than their American-made counterparts.

Perhaps more subtly, even while steel workers were being laid off in Pittsburgh and Gary, and auto workers in Detroit, if you were in the computer industry on one of the coasts, things were looking pretty good. It has been said that ideas need new space, and so it was with postwar America. Although the manufacturing Midwest suffered, there were poignant examples of workers, industries, and regions, such as what we now call Silicon Valley near San Francisco and Route 128 around Boston, which noticeably thrived, not in spite of globalization but because of it. And as people stopped focusing on the postwar industrial powerhouses of steel and automobiles and instead started focusing on the success stories of Silicon Valley, Boston's Route 128, North Carolina's Research Triangle, as well as Austin, Texas, and Madison, Wisconsin, they realized that these places, their industries, and their people had one thing in common: they were all about ideas, or what economists call *knowledge*. When one drives around any of these regions, the absence of large factories is rather striking. Yet these have ranked among the most successful regions of America in the last decade or so. How is this possible?

After all, if factories, machines, and assembly lines were part of the physical capital key to economic success, how could these regions and industries, as well as workers, who didn't seem to have much of this assumed key factor, physical capital, at all, become so successful? Whatever Silicon Valley had, it didn't have plants and factories. Nor did Research Triangle Park, Route 128, Austin, or Madison. If they didn't have physical capital, what did they have? These people didn't work with machines in factories, as many of their fathers had in other regions. They worked with their heads developing *knowledge*.

It was becoming increasingly clear that ideas and knowledge were now at least as important or perhaps even more so than the physical capital that had so dependably served as the engine of growth, jobs, and prosperity in the post–World War II era. Scholars responded to this increasingly apparent insight by beginning to expand their characterization of what matters for growth so as to take account of knowledge and ideas as the driving force.[1] Economists called this new understanding the *endogenous growth theory*.[2]

Western Publishing, the printing plant where I worked in Poughkeepsie, closed, as did most book and publishing factories in the United Sates, decades ago. Pittsburgh, once the proud capital of the steel industry, no longer has a single steel mill. Gary, Indiana, which still has steel mills, may wish that it were Pittsburgh. The new jobs replacing the book factories, auto plants, and steel mills of America are as different from my old factory job, and most old factory jobs, as day from night. Many jobs today, and certainly most of the jobs that pay enough to sustain a middle-class family, require thinking. They require workers to constantly think, question, and challenge. This is true of the jobs that remain at the auto and steel plants; due to these plants' technology, these jobs require not just technical but also thinking and decision-making skills.

Such jobs might involve high technology—for example, computers, software, biotechnology, life sciences technology, nanotechnology, or information technology. But not necessarily; many people in service and design industries work with ideas. And these jobs are not limited to just working with ideas; often employees work with other people. Ben and Jerry's ice cream was a great idea that Ben and Jerry thought up, partly from working with other people. So was Starbucks. As Albert Einstein observed, "imagination is more important than knowledge." Perhaps the most important realization about the knowledge economy is that it is about a lot more than just knowledge, especially technical and scientific knowledge. Rather, so-called softer skills and capacities, for example, creativity, the ability to communicate, and emotional intelligence, may all be a part of what economists have labeled *knowledge*.[3] It is exactly these softer skills, which involve working with ideas, not physical capital, that provide the basis for innovation, which in turn is the key to having a high standard of living. As Herbert Henzler, chair of the Bavarian Research Agency and honorary professor at the Ludwig-Maximilians-University of Munich, points out, "innovation is the essential factor for economic growth and job creation."[4]

In her book *The Spark: Igniting the Creative Fire that Lives within Us All*, Lyn Heward suggests that it is creativity, or what she calls the spark, that matters for success.[5] By contrast, in the old manufacturing era, jobs were routinized, standardized, and mechanized. It is true that the very nature of assembly-line work required a team of workers, sometimes even an army, as in the case of automobile production. But the interaction among these workers did not really matter. The main thing was to avoid fights and disputes—anything to keep from shutting the line down.

How different work and interactions between and among people are in today's knowledge economy! Not only are technical or scientific knowledge valuable but also emotional intelligence—how one relates, engages, and interacts with others. It is not just about selling to customers; it is about working in teams and groups, with ill-defined contexts and missions, but always with one clear goal: to do things that have never been done before, that is, to *innovate*. Thus the capacity to generate ideas, creativity, and the ability to work with others emerge as the key assets in the knowledge-based economy, replacing the brute strength, blind obedience, and corporate conformity of the earlier managed economy. Managing in the managed economy was relatively straightforward: one knew what to produce, how to produce it, and who should produce it. However, if it is not known what exactly should be produced, or what precisely constitutes the service and its delivery, or how it should be produced or delivered, and what kind of people or workers can best generate such an unknown good or service, management is anything but easy. Thus management and strategy in the knowledge economy poses new challenges for managers.

Figure 5.1 compares the mean annual income of Americans without a high school diploma, with a high school diploma, with a college degree, and with an advanced degree. Well-educated Americans have always earned more than high school dropouts. Over time, the real earnings of high school dropouts and those not completing college have decreased, while the real earnings of Americans with advanced degrees have increased. That is, the income gap between the educated and uneducated has increased over time, especially in the 1990s. In addition the role of knowledge in the American economy has dramatically increased in importance, particularly as measured by the explosion that has occurred in the number of people with doctoral degrees who are employed in industry, which now exceeds the number of such people employed in academia (see fig. 5.2).

A major conclusion of chapter 4 was that the dramatic change that globalization made possible was a reduction in the cost of moving physical capital across national borders so as to locate a manufacturing enterprise virtually anywhere in the world. Why should this be less true for knowledge capital, or working with ideas? In fact, since working with ideas usually does not involve investing in large physical assets, knowledge capital should be more affected by globalization. Observing the way information can be transmitted across geographic space via the internet at high speed and for virtually no cost, fax

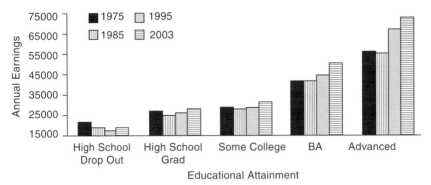

Figure 5.1 Mean earnings of workers 18 and over by educational attainment, 1975–2003. Adjusted for inflation.

machines, and the electronic "communication superhighway," in 1995 *The Economist* proclaimed "the death of distance."[6] New communication technologies triggered a virtual spatial revolution in terms of the geography of production. According to *The Economist*, "the death of distance as a determinant of the cost of communications will probably be the single most important economic force shaping society."

While the telecommunications revolution reduced the cost of transmitting information across geographic space to virtually nothing, at the same time, the microprocessor revolution made it feasible for

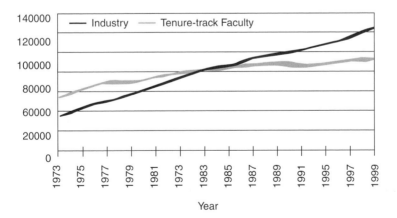

Figure 5.2 Number of PhDs by sector, 1973–99 (for those 5 or more years since PhD and aged 65 or younger). All science and engineering fields. Source: Stephan, 2006.

almost everyone to participate in global communications. At the dawn of the cyberspace age, it was widely assumed that ideas and knowledge would be subjected to the same forces of globalization as physical capital and labor, only faster. In a world of email, fax machines, and cyberspace, how could the workforce working with ideas have exploded, along with the emergence of entire regions, such as the Silicon Valley and Research Triangle Park?

The explanation of this seeming contradiction posed by the emergence of competitive advantage based on knowledge and ideas in an era where the telecommunications revolution has drastically reduced the cost of communication lies in a distinction between knowledge and information. *Information*, such as the price of gold on the New York Stock Exchange or the value of the copper in London, is easily codified and has a singular meaning and interpretation. On the other hand, *knowledge* is vague, difficult to codify, and often only serendipitously recognized. While the marginal cost of transmitting information across geographic space is virtually zero because of the telecommunications revolution, the marginal cost of transmitting knowledge, especially tacit knowledge, rises with distance.

This distinction between tacit knowledge and information hit home when I was living surrounded by the Berlin Wall in the West Berlin of the 1980s. The nightly television news featured two East German border guards who had safely escaped across the Wall to the freedom of the West. Such escapes by East German border guards were rare. The East German communist authorities had long since learned how to take the necessary precautions to deter such traitorous escapes by their border guards. They paired guards from different regions to ensure that they would not previously have been friends, and would have little in common. This was to minimize the likelihood of any collusive agreement about an escape plan being developed. Similarly, the guards were kept together in units only for short periods. The most draconian measure was an absolute order to shoot to kill in the event that a comrade should attempt to defect. To sweeten the reward, compliance with this order was typically rewarded with a promotion, while border guards suspected of shooting to miss were summarily punished.

Thus, the question of how these two young men could navigate their way across the Wall and through the maze of disincentives was of considerable interest to the public. I still clearly remember their explanation: "I looked in his eyes and he looked in mine. We both saw the same thing. Without uttering a word, we simultaneously threw down our guns and started running."[7] What was communicated when the two young men looked in each other's eyes was tacit knowledge. How such sentiment was simultaneously transmitted in an alarmingly hostile situation is rooted in the human spirit and capacity to read, process, and interpret nonverbal communications, including facial expression, body posture, previous behavior, and even intuition based on looking deeply into someone's eyes. The meaning contained in such nonverbal tacit communication is not only noncodifiable but also requires face-to-face communication. Any misinterpretation in this situation could easily have resulted in being summarily shot. Such sentiment could not have been transmitted without being confronted by the immediacy of looking into each other's eyes. Even with the internet, it is impossible to do this over any distance.

Many of my friends and colleagues have had the unpleasant experience of having an e-mail message misunderstood or misinterpreted. The problem arises from literal interpretation of codified messages. When the content is communicated through face-to-face interaction, a host of nonverbal communications—ranging from facial expression to body language, including tone of voice and intonation—modify and qualify the actual content of a message, rendering perhaps a different meaning than would be understood solely from the codified message. Everybody knows that if you have something really important to communicate, it is best to try and do it face to face. Second best is verbally over the phone. As for e-mail, even the old-fashioned hand-written letters revealed something through the handwriting and style.

When only the cold, hard facts matter, email is ideal. There is no need to allow any (wasteful) emotion to get in the way while telling somebody the capital of Brazil, the amount of rain in Paris yesterday, when Johann Wolfgang von Goethe lived in Weimar, Germany, or what movies are playing when at the local multiplex. All of this information can be accessed equally well with no disadvantage regardless of where you are located on the globe.

However, when it comes communicating ideas, especially tacit knowledge, the internet, or any type of mass communication, becomes less useful. Thus, when it comes to knowledge and ideas location matters. The actor Woody Allen once quipped that "90 percent of life is showing up." This may have always have been true, but in the knowledge economy it may be that 90 percent of life is showing up at the right place, because being in the right place and at the right time means being positioned to access and take advantage of knowledge spillovers. It means being in a position to win. In learning from the creativity of the performing team of the Cirque du Soleil, longtime executive Heward points out, a virtue of physical proximity in the impact of communication is eye contact: "people can tell if you're not there."[8] "They say two things get them excited. One is colleagues who get you in the right frame of mind. The second is the crowd. They say the crowd will always pull you through."[9] Both colleagues and crowds require close geographic proximity to access the energy and the immediacy and to direct attention. Location and geographic proximity matter. You must be there.

In the capital-based managed economy, a factory worker in Detroit might have moved to Pittsburgh, switching from an auto plant to a steel mill. Why would he do that? The answer was typically pretty simple—for a higher wage. If he saw that the wage at the mill paid a couple of dollars more per hour, he would consider moving. Evidence consistently showed that workers were motivated by wage differences. Wage differences were static; professors measured the difference between Detroit and Pittsburgh in terms of "static wage differentials," and these differences were what made different cities more or less interesting to workers. In Upton Sinclair's hotly debated novel *The Jungle*, the families who were displaced and thrown off farms and the immigrants who were herded through Ellis Island didn't make their way to Chicago because they liked the meatpacking stockyards;[10] in the jargon of the economists, it was all about static wage differentials.

However, if work is based on knowledge, ideas, emotions, and creativity, the advantages and disadvantages of different cities center not on wage differences but on the quality of life. This is why so many graduates of the midwestern universities head for the coasts. My students tell me: "I could get a pretty good job here in the Midwest, but if I go out to the coast, I'll really get an opportunity to learn." What does this mean? Sure, the weather might be better, and it might just be time for a change of scene, but I don't hear these excuses a lot. They certainly are not going for higher pay, at least when cost of living is factored in. The fact is that many young graduates share residences, scrambling to make ends meet. Communal living is not as much fun as is portrayed in the long-running and greatly loved sitcom *Friends*. In fact, had these compelling sitcom characters stayed home or located in America's heartland, they could have earned more, at least after factoring out the cost of housing, and had plenty of living space.

Today's youth go to the place where they can meet the right kind of people, get the right experiences, and access the critical ideas and insights that spur their learning. After all, that is why they went to college in the first place and, subsequently in an increasingly number of cases, to graduate school as well. But that learning doesn't stop with graduation from the university. Rather, the choices that people make about whom they work for and where they live determine their access to knowledge and ideas and therefore their ability to keep learning.

At one time it was fashionable to say "You are what you eat." While this might or might not be true, it is certainly true now that you reflect your surroundings. In the knowledge economy, what you know is highly shaped and influenced by who you know. What you know is conditioned and dependent on what the people around you know, and your own ability to access and absorb that knowledge. If you wanted to be a movie star or screenwriter, you moved to Hollywood. Many of the people working in the industry have to be there to learn about the business. Because of the tacit nature of film industry knowledge, living in Hollywood has proven to be important for gaining access to that knowledge and developing the personal connections and networks needed to be successful.

It's not just Hollywood and film. Everyone knows that Microsoft is located in Seattle because it is Bill Gates's hometown, but when he dropped out of Harvard, he didn't head directly home. Rather, he made a detour to Albuquerque, where he studied the Altair computer. The company was a leading manufacturer of kits favored by hackers and hobbyists experimenting with computers. Gates justified his detour by pointing out that he needed first to learn more about the industry.

In 2004 General Electric located its new Global Research Center in Munich, Germany. The reason? As Armin Pfoh Leter of the Global Research Center explained, "Munich was the only city which offered us a location on the campus of the university."[11] As a dream team of noted economists led by the eminent University of Chicago economist Edward Glaeser observed, "intellectual breakthroughs must cross hallways and streets more easily than oceans and continents."[12]

To factory workers in the capital-driven managed economy, the virtue of one firm, industry, or region over another was relatively simple—higher wages. Who you were working with or might make friends with did not matter. In the mass-production assembly line, you performed your preprescribed repetitive task with reliability and dependability. However, if your work is based on your ability to conjure new ideas, along with using those ideas to identify and solve problems, you view your coworkers very differently. Your very livelihood depends on your ability to imagine the right ideas at the right time, and to do that, you need help. The value of your own ideas and knowledge is conditional on and is shaped by those around you. So while it matters what you bring to the table, your ability to learn from others in your environment also matters. People with the capacity to recognize and understand important insights from others will augment their knowledge more than those who ignore or lack that capacity.

Thus, for people working with ideas and knowledge, being in the right place at the right time really matters. It matters not because of any static wage differentials that might exist. Rather, the opportunity to learn and augment human capital and knowledge will greatly influence such a person's future. The value of your ideas will be highly shaped by those around you, and if you are in the right place, those around you will have more and better ideas, thereby enabling you to learn more, and perhaps ultimately earn more as well.

This is certainly true of Michael Hatfield, who studied engineering at Rose Hulman Institute of Technology in Indiana. Although he loved and continues to love Indiana, after graduation, he moved to San Francisco. The reason? "That's where all of the top people were in communications technology." By being in the vicinity of the information technology engineers and scientists of the Bay Area, he was able to build on what he had learned in his formal education at Rose Hulman (where he now sits on the board of trustees), and he founded California-based Calix, a company that creates fiber optic network products for use in telecommunications, which became one of the most important producers of broadband technology.

So it was with Jack Harding, the founder, president, and CEO of eSilicon, also in the San Francisco Bay Area, and former CEO of Cadence, one of the largest semiconductor firms in the world. Upon graduation from Drew University in 1977, Harding aggressively sought out a sales position at IBM. Why? According to Harding, it was "because I knew I would get the best training in the world with IBM."[13] Harding choose his route not thinking about static wage differentials but rather about where he could best augment the human capital in which he and his family had already invested so much.

Jack Harding and Mike Hatfield started from very different places and took very different paths to end up at different places as well. But they have one thing in common: they decided to go where the right people were—the people with the ideas, experience, and knowledge they realized would help them make the next step.[14]

Rather than wage differentials, when you work with ideas and knowledge, it's all about "knowledge differentials," because it helps to be in the same place as the right people in order to interact, understand, and communicate.

Archie Bunker of *All in the Family* best exemplifies the worker caught by the shift from the capital-driven to the knowledge-based economy. Of course, knowledge and ideas have always mattered for economic growth. However, after World War II, the blue-collar workers producing goods on America's assembly lines did not work with ideas or do much thinking at all. This was certainly typified in the perhaps lovable but certainly racist, bigoted, and narrow-minded Archie Bunker. Like many American men of his generation, he was grateful for the job at the factory, but got his joy after work at the bar, the bowling alley, and, occasionally with his family. Ideas and knowledge did not matter in his world. On the other hand, his daughter and son-in-law studied at the university, and clearly had a different orientation. America was at the crossroads, moving not only away from bigotry and narrow-mindedness to tolerance and openness but also from working in factories with machines to working with ideas and knowledge.

If being in the right place at the right time matters so much for accessing knowledge and ideas, this explains an important development that has emerged along with the increased importance of knowledge as an economic force. Related to chapter 4, the fact is that even in a global economy, economic activity based on knowledge and ideas cannot be easily and costlessly transported to lower cost parts of the world. In fact, because capital-based work can be easily shifted to lower cost locations, this has actually increased the relative importance of work and economic activity based on ideas in developed countries, first and foremost in the United States. Thus, the competitive advantage of the United States has shifted and is continuing to shift toward economic activity based on knowledge and ideas and away from economic activity where no or little thinking is required. If the task is repetitive and routinized, it can simply be outsourced or offshored to cheaper locations in India, China, eastern Europe, or Latin America. Thus, the competitive advantage of individuals, firms, and regions in high-cost locations, such as America, is to take advantage of their educational opportunities, their culture and tradition embracing freedom and exploration, and their social environment emphasizing creativity. As Lester Thurow observes, "the world is moving from an industrial era based upon natural resources into a knowledge-based era based upon skills, education, and research and development."[15]

As any introductory economics student will tell you, if you are competing in the same market for work with millions of unskilled and uneducated workers around the globe, desperate for any work opportunity, and grateful for any they might receive, your wages are doomed to fall and keep falling. As the Europeans learned the hard way, trying to maintain or even increase the wages of nonknowledge workers in a global economy results in increasing unemployment.

Thus the very nature of knowledge and new ideas—people's propensity to require close physical proximity with each other to access and absorb them—provides a natural shield against the forces of globalization that would otherwise push wages and living standards downward. As *Business Week* points out, the Earth may not be flat when it comes to soft skills, which, although they are not the same thing as technical or scientific knowledge, are still an important type of knowledge: "What's missing is the soft skills: How do you cope with change, how do you motivate people and how do you work in teams?"[16]

Is the West doomed to stagnation and increasing unemployment? Perhaps not everything can be located costlessly around the globe. In particular, ideas, or knowledge, or thinking, require face-to-face proximity. Not only do you have to have the right education to access new ideas, but often you need to be located where other people are working on similar ideas. It doesn't matter how cheap labor is in southeast Asia or China; in order to compete in knowledge industries, both education and human capital are required, as well as geographic proximity to the right ideas in the right place. The last two decades have seen the emergence of highly competitive, productive clusters that are virtual job machines: California's Silicon Valley; Germany's Munich; and Finland's Helsinki. Perhaps the world is not so flat after all, particularly if you have a highly educated, creative, and motivated workforce benefiting from the highest social investments in the world—investments such as universities, research institutes, and the arts. As Dalia Marin, professor of economics at Munich's Ludwig-Maximilians-University, concludes, "where R & D goes, innovation and growth follow."[17]

An unexpected implication of the shift from physical capital to knowledge, or from machines to ideas, as the driving force for economic growth and competitiveness is the emergence of local and regional clusters of knowledge-based economic activity. Being in the right place actually becomes more important in the global era. This draws on a certain paradox of geography in the global era: even though the earth appears flatter, the importance of particular places as a source for knowledge, ideas, and creativity has increased significantly. Not only has *The Economist's* prediction of "the death of distance" been proven untrue, but the complete opposite has emerged. Places such as Silicon Valley, for software and information technology, San Diego, for life sciences, and New York, for finance, have become more, not less, important as a result of globalization.

For example, *Fortune* magazine has pointed out that "business is a social activity, and you have to be where important work is taking place."[18] A large survey of executives based in America's sixty largest metropolitan areas ranked the Raleigh/Durham metropolitan area as the best city for knowledge workers and innovative activity.[19] The reason was that

> A lot of brainy types who made their way to Raleigh/
> Durham were drawn by three top research universities. . . .
> U.S. businesses, especially those whose success depends on
> staying at the top of new technologies and processes,
> increasingly want to be where hot new ideas are percolating.
> A presence in brainpower centers like Raleigh/Durham pays
> off in new products and new ways of doing business. Dozens
> of small biotechnology and software operations are starting
> up each year and growing like *kudzu* in the fertile climate.[20]

Silicon Valley, the original high-tech cluster, is widely considered to be the most important, and eSilicon founder and CEO Jack Harding says:

> There are durable reasons why we lead the country. Silicon Valley, as a hotbed for entrepreneurial success, combines: (1) the most experienced concentration of risk capital in the world; (2) a vast, deep relationship with its region's higher-education institutions, whose leaders understand and participate in our innovation model; and (3) friendly local government infrastructure that understands it must excel in support of Silicon Valley's unique and thriving climate for innovation.
>
> Further, as ground zero for this architecture for innovation, we attract a diverse, sophisticated and motivated workforce from around the world. Here at eSilicon, a small company of about 100 people, we have nearly 20 nationalities represented—clearly not a sign that Silicon Valley is fading. There's a technical and cultural integration here that results in better business practices, better products and a better understanding of how to market these products on a global basis. I'd suspect that there are few, if any, other communities where everyone, from the CEO to the bench engineer, understands and is singularly motivated by the innovation model: how it works, where its risks lie and what its rewards are.[21]

The phenomenon is not just headline-grabbing regional knowledge clusters like Silicon Valley and Research Triangle Park. It also involves less well known but no less impressive technology clusters, such as life sciences in Madison or software engineering in Austin. Such regional knowledge clusters are no longer exclusive to the United States. There is software engineering in Ottawa and Bangalore; information technology in Stockholm; and biotechnology in Cambridge, England, and Jena, Germany.

Such regional knowledge clusters are not just about high technology and science, either. Country music clusters in Nashville, Tennessee. Production of pop music is centered in Los Angeles and New York, with recently emerging clusters in Stockholm and Dublin. Cutting-edge fashion designers cluster in Milan, Paris, Tokyo, and

New York, while finance is dominated by Frankfurt, London, New York, and Hong Kong.

Public policy has not played a passive role in the shift away from physical capital and toward idea- and knowledge-based economic activity. When it became clear that economic activity based on ideas, knowledge, and social interaction was generating growth, jobs, and prosperity, politicians and policy-makers switched away from promoting investments in physical capital to promoting knowledge capital investments. Since the 1990s, there has been a growing concern about investments in education at all levels. The mechanisms and incentives to promote research and development, and to attract talented knowledge workers, have become a primary concern for many communities. Upon his election in 2000, George W. Bush declared himself "the Education President." It is doubtful that any of his opponents in that campaign or his predecessor, Bill Clinton, would have contested the primacy of education in shaping America's future. Similarly, the Organization for Economic Cooperation and Development (OECD) is so concerned about the role that investments in primary and secondary education play in generating economic growth that it recently commissioned a study, now called the Bologna Report, which benchmarks educational attainment across a broad spectrum of OECD countries. The less-than-desired results for certain countries, such as Germany, have triggered waves of introspective questioning and the beginnings of educational reforms. If knowledge and ideas matter for economic growth and jobs, then education, schools, and research will shape the future. Thanks to globalization, brains have replaced brawn.

6

The Wall

Some say you don't know what you've got till it's gone. There's a reason for them saying it. And what is true with life and love, nature and paradise is unfortunately at least as true with ideas. Not with just any idea, but actually with what has in more than a few cases proven to be the better and more valuable ideas. At first glance, this doesn't seem to make sense. Why would anyone—society in general, firms, institutions, or individuals—be so quick to let any valuable idea, let alone the most valuable ideas, simply get away? After all, who wouldn't recognize a good idea when they see one? In fact, as this chapter will make clear, dealing with ideas and deciding between the good ones and bad ones is anything but trivial.

In chapter 5, we saw that in the era of globalization, knowledge and ideas are the keys to economic success. If knowledge is so important, at least in the sense of having a creative, well-educated workforce enjoying access to state-of-the art research at companies and universities, then Europe should rank among the most powerful locomotives for growth and job creation on the planet. Investments in European knowledge and human capital made Europe an expected winner from globalization.

But, as we all know, it didn't quite work out that way. Europe is burdened with stagnant growth, nagging unemployment, and bleak prospects for future employment. Economic growth, job creation, and a brighter standard of living typically rank as the most important policy priorities across Europe. Students and labor unions did not strike in Paris during the spring of 2006 without reason. They had a clear reason and a clear, if not perhaps possible, goal. The motive was fear: the strikers felt that their futures lacked the same opportunities and guarantees their parents and grandparents futures had held when they were the same age. The strikers' goal was to try and prevent the French government from eliminating the job protections that older workers had used to ensure lifetime employment with one company.

Back in 2002, I was invited to a conference at the Swedish Ministry of Economics focusing on why Sweden had suffered a decade of stagnation, low growth, and rising unemployment. Armed with the latest theories about growth in the "new economy," I marched into Stockholm, advising the minister of economics that if it was growth and jobs he needed, the answer was to invest, invest, and invest in knowledge—particularly in university research and human capital. My host shook his head, and suggested that surely the professor must be right, but it was hard to believe, and certainly even harder to sell to the citizens, the taxpayers, on this strategy, because by all accepted international measures and benchmarks, Sweden had the largest investments in research and human capital in the world. (In second place was Japan, which hadn't done any better.)

It was at this conference that I first heard about what the Swedes called the Swedish Paradox: a high level of investment in research and development, in the universities, and in human capital,with the anticipated return in terms of growth and jobs, what the public so desperately wanted,remaining exactly that—anticipated. Romano Prodi, then President of the European Commission, must have been so impressed by the Swedes that shortly afterward I started reading about the European Paradox. Europe ranked among the best in the world in terms of research, universities, and human capital, but the jobs and growth remained elusive.

Why? What went wrong? What could Europe do? Investments in science, research, and human capital do not do the taxpayers much good if the investments do not translate into jobs and growth. There is no shortage of educated, scientific, and engineering-trained, as well as cultured, creative and dedicated, people in Europe. But what if European companies do not pick up the product of all of this education, culture, research, and creativity—these Europeans' new ideas and insights? Why wouldn't this happen, you might ask? Why would a great successful company ignore its best asset—the ideas of bright, creative, and talented workers? Well, they wouldn't do it on purpose.

Had Europeans looked across the Atlantic earlier, the answer would have been obvious. In the late 1970s, Senator Birch Bayh realized that while investment in research and science was necessary for knowledge-based economic growth, it was not sufficient: "A wealth of scientific talent at American colleges and universities—talent responsible for the development of numerous innovative scientific break-throughs each year—is going to waste as a result of bureaucratic red tape and illogical government regulations."[1]

What Senator Bayh described is what scholars now call the *knowledge filter*.[2] It stands between investment in knowledge, science, and ideas on the one hand and commercialization, which ultimately leads to economic growth, on the other. The knowledge filter impedes and slows the spillover of knowledge and ideas, thus preventing ideas from becoming goods and services that we can buy at the store—the same goods and services that fuel economic growth. Senator Bayh found the magnitude of the knowledge filter daunting. "What sense does it make to spend billions of dollars each year on government-supported research and then prevent new developments from benefiting the American people because of dumb bureaucratic red tape?"[3] That is, the billions of dollars pouring into investments in research, science, and education did not automatically result in inventions, innovations, or new and better products, often because the same laws that funded the new knowledge prevented the knowledge from being used outside of the government.

This is just as true for Europe. According to Garching Innovation,

> Would you build a car without wheels? Presumably not. But something similar happens every day in Germany, at least when Research and Development is involved. We are investing around 17.5 billion Euros in publicly supported science and research. About half of that investment, around nine billion Euros, is in basic research, which, even though it could of course be improved, is still at the cutting edge by global standards. However, we lack the 3 to 4 percent of this

investment [that is] required to transform these investments into new and innovative products. It is as if you . . . invest[ed] a huge sum of money to develop a new automobile, but in the end realize[d] there are not sufficient funds to purchase tires.[4]

The knowledge filter impedes knowledge spillovers and commercialization based on investments in research, science, and education at universities and scientific institutions. But research at universities and other public research institutions is not the only dimension where the knowledge filter blocks investments in knowledge from becoming commercialized. The knowledge filter also exists in at least two other key dimensions. One of these is in the private sector, where the knowledge filter appears to be pervasive. Consider what happened in Heidelberg, Germany, a few years back. A group of young employees at IBM came up with an idea for business software. Their boss, however, and their boss's boss turned this idea down because they didn't think there was a market for the software. In addition, IBM was the wrong firm for this idea, because it made mainframe computers, not software. So these three young men tried to obtain funding to start their own company. They approached the three large German banks—Dresdner Bank, Deutsche Bank, and Commerzbank—but their request was again turned down. These banks thought that because IBM had already rejected the idea, it must not be a very good one. Fortunately for Germany, through a personal connection at a local bank near Heidelberg, the three eventually found funding to start SAP, which is now one of Germany's largest firms, with the equivalent of 35,873 full-time employees in 2005.[5]

It might be surprising that such a knowledge filter exists in the private sector. Why don't the great private corporations take advantage of the ideas and knowledge they have invested in creating? This doesn't sound very rational, and economists are always looking for rationality in behavior. Why would Xerox invest so many dollars in top scientists and engineers to do research on products in their laboratories that would prove crucial for the personal computer, only to decide not to use the results? If they weren't going to do something with the marvelous new technologies emerging from Xerox Park, why do it at all? After all, a large company like Xerox would not purchase a new machine and then leave it unused or trashed. Although I am sure this happens occasionally, it must be an exception and not the rule. Most of the time, companies know what the machine is for, why and how it will be used, before it makes the purchase. Otherwise, why buy it at all?

However, the situation is radically different when it comes to new ideas. New ideas suggest doing something different from before. Whether that something ultimately proves to be valuable or not is unclear. This is to say the product of working with an idea is less certain than the product of a machine.[6] Knowledge capital is inherently less certain than physical capital.

Back when I worked in the printing plant in Poughkeepsie, it was pretty obvious what a machine could and could not do. The binder could bind, the printer could print. Thus, the value of these machines, or physical capital, was more or less known, depending on market conditions, which in an established, mature industry tended to be relatively stable. Similarly, when I worked at Dunkin Donuts while in high school, it was pretty obvious what the various machines and instruments, ranging from dough-mixing machines to caskets for boiling the doughnuts—that is, the physical capital—could do. It was also pretty clear that although the building could house a broad variety of businesses or even residences, the machines and equipment limited what could and could not be made inside the doors labeled Dunkin Donuts: we were not going to be selling furniture.

Not so with ideas, or with knowledge. If a designer has an idea for a new fashion, it is not at all clear how it will be received. Once Ford had an idea for a new car, the Edsel. Obviously, company experts predicted that it would be popular, otherwise Ford would never have designed, developed, manufactured, produced, and marketed it. But Ford's experts were wrong: the public neither liked nor wanted the Edsel, and an awful lot of money invested in an idea that proved to have very little value. One might wonder "What were they paying those experts and executives for, anyway, to dream up a new model that the public didn't want?" At least when Ford purchased machinery to manufacture the Edsel, they knew what they were getting and how it could be used.

Back in 1985, Coca-Cola made the decision to alter its flagship product, making it sweeter. The New Coke flopped, and the company spent millions of dollars restoring its original brand. Most of us today would think "Whoever thought that one up must have been crazy." However, it was not just one person or a handful of people who thought

New Coke was better: the senior managers and board of directors had to approve such a significant change. It was just like the Edsel and countless other ideas that turned out to be not such a good idea after all or even a downright bad idea.

A few of us have thought "What the world needs is a better . . . X." More likely, many of us have thought "What my company needs is a better . . . X" or, even more likely, "What would be better for me is . . . X." I would guess that virtually all of us have experienced a moment when that something better turned out not to be so good after all. The point is, trying out something new involves more uncertainty than sticking with the tried and true and replicating the past. This means that working with ideas and trying something new is not only inherently more uncertain but also inherently riskier. So it has been at Ford with the Edsel, at Coca-Cola with New Coke, and at countless other companies that have pursued an idea that started out as the inspiration, dream, and vision of one or a handful of people and spread with approval and enthusiasm, until the launch of a new action or product . . . and ultimately failed.

When I was three, I, too, had a brilliant idea. Why not ride my tricycle down the stairs leading to the basement? Unfortunately, implementation of this idea ultimately required visiting the emergency room, where, thankfully, doctors made sure I lived to tell the story of my great innovation.

Who says that younger people have better ideas?

It's bad enough that economic activity based on creative ideas and knowledge is inherently less certain than simply cranking items off an assembly line, as in the capital-based managed economy. Knowledge-based economic activity is also highly asymmetric.[7] This means that what one person thinks, knows, and understands, others do not automatically understand, and to share knowledge is a difficult and challenging task, often involving a lot of effort and investment.

Various kings and queens in Europe repeatedly denied Christopher Columbus funding and royal approval for his famous voyage. Of course, the envisioned journey was uncertain: maybe the Earth really was flat. Columbus, of course, like all of the great explorers, was less risk averse, but he also knew from on-the-job experience that the expected outcome of sailing west was not as dangerous as everybody else believed. His beliefs and expectations for the voyage were shaped by asymmetric knowledge and information. To have the same optimism and certainty about the voyage's destination, European royalty would have had to share Columbus's experiences and learned what he had learned. Sharing life experiences with others is difficult and challenging, if not impossible, in many cases.

Elvis Presley shared Columbus's struggles. As a young musician, Elvis got a big break to perform at a nightclub in Nashville. While his band was rehearsing, the nightclub owner came by and asked, "What are them things there, son?" Elvis responded, "Drums, sir." To which the nightclub owner retorted, "Get ridda' 'em. We don't use drums down here in Nashville." At least one version of the story has it that the great country singer Patsy Cline, who was sweet on Elvis at the time, simply whispered in his ear, "Honey, you just keep on a-doin' what you're doin'." And he did, creating a whole new genre of music. Elvis was doing something different, based on an idea that obviously made sense to him but was less compelling to the nightclub owner. Had the owner been in Elvis's shoes, experienced everything and done everything Elvis had experienced and done, he might have been using drums as well. But the club owner hadn't, and Elvis could not easily and simply share his knowledge.

Information, on the other hand, is easily shared. If someone asks you where your city hall is, or if the library is open Tuesday night, the information might be asymmetric—you know, and they don't—but the cost of transacting, or communicating, such asymmetric information is trivial and easy. You tell them, and then they know. One of the reasons must of us gladly share such (asymmetric) information is that the cost of transacting it is trivial, easy, and negligible. It barely requires much more than a nod, a smile, and a simple pleasantry—certainly no more than a second or two.

On the other hand, communicating ideas, and why you think they might be good or bad, is usually quite the opposite of communicating information—such transactions must be burdened with explanations, context, and nuances. Why? Because we do not all know the same things, have the same set of experiences, and have the same personality that drives our instincts, intuitions, and gut feelings. Our paucity of common values does not make it any easier. Perhaps that's why all of my great ideas, like the one where my kids prepare and serve breakfast every weekend, are not automatically embraced with overwhelming enthusiasm in my own household. My campaign to change our breakfast habits has been ongoing since the mid-1990s.

One of the best examples of the ease of communicating information as opposed to the difficulties in communicating knowledge can be found in the national security agencies. After September 11, investigators discovered that the terrorists had enrolled in American flight schools and that their instructors had been concerned that the students were more focused on flying and take-offs than on landings. The information was communicated to national security officials, but the knowledge of what this meant could not be communicated: it was too difficult to transmit the knowledge, understanding, and implications of what might happen across different national security agencies, until after the shock of terrorist-flown jetliners crashing into the Twin Towers made the consequences very clear.

Thus, making a decision whether to pursue a new idea or not is anything but easy. It is especially difficult for individuals. I've had countless sleepless nights, staring at the bathroom mirror, asking myself, "Should I or shouldn't I?" I've wondered about job changes, picking an apartment, asking a girl out on a first date, and more. I doubt I am alone in my sleepless ponderings. These decisions became even more complicated once I got married, and the complexity increased once my first child was old enough to express his opinions. Group decision making is pretty complicated and rarely done quickly.

Organizations are nothing if they are not groups. Yes, they have a structure, and yes they have a chain of authority, with well-designated governance structures. But in the end, they involve groups of people, clearly not all possessing the same degree of decision-making authority, but each with different personal and professional experiences, resulting in different instincts and opinions.

We saw in chapter 3 that the modern corporation was designed to make production in the capital-based economy as productive and efficient as possible. A chain of command facilitates production on the shop floor and on the assembly line. The hierarchy and decision-making process is designed to identify and obtain information about production at the bottom of the organization, then process it upward, each layer in the hierarchy adding its own input and assessment. Once decisions were made at the top, sometimes based on information from the shop floor, they would then be sent downward through the managerial hierarchy, and ultimately implemented on the assembly line. Thus the organization was designed for production in the capital-driven economy.[8] After all, the managerial revolution was based on the emergence of the corporation as the entity to harness mass production. There has not yet been another managerial revolution.

Organizations excel at replicating the past but have a harder time dealing with change. Making decisions about new ideas based on insight, experience, creative impulse, and instinct is a major challenge when groups are involved. Perhaps the best thing going for Columbus was that once he convinced Queen Isabella to support and finance his voyage, there was no additional bureaucracy to confront. Had Columbus been required to submit his request to a typical modern bureaucracy, it seems doubtful that his trip would have been supported. Studies show that as group size increases, decisions tend toward the status quo. Ideas that do not require much change are more likely to be approved, while those proposing radical change, charting out bold new courses, are more likely to be rejected. Thus organizations, especially large ones, seem doomed to incremental change, staying close to the tried and true.

David Halberstam reports how in the U.S. automobile industry during the era of the capital-based managed economy, ideas and insights from engineers, especially young and idealistic engineers, for improving cars were largely ignored. The annual new model introductions were

> actually a kind of pseudo-change. The industry's engineers were largely idle, as their skills were ignored. Thus, during a time when the American car industry might have lengthened its technological lead on foreign competitors, it failed to do so. Instead, the industry fiddled with styling details, raising and lowering the skirts, adding and augmenting fins, changing color combinations. Fins, the most famous automotive detail of the era, represented no technological advance; they were solely a design element whose purpose was to make the cars seem sleeker, bigger, and more powerful. . . . That failure would come back to haunt the entire industry in the seventies.[9]

Thus, the American auto industry was characterized by a self-imposed knowledge filter. Innovative ideas were there, generated by the floods of talented young engineers who flocked to Detroit for their imagined dream jobs. But management rejected substantive innovations in the auto industry with alarmingly predictable consistency and regularity. Halberstam reports that "young (automobile) designers who went to work for the company in the mid-fifties . . . were stunned" by the continual rejection of ideas for substantive innovative improvements and acceptance only of the superficial and increasingly gaudy design changes.[10]

My friend Steven Klepper, a professor of economics at Pittsburgh's Carnegie Mellon University, is convinced that Henry Ford succeeded beyond everyone else's wildest imagination because of his overwhelming focus and singular tenacity toward achieving one goal—providing a standardized, mass-produced automobile that would be affordable for virtually every American household. Klepper believes that this led to Ford dismissing many good ideas and suggestions made by his own employees. If an idea or suggestion did not support Ford's vision 100 percent, he didn't want to hear it. The same single-minded drive, focus, and tenacity that generated Ford's success also contributed to creating Ford's own knowledge filter. Ultimately, Klepper concludes, this knowledge filter led to the downfall of the American automobile industry.[11]

Organizational bureaucracies in large corporations are almost guaranteed to favor the status quo over any kind of change. As William H. Whyte observed in his chapter entitled "The Fight against Genius" in *The Organization Man*, the bureaucratization of decision-making in the context of the large organization leads to, the following tendencies:

> (1) scientists would now concentrate on the practical
> application of previously discovered ideas rather than the
> discovery of new ones; (2) they would rarely work by
> themselves but rather as units of scientific cells; (3)
> organization loyalty, getting along with people, etc., would
> be considered just as important as thinking; (4) well-rounded
> team players would be more valuable than brilliant men, and
> a very brilliant man would probably be disruptive. Lastly
> and most important, these things would be so because people
> believe this is the way it should be.[12]

Why don't large organizations try and avoid this decision-making trap and reduce the number of people involved in making decisions? The problem is knowledge: if the new idea involves uncertainty, the decision-maker may lack sufficient expertise to competently make a decision. Do you consult only one doctor when confronted with a major medical decision? Probably not, no matter how much you trust your doctor. Common practice is to seek a second, if not a third, opinion. Not surprisingly, it is not uncommon for experts to disagree on how to proceed with major problems and treatments. Similarly, executives in large organizations consult others each of whom brings his or her own particular background, competence, experience, intuition, and expertise to the situation. There is safety in numbers, and safe decisions tend to emerge more often than not from large organizations.

But safe decisions are not always the best ones.

In the 1960s and 1970s, IBM had the most daunting collection of scientists and engineers that any one company had ever assembled. Scientists and engineers had graduated from the Massachusetts Institute of Technology (MIT), California Institute of Technology (Cal Tech), and other top universities. It was IBM that had broken through the computational world and introduced the mighty IBM 360 in 1964, the machine that revolutionized the world. In 1986, Bill Gates approached IBM to see if it would be interested in buying part of a struggling Microsoft. IBM was not interested and turned Gates down—a "chance to buy 10 percent of Microsoft for a song in 1986, a missed opportunity that would cost $3 billion today."[13] IBM based its decision on the grounds that "neither Gates nor any of his band of thirty some employees had anything approaching the credentials or personal characteristics required to work at IBM."[14] Even as recently as 1991, IBM believed, as was written in an executive's memo, that "the technical superiority of IBM's OS/2 and Presentation Manager over DOS and Windows 3.0 is universally unquestioned."[15]

IBM was a victim of its own knowledge filter. It would seem sensible, even today, not to give credibility to a college dropout, albeit from Harvard, and his "band" of young and unaccomplished software employees. IBM became the world's number one company, at least according to Peters and Waterman assessment in the book, *In Search of Excellence*, by hiring only the best from the best.[16] It was the uncertainty associated with an idea combined with asymmetries that led IBM to lose one of the best business opportunities of the last century because of its self-imposed knowledge filter. Gates and his "band" of thirty could see it, while thousands of the best and the brightest at IBM could not.

We already know that the knowledge filter can impede private firms from investing in ideas and knowledge, while publicly funded research also does not automatically result in new commercial products. In addition, there is another, more general, type of knowledge that is vulnerable to the knowledge filter. The previous chapters have made it clear that simply replicating the past is not an effective business strategy in the age of globalization; for people to enjoy a "livable wage" and a stable or improving standard of living, they need to be working with ideas, employing their minds, and involved in making decisions about the future. They need to be engaged in economic activities that do not yet exist and cannot be easily replicated or standardized and subsequently outsourced or offshored to a lower cost location. This puts a decided pressure on people to move away from the known toward the unknown. *Fortune Favors the Bold*, as the title of Lester Thurow's recent book declares.[17]

In fact, Western society makes massive investments to facilitate people's capacity to not just survive but actually thrive in the knowledge-based globalized economy. Western societies, including the United States, make massive investments in education, ranging from your local elementary, middle, and high schools to universities across the country. Investments in education have multiple purposes, to be sure, and I do not believe current investments are enough. In a global economy where the future is based on knowledge and ideas, increasing educational spending, investing in the capacity of people to understand and work with ideas, is at the core of the national competitive advantage. But the capabilities and competencies to compete and thrive in the globalized knowledge-based economy are not obtained just from formal education. As Richard Florida persuasively argues and documents in *The Rise of the Creative Class*, cultural creativity also plays a critical role.[18]

Society makes substantial investments in culture, however narrowly or broadly defined. Investments in culture span a broad dimension of activities and events, as they should. Richard Florida found that societal investments not only in opera houses and museums but also in sports stadiums, music arenas, city centers and waterfronts, and even television programs were important. I will admit that not all of these cultural investments appeal to me or even make sense to me, but as we have seen, private sector investments don't always make sense either, particularly in the 20–20 vision afforded by hindsight. Not all investments are understood by everyone, nor will all invest-ments be successful. However, our understanding of these investments has changed. In the capital-driven managed economy, knowledge and educational investments were considered more of a luxury afforded by economically successful societies. Although such investments were needed for political and social reasons, few thought of them as sound investments for future economic growth. In the globalized knowledge-driven economy, this changes. Knowledge, creativity, developing a finely tuned, nuanced instinct or intuition, and capacity for dealing with and even thriving on change greatly alter the economic justifica-tion for investments in knowledge, human capital, and culture.

Just as we saw with private corporations and university research, investments in education, human capital formation, and culture are not automatically transformed into new products, innovation, and economic growth. Again, the knowledge filter stands between these investments in people and their human capital. Human capital is the capacity of people to be creative and to think, dream, and develop new ideas.

One quick look at Europe, particularly northern Europe, reveals populations blessed with impressive public investments in education as well as health, social services, and culture—all of which helps improve human capital. No one can accuse Europe of ignoring or minimizing cultural investments. As the European paradox suggests, Europe has a well-educated labor force that benefits from the large cultural investments. I can testify that European society emphasizes freedom, creativity, spontaneity, originality, and autonomy, along with tolerance for others, respect for diversity, and social capital, or the capacity to interact and engage others in a meaningful way. Foreign tourists are blown away by Europe's rich cultural traditions. Europe benefits from a rich heritage based on the intellectual and cultural traditions of the Enlightenment. Europe seems to have it all.[19]

So why the European Paradox? All of these investments and assets, along with Europe's rich cultural and intellectual heritage, which are the envy of the rest of the world, still do not seem to generate economic growth. One hypothesis or interpretation is that despite modern economic growth theory, knowledge and ideas are not that important for creating jobs and growth. An alternative hypothesis is that Europe suffers from the same impediment as Ford and IBM: the knowledge filter. Public investments in knowledge and culture are not automatically translated into what society wants and needs; the filter hinders the harvesting of the results. The future bountiful standard of living, job creation, and economic growth remains stuck on the wrong side of the filter.

There are no shortages of factors contributing to the creation of the knowledge filter. Some are legal; others are institutional; others are rooted in culture, tradition, and history. As one of my kids says, "I'm just the way I am." Still, countries like Germany are increasingly concerned with their inability to turn their large biological, chemical, and health science investments into a viable and thriving life science and biotechnology industry. One simple explanation is obvious: a nervous Germany has meticulously legislated and restricted what can and cannot be done in terms of genetic experiments and testing. After all, the virtually unlimited freedom to impose such testing on human subjects in the Nazi regime is not only part of the national shame but contributed to the death of millions. Germany, for understandable and justifiable reasons, has not been in a hurry to allow genetic testing and experiments to form the basis of its life science and biotechnology industry. Thus, in order to meet a social and political objective, a legal and institutional knowledge filter has been imposed. A cultural and social knowledge filter has also been in place, reflecting the societal concerns about genetic testing and experiments.

A very different and certainly much less technology-oriented knowledge filter was visible during my years living in Berlin in the 1980s and 1990s. At that time, when I was especially exhausted from family life with young children, I yearned for home-delivered pizza, a yearning shared by many Americans living in Germany. I am equally sure that many pizzerias wanted to deliver their pies to willing consumers; it must have occurred to more than one that there was money to be made in offering such a service. However, at that time, the laws prohibited delivery services, at least from restaurants. America's Domino's Pizza rose in the 1980s, filling a previously unknown need for home- and office-delivered pizza. However, the laws preventing one company from getting an unfair advantage prevented Germans from having pizza delivered in 30 minutes, or even an hour. The desire to prevent unfair competition was also behind the weekend laws, mentioned earlier, that required all stores to be closed by certain times and on certain days and ensured that store employees could spend the evenings and weekends with their families, and the firms would not face competition from those with less respect for traditional and historic norms. Although these are not profound examples of the knowledge filter, they are typical of the myriad minor impediments to acting on a new idea. Thankfully, these rules have been changed—and pizza can now be at your doorstep in minutes, at least in Berlin, as throughout most of Germany. Knowledge filters permeate and affect all spheres of life, not just pizza. Rampant in our day-to-day mundane transactions and impediments, filters are often hard to distinguish and understand. Burdened with centuries of knowledge filters, Europe manages to choke off its investments in creative, knowledgeable, and skilled people before getting out of the starting gate, thus stifling much needed innovation, economic growth, and job creation.

Of course, Europe isn't the only place with a knowledge filter. America has strict restrictions involving stem cell research. While there may be perfectly valid social or political reasons for such restrictions, it should be clearly and widely recognized that such restrictions are, in fact, a knowledge filter that renders science and research investments less effective at contributing to economic growth and jobs. The public and policy-makers decide whether such knowledge filters are worth living with. There is clearly a trade-off between the dismantling and reducing the knowledge filter and other conflicting social and political values. It's important to remember that some knowledge filters are not bad or undesirable. There may be important and valuable social and political reasons contributing to a knowledge filter. However, I believe it is important to recognize what the cost of that knowledge filter is to society when these decisions are made.

Another U.S. example involves the increased barriers and difficulties set up after September 11, 2001, that prevent foreign scientists, engineers, researchers, and students who want to enter to the United States to study and work. Similarly, it became more difficult for companies to get the necessary approval to buy and sell some products abroad. This hinders the ability of American companies to innovate and grow. Thus, homeland security imposed a large knowledge filter preventing the growth of our economy and creation of new jobs. This is not to say that homeland security is a vacuous goal; but it does come at the cost of a more imposing knowledge filter, which impedes economic growth, job creation, and reduces the standard of living.

One of the founders of Sun Microsystems, Andy Bechtolsheim, found his ideas, dreams, and visions blocked by Germany's knowledge filter. He was unable to find the money and right employees for his envisioned computer company. Fortunately for the world, he managed to secure funding for his idea. Unfortunately for Europe, he found it in California. This is a common story, with two variants. Either people with ideas, dreams, and visions give up when they run into knowledge filter walls—or they overcome and succeed. Success doesn't always come at the hands of the original innovator; sometimes somebody else, often in a different context—whether a different company, region, or even country—hits on the same idea. In such a case, the world doesn't suffer so much, but the organization making the original investments that enabled the person to create the new idea does, and that organization could be a firm, a city, a state, or a country.

It is the same with knowledge and ideas. It is not just that the ideas, dreams, and visions may be lost by society forever, but that in a world of global competition for knowledge, ideas, and ultimately innovation, ideas are likely to surface and be tried somewhere else. This is clearly a concern in Indiana, and throughout the American Midwest. Indiana, like other midwestern states, makes large investments not just in universities and research institutions but also in culture and education. It is also home to many great corporations that have armies of capable employees. Like many midwestern states, Indiana does not want to squander its investment in knowledge and people, yet the state suffers from brain drain. Many of the best and brightest simply say thanks for the state-supported education and then pack up and move, often to one of the coasts. Over the years I have repeatedly heard and read in newspapers various proposals to reduce investments in knowledge: schools, research institutions, cultural facilities, and universities have all faced the knife. After all, if the rewards of investments cannot be reaped, shouldn't they be reduced or reallocated toward areas with greater returns? Alternatively, some have suggested, presumably tongue-in-cheek, that the state needs to erect a wall keeping recipients of these investments from moving.

It's already been tried. After signing the Potsdam Treaty following the capitulation of the Nazis at the close of World War II, the western

Allies were granted a portion of divided Berlin, deep in the heart of eastern Germany, which was to be controlled by the Soviet Union. In the Soviet parts of Berlin, communism was imposed. The Soviets felt that people should earn according to their needs, not according to their abilities. Thus wages were virtually identical for all workers in East Germany, regardless of their training or education. This meant that doctors or engineers earned the same as street sweepers and factory workers. But in the 1950s, doctors, engineers, and other skilled workers in East Berlin avoided the Soviet pay scales easily by walking, taking buses, and riding subways into West Berlin and working for private companies instead of state-owned East German ones. Communist leaders and officials were outraged: how dare these East German comrades, who had not protested when they were the recipients of state-financed education and training, not to mention access to universally low-cost housing, food, and beer, simply cross over to West Berlin to enjoy better wages!

This betrayal deprived their East German comrades from benefiting from their government's investment in their training and education. In August 1961, with assistance from the Soviet Union, East Germany hit upon a solution: to erect the "Anti-Fascist Protection Barrier"—what became known as the Berlin Wall. It was one way to ensure that the government's investments made at home stayed at home. Among other things, the Berlin Wall was a grotesque knowledge filter, hindering the knowledge, ideas, creativity, dreams, and aspirations of East Germans from being pursued and realized in West Berlin. Given the results of that Wall, it doesn't seem like a viable option again for the future.

Society wants a return on its investments and inheritance in knowledge. This is true in Indiana, throughout the Midwest, in the entire United States, and in all countries. But the knowledge filter hinders existing firms from using investments in knowledge and ideas in the market. In cities, regions, and countries, taxpayers are growing impatient with stagnant economic growth. They make substantial investments in the creation of knowledge societies, or what Richard Florida terms the *creative class;* but in the presence of an imposing knowledge filter, sometimes knowledge and creativity are not enough. Thus, in our globalized economy, the returns from knowledge investments in terms of jobs and growth have continued to be elusive. Society is not satisfied with wonderful and inspiring investments in knowledge and culture; it demands a return, especially in terms of jobs and economic growth.

Instead, as the student protests in France during the spring of 2006 demonstrated, fear pervades—fear that the future will be worse than the past. Given France's investment in the current generation's education and culture, it is somewhat ironic. What do they want?

What they want, and need, just as the East Berlin skilled workers wanted and needed decades earlier, is to penetrate the knowledge filter. The missing link that can penetrate the knowledge filter, thus spurring economic growth and creating the much-desired jobs, is the topic of the next chapter.

7

The Road Less Traveled

Chapter 6 explained how economic activity based on ideas, creativity, and knowledge is radically different from that of the factory- and machine-based economy. Although people can agree on what any particular machine, assembly line, and factory can do, consensus is rare when it comes to new ideas. Different people evaluate ideas differently. Try this at home: suggest a new idea to your family and see what the reaction is. In my experience, one is greeted by a diversity of reactions. What your son or daughter thinks is a great idea your partner will think is a dud.

It is the same at the office. When one worker has a better idea how to do something, he cannot just do it. Rather, he needs approval from his boss and his boss's boss. He may also want compensation in some small way, if he believes his idea will significantly improve the organization. However, just like at home, his boss and his boss's boss may be less excited. The idea is more likely to be rejected as more people and committees are needed to approve implementation. As I pointed out in chapter 6, group decisions push toward incremental change, usually avoiding the bold and radical.

It is ironic that our traditional values inherited from the managed economy often lead to people losing their jobs. Making waves with new ideas, insights, and recommendations, once avoided by past generations, keeps the company fresh and innovative, thus ensuring future employment. Not saying anything is conducive to the stagnation that in a globalized economy leads to job loss when the company relocates or goes bankrupt. The forces of a globalized economy dictate that in high-cost locations, like North America and Europe, engaging in routinized work activities and in offices, the standardized and repetitive work found on assembly lines and in offices, is likely to prove fatal. However, it is not the corporation that dies: it is the worker who loses her job and the community that loses its tax base. In the era of the globalized economy, when corporations outsource and offshore work in order to remain competitive, the company that fails to keep up with the global pack has a limited life expectancy.

Workers must engage in work that is new and different, work that cannot be done on a distant assembly line, in order to improve job prospects and wages. Corporate organizations regularly outsource and offshore work that can be standardized and routinized, meaning that employees at home are likely to be out of a job. Thus, when it comes to ideas, insights, dreams, and suggestions—just do it. Or perhaps, more accurately, just do it, and improve on it. This is why athletes prefer playing on a losing team to warming the bench with a winning team. Although everyone prefers winning to losing, it is better to improve your skills by playing the game and losing than sitting around doing nothing.

But what happens when a worker wants to do something different, something she perceives to be an improvement, and her firm or organization turns her ideas down? Confronted with rejection of her idea, what will a worker do? In most cases, workers do nothing. They lick their wounds, recover from the blow to their egos, nurse their bruised self-esteem, and then forget that they ever suggested anything. They go back to work doing whatever they were doing before.

But not always. Sometimes they will choose the road less traveled. Some years ago, Robert Noyce had an idea. He was working at Fairchild Semiconductor, a pioneering semiconductor firm based in California. His idea was not about a way to improve the product but about how the people working at Fairchild should be treated— organization and management. In particular, Noyce thought that if the pay of Fairchild workers was tied to the company's performance, they would feel more connected to the company and would behave differently. Among other things, he proposed offering stock options to all employees of the company. But Noyce ran into a knowledge filter—the owners of the firm, Fairchild Camera and Instrument, back in Syosset, New York, did not think this was a good idea.

> Noyce couldn't get Fairchild's eastern owners to accept the idea that stock options should be part of compensation for all employees, not just for management. He wanted to tie everyone, from janitors to bosses, into the overall success of the company, . . . This management style still sets the standard for every computer, software, and semiconductor company in the Valley today, . . . Every CEO still wants to think that the place is being run the way Bob Noyce would have run it.[1]

Noyce's idea, his vision, of a firm was to forgo the dress codes, reserved parking places, closed offices, executive dining rooms and other trappings of status that were standard in most traditional American corporations. After he tried to persuade the owners and was flatly rejected, rather than take the rejection and get back to work, Noyce teamed up with Gordon Moore and started Intel.

Or consider Ted Hoff's idea. Hoff, working at IBM in the 1960s, realized that it would be possible to manufacture a microprocessor. A microprocessor has been described as a computer on a chip, in that it has a central processing unit (CPU), is programmable, and can readily be connected to memory chips and input-output devices. Excited, Hoff shared his idea with his employer. At the time IBM ruled the Earth much as *Tyrannosaurus rex* once had, but with mainframe computers instead of sharp teeth and claws. IBM rejected Hoff's proposal because they did not think it had a viable future. The most important company on Earth knew that the future was about large mainframe computers, not the silly microprocessor dreamed up by Hoff.

Licking his wounds from being rejected by his own employer, Hoff took his idea to Digital Electronic Computing (DEC), the other major computer company at the time. He was shown the door with the same answer. "IBM and DEC decided there was no market. They could not imagine why anyone would need or want a small computer; if people wanted to use a computer, they could hook into a time-sharing system."[2] Hoff had run into two knowledge filters at two different companies. Fortunately, Hoff was not deterred by IBM and DEC's assessment. He went to work with the then newly formed Intel and contributed his knowledge, thus helping make Intel the world's leading producer of computer chips.

Steven Jobs is also no stranger to the knowledge filter. When he and his partner Steve Wozniak thought that mass-producing personal computers might be a good idea, Jobs approached seventeen of the leading computer and technology companies, including IBM, Hewlett Packard, and Xerox.[3] All seventeen turned him down, asserting that the world was not interested in personal computers. Existing mainframe computers would provide all the needed computing power. The fundamental conditions inherent in the uncertainty of knowledge and ideas were clearly at play, resulting in a formidable knowledge filter blocking the personal computer. IBM, with all its army of the world's leading scientists and engineers, was proven to be wrong.

College dropout Steve Jobs was able to see something that IBM and other great computer companies did not. Jobs's life experiences, starting with dropping out of Reed College, journeying across India meditating, and ultimately joining the incipient hacker computer community in the San Francisco Bay Area gave him experience, knowledge, and context that was invisible to IBM's expert management team, which consisted of upper-middle-class East Coasters with lifetimes of experience in the industry.

How could college dropouts in their garage beat the army of IBM scientists and engineers with a decades-long track record of savvy business decisions and success? That's the trick about working with ideas: it isn't just knowing how to make something, it's understanding where the world is going next. It's about the basic conditions that make economic activity based on ideas and knowledge radically different from that based on factories and machines—uncertainty and asymmetries. Nobody, including Jobs, knew how well the personal computer would do. It wasn't even clear that the public wanted to bring one home, so this was the uncertainty. However, based on his life experiences, Jobs felt that it had potential. IBM executives disagreed.

For these corporate executives to really understand what Jobs thought and felt and why he was so passionate about his vision, they would have to have been in his shoes. But coming from middle- and upper-middle-class communities, with engineering degrees from America's top universities, they were a far cry from being able to understand, let alone even fathom, what this young, bearded college dropout was so passionate about. That's asymmetry.

IBM wasn't the only victim of the knowledge filter. As already noted, sixteen other computer and technology companies didn't want to be the world's first mass producer of personal computers—including Xerox. Xerox was founded by Chester Carlsson after Kodak rejected his idea to produce and sell a copy machine—a completely new concept. Kodak felt that a copy machine would not earn very much money because few, if any, people needed documents copied by a machine. In addition, Kodak executives knew they were in the photography business, not the photo-copying business. Thus, it was perhaps no small irony that Xerox rejected Jobs's proposal to produce and market a personal computer because few, if any people would purchase a personal computer, plus they were in the copying business, not the personal computer business.[4]

A more contemporary example involves Jack Harding, who as president and CEO of Silicon Valley's Cadence Design Systems in the 1990s, then the world's largest supplier of electronic design products and services, including semiconductors, realized that his business was facing a limited future because of how the market was changing. Faced with a board of directors rejecting his proposed changes, Harding opted to start a new firm, eSilicon. By 2005, five years after founding, eSilicon had Kodak and Microsoft as clients, had turned a profit, and ranked as one of the fastest growing U.S. corporations. Noyce and Hoff's Intel, Jobs's Apple, and Harding's eSilicon are prime examples of how one person can penetrate the knowledge filter by becoming an entrepreneur and starting their own company.

Intel, Apple, and eSilicon are much like SAP, the business software company discussed in chapter 6. All of these companies have pene-trated the knowledge filter—all via entrepreneurship. Today these firms employ thousands of the world's brightest and most creative people, fueling economic growth and employment. Thus, *entrepreneur-ship* is the missing link generating growth and jobs. If existing corpora-tions cannot or will not supply desperately needed jobs, little is accomplished by trying to appeal to these corporations' hearts and souls, pleading for help on the basis of social responsibility to the home community. Companies find themselves locked in the midst of a global race for competitiveness and are focused on accessing cost-effective workers, regardless of where they are located.

Europe's highly creative, innovative, and talented workers are not being hired for the same reason America's creative, innovative, and talented workers are not being hired. In the globally competitive world, European companies look elsewhere for low-cost employees, and no amount of pleading on the basis of social responsibility will change this. So if the great European companies cannot supply the jobs that set the talents of Europeans free, entrepreneurship is the missing link that sets people free, generating jobs and economic growth that would have otherwise been lost.

Why is entrepreneurship needed to set the talents and aspirations of people free? Aren't the existing corporations, including some that have demonstrated breathtaking success, such as Google, Microsoft, and Intel, sufficient? After all, they have a proven track record. As chapter 6 explained, the problem is the knowledge filter. It seems that wherever there are ideas in play, there is a filter. It may even be that the more important a role new ideas play, the larger will be the filter within an organization. After all, no single firm, or organization, can do everything.

This explains why IBM is involved in so many examples of a knowledge filter blocking new ideas. It is not a coincidence. By the 1960s, IBM had amassed the largest army of awesome scientific and engineering minds ever assembled in one place. IBM designed and produced the IBM 360, an amazing mainframe computer that revolutionized the way businesses, governments, and other organizations used information. When I started high school, I learned math using an abacus—admittedly, for historical and demonstration purposes. In 1972, when I started college, we used an IBM mainframe computer for computations. It is no secret that the Japanese admired and respected IBM beyond all other corporations and emulated it to develop their economy. In their bestselling book of the early 1980s, *In Search of Excellence*, Tom Peters and Robert H. Waterman Jr. identified the top fifty American corporations on the basis of past performance and future promise,[5] and IBM ranked above all others. It was the best of the best.

With the luxury of hindsight, is it apparent why IBM suffered from such an imposing knowledge filter? One answer: because of its very success. Having amassed such an impressive army of scientists and engineers, made enormous investments in research, and set the world standard for computational technology, IBM was generating many ideas involving many different people. Many of the ideas that were generated there were a direct result of internal research, as was the case with Ted Hoff and his microprocessor. Other ideas were generated externally but found their way to IBM's doorstep, like Steven Jobs's personal computer. IBM also had the opportunity to own Microsoft. IBM had the microprocessor, the personal computer, and the Windows operating system within its grasp—technological developments more valuable than the mainframe computer—but *IBM let the ball drop*. IBM let these ideas crash helplessly into its own knowledge filter.

Remember that IBM was bombarded with a myriad of ideas, proposals, ventures, schemes, and visions every day. Which were credible? Which visions should they invest in? If the question were about purchasing a new machine or building a new factory, the answer might have been easier, more straightforward. But it wasn't about purchasing physical capital; it was about making a decision to act on knowledge and ideas, which ultimately means dealing with greater uncertainty and asymmetry. IBM's massive investments in knowledge, research, and science drawing on the passions, experience, and talents of smart, educated, and ambitious people generated a plethora of new ideas and insights. Even the best managed company will find it difficult to separate all the wheat from the chaff, to identify all the good ideas and separate them from the rest accurately. As the country singer, Kenny Rogers sings in "The Gambler," "You got to know when to hold 'em, / know when to fold 'em." It's not easy in poker, which involves calculable risks. The world of ideas, which is fundamentally uncertain and asymmetric, is far more challenging. Thus a knowledge filter is inevitable.

IBM didn't do itself any favors or put itself in a position to win in an economy where moving boldly in new directions pays and sticking with the status quo does not. IBM was positioned to win in the managed economy, where its production of mainframe computers situated it to dominate. The world changed while IBM wasn't looking, and new possibilities opened up. It is ironic that many of the ideas and ultimately new technologies that generated these new possibilities and directions emanated from IBM's own investments in research and development. The company was a victim of its own knowledge filter. Knowledge filters are not unique to IBM. Virtually every company suffers from one. What was unusual about IBM was that due to the magnitude of its knowledge investments, the ideas repelled by its knowledge filters had a significantly greater value compared to those of most other companies.

By putting itself in a position to win in the managed economy, IBM doomed itself to stumble in the globalized entrepreneurial society. IBM was a prototype company of those Whyte described in *The Organization Man*. Loyalty, teamwork, and fitting in were the highest priorities. Until its crisis of the late 1980s, IBM stuck rigidly to a personnel and human resource policy that doggedly reinforced conformity and homogeneity. My father was a research engineer with IBM. He contributed to the development of the IBM 360. His IBM, during the managed economy, was filled with white, middle-class men who dressed, looked, and acted remarkably like him. In striving for a human resource policy of hiring the best of the best, IBM hired from a narrow set of universities. Such strategies and policies created an organization where people didn't just dress and live the same way, they thought the same way. IBM's motto, "THINK," implored its employees not just to think but to think the IBM way. The strategy excelled: IBM produced and sold the world's best mainframe computer. However, IBM's homogeneity was its knowledge filter. Only after it had missed several major computing innovations—including those already mentioned—did the company's leadership realize that it had a structural problem. It recognized that it was suffering from its own knowledge filter and was missing out on the benefit of its investments, which had spawned entire industries that IBM now viewed from the sidelines. IBM often remained a distant observer of the results of its innovations and investments. For example, the disk drive industry, generated from IBM knowledge, is a prime example of how the company missed the boat. Former IBM employees who saw the opportunity to manufacture disk drives had to leave the firm to do so, keeping not only the knowledge IBM had invested in but also the resulting profits.

Trying to recover from its missed opportunities, IBM committed to developing the personal computer. However, IBM's executives recognized that its knowledge filter was so impermeable that the executives, scientists, and engineers working in IBM's traditional stronghold, the mainframe computer, were choking off the new product. Thus, when the company's leadership realized that it had to catch up in the personal computer market, they chose to do so in Boca Raton, Florida, far away from corporate headquarters in White Plains, New York.

Both Steven Klepper and Rajshree Agarwal have documented how spinoffs help bring ideas that have been rejected by parent firms to the market—something that doesn't just happen in one or two industries but in industry after industry. Klepper's research underscores workers' frustration when their best ideas and proposals slam into a knowledge filter. Agarwal notes that many of America's most important companies and industries were started when frustrated workers pursued their ideas and started their own firms. Thus, while IBM may be the most prominent example of a large, successful firm victimized by its own knowledge filter, my point here is that all such companies serve as incubators for new firms and industries. As long as there is entrepreneurship, there is a link into the future.

It is not just in the context of the private sector where entrepreneurship can serve as the missing link to innovation and economic growth. Entrepreneurship provides the missing link to innovation and growth in virtually every context where people have ideas and where the startup of a new firm is not blocked or impeded. For example, American universities are hotbeds for generating new knowledge and ideas. If factories generated the manufacturing goods in the capital-driven managed economy, universities and research institutions are the idea factories in today's knowledge-based economy. Society's massive investments in university research and education are not automatically transformed into new products, innovations that lead to growth and jobs; again, a formidable knowledge filter must be overcome. Much research is so technical and advanced that it takes more than just a Ph.D. in the basic scientific discipline to understand the ideas; it takes incredible specialization within a narrow specific area even to begin to comprehend what the science and possibilities might be. It may also require a keen sense of market possibilities as well. Thus, the knowledge and ideas that emanate from university research are obscured by the fundamental conditions, already mentioned, that render knowledge capital distinct from physical capital: high uncertainty and asymmetry. Thus, no existing firm may be suited to understand, implement, and commercialize new knowledge generated by university research. After all, if a company like IBM couldn't recognize the value of its own ideas, it should be no surprise that it would have more trouble recognizing the value of new ideas from outside the firm. More than one great firm has suffered from the "not invented here" syndrome: if the idea didn't come from the firm, it must not be a good idea and therefore not be worth pursuing.

For all of Intel and IBM's technological prowess and success, they did not develop a successful internet search engine. The point is that these technological and business powerhouses never really tried; they were too busy paying attention to their core products to be distracted by the untried idea of a new search algorithm that was floating around a university campus. The idea, developed by a couple of college kids working with their professors at Stanford, became Google. Even before the search engine started working, the media was peppered with reports and prognoses of the inherent flaw in the startup's business plan: the basic service—providing free and unrestricted access to the search engine—did not seem to have a viable revenue source.

With 20–20 hindsight, we know their revenue source was ingenious and profitable, creating a whole new way to advertise on the internet. The millions of dollars Google generated benefited not just its founders but also Stanford University. Google is not an isolated example. The most brilliant success story in the biotechnology industry, Genetech, was a spinoff not from private firms but from the University of California at San Diego.

The investments made by society in ideas and knowledge extend way beyond those made by firms and universities. Ideas are generated every day by all kinds of people with all kinds of backgrounds, reflecting a vast array of experiences. Society makes vast investments in education, providing a safe environment, as well as a broad spectrum of cultural and social experiences.

Ben and Jerry's start was not so different. Their recipe for ice cream certainly was not innovative or high-tech—it was obtained from the extension service of The Pennsylvania State University. They were two starving hippie dropouts from New York City trying to scratch out a living in bucolic Vermont. Starting an ice cream business reflected an instinct and willingness to try something new and different and did not require science, research, or high-technology investments.

Entrepreneurship connects a vision held today with the future. It is the common denominator among all entrepreneurs. Entrepreneurship is the activity required to implement and attempt to realize a vision, thereby altering the future. If there is no vision, there is no entrepreneurship. If there is a vision but no action or activity, there is also no entrepreneurship. But what if there is first a vision followed by action for change within an existing firm or organization? Is that not entrepreneurship? This is a question that has plagued entrepreneurship scholars.[6] Some scholars have chosen to use the terms *intrapreneurship* or *corporate entrepreneurship* for change, or innovation, that is implemented by an existing organization. At any rate, there is one thing, for sure, that, whatever you call it, is important and holds the key to our future, and that, of course, is innovation.

If all of the existing organizations could effectively move us into the future, there would be no particularly interesting or important role for entrepreneurship—at least the version that is restricted to the creation of a new organization. That would mean that sufficient innovation was being generated by existing organizations. If there was a deficiency of new, viable ideas, the problem would be in terms of people. But there is no deficiency of people with interesting and creative ideas.

The problem is not with individuals' education, experience, or creativity, but with the fact that knowledge filters inhibit individuals from reaching their maximum potential. People have ideas, aspirations, insights, and visions about how to do things differently or better, ways to improve our future and allow countries, states, cities, towns, and even neighborhoods to compete globally. Unfortunately, just doing it, putting the idea into action, all too often gets hung up in knowledge filters.

What's a person to do? Consider John Burton Carpenter, a man with a vision. One day, while he was living in New York City and working as an investment banker, it snowed. Snow in New York City is different from anywhere else, as it transforms the world's grandest city into a winter dreamland. Carpenter, who now goes by the name Burton, had recently stopped skiing and started experimenting with using one board to go down the mountain instead of a pair of skis. That day, he said, "as I saw the fresh snow flakes on that day in Manhattan, I had only one choice—to quit my job as investment banker."[7]

Burton started experimenting with snowboards during an era when there were no snowboards. Skiers in the 1960s and 1970s saw only a reflection of themselves. The idea of hurling down a ski slope on a board was unthinkable: Ski slopes were, after all, named ski slopes. He may have had a dream that snowy day in Manhattan, but it was sketchy. He knew that he loved snow. He also loved what we now call snowboarding.

Why didn't the giants of the winter sports industry who produce skis simply see the opportunity in the incipient snowboard market and start production themselves? To quote William Shakespeare, "the fault, my dear Brutus, lies not in our stars, but in ourselves." Burton tried, but ski companies simply weren't interested in producing boards for sliding down the mountain. It was the knowledge filter that effectively impeded the transfer of knowledge—the idea that snowboards were wanted by consumers.

So Burton moved to Londonderry, Vermont, and started Burton Boards, manufacturing the snowboards himself. In hindsight, now that snowboarding is a multimillion-dollar global business and an Olympic sport, Burton confesses, "I had not the least idea. Even my wildest dreams were far away from what snowboarding has become."[8]

Burton believed that people would find snowboarding fun, and that they might want to buy their own snowboards. His shop was in the garage. His living room was the showroom. In fact, Burton points out that his vision was a little overoptimistic in the beginning. "I had inherited a little money from my mother and had been experimenting with building snowboards. . . . Unfortunately, [I was] a little too optimistic. According to my calculations, my three employees and I could build 500 boards. We sold only 300 boards in the first season, and so I was suddenly $100,000 in debt."[9]

Like Burton, his coworkers were experimenting with building a snowboard and were as possessed as he was. To try to make ends meet and keep his struggling business alive, Burton worked two jobs the summer of 1978: as a waiter and tennis instructor.

In fact, skiers did not automatically embrace Burton's new snowboard. He traveled from resort to resort, showing winter enthusiasts the wonder of snowboarding and selling only seven hundred in the second year. After that, as Burton points out, "the market took off." And the rest is history. Burton created not only an Olympic sport, a successful product, and a firm but also an entire industry, creating thousands of jobs. Even as globalization has resulted in a massive loss of jobs in industries previously thought to be the heart and soul of America, entrepreneurs like Burton have helped lead the country into a future that is different, and unanticipated, but promising.

Although Burton's ideas did not come from formalized research, science, or technology, Burton is a product of America, its education system, its universities, and its culture. He was shaped by the swirl of events, interactions, and experiences around him. It might not be correct to assert that America created Burton, but it is surely correct to assert that Burton found his path in America. And what did he give back to America? He gave back the thing that all developed countries and communities so desperately desire: jobs and a way into the future. Although it was in a way that no one had anticipated—manufacturing and selling snowboards—it is hard to argue with the results. Finding surprising paths to economic growth and job creation is the nature of entrepreneurship and what entrepreneurs give back to society.

Other intriguing examples of nontechnological entrepreneurship abound. Consider the case of Yngve Bergqvist, a young Swede who loved nature and the outdoors, who found himself leading adventure tours in the Swiss Alps, taking people hiking, climbing, riding, and whitewater rafting. In 2001, I heard him explain how this led him to believe that there was a demand for authentic natural experiences. Authenticity seems to be the opposite side of the globalization coin. As the world becomes more globalized and integrated, the harder it is to find authentic experiences, and the more people yearn for such authenticity. Coming from Sweden, he had the idea of building a hotel out of blocks of snow and ice that would be located far in the north of Sweden, not far from the Arctic Circle. Guests would have the opportunity to enjoy an authentic Nordic experience, spending the night wrapped in reindeer blankets and hunkered down in the ice hotel. When Bergqvist approached some of the large hotel chains about undertaking such a venture, his idea was rejected and he was told: "people don't want to rough it in the frozen Swedish tundra, freezing on the ground. They want the comfort and amenities of a Hilton or Marriott." But Bergqvist's experiences leading whitewater rafting and climbing tours made him think differently. It was true that an ice hotel was not for everybody, or even for most people. But Bergqvist had seen with his own two eyes that there were enough people who would be eager and willing to pay for such an authentic natural experience. The percentage of interested people might be pretty small, but after all, the world's population is so large that it wouldn't take a very high percentage to make the ice hotel a resounding success. So, after accumulating a number of rejections, he just built it himself.

Upon hearing him recount his story in May 2001, I rushed up afterward to the stage and told him I really could imagine my wife would enjoy such an adventure but I feared that it might be beyond the means of a college professor. He said no, actually, the nightly rates were quite reasonable. I was so excited that I wanted to change our travel plans immediately to include a night in his ice hotel. He looked at me like I was crazy. "But it's melted!" It melts each spring, and a new hotel is built each winter. That's an entrepreneur!

Innovation is the key to moving proactively into the future rather than allowing a globalized economy to victimize us. We know now that a secure future needs something new, different, and better, at least as defined by the (global) market. Sticking to the same old same old may be known and comfortable, but, thanks to globalization, it is also increasingly known and comfortable in other, less expensive, parts of the world. If the same old same old can be done in Mexico or South America, not to mention Romania or Poland, or China and India, it will continue to be done, just not in the same old place. Innovation is a way of taking advantage of globalization's opportunities rather than being victimized by its liabilities, and entrepreneurship is a key way to innovate.

Entrepreneurship is about two things. First, it is about starting a new activity, organization, or firm. If you can't pursue your ideas, your dreams, your insights within an existing organization, it's about moving someplace where you can. Use it or lose it. Second, it is about moving into the future. Lots of people have ideas about how to do something differently, a way to make something, however big or small, look different from today. However, it is not enough to just have a vision. As the German writer Johann Wolfgang von Goethe observed some two centuries ago, "Es ist nicht genug zu wissen, man muss es auch anwenden; es ist nicht genug zu wollen, man muss es auch tun." (Knowledge alone does not suffice, it must also be applied: wanting is not enough, one has to actually do it.)

8

Not Your Father's University

In the 1900s, a wall divided universities from the community. The ivory tower might have been invisible, but it was keenly felt by those on each side. Professors and students were proudly and happily cut off, isolated from society behind university gates. Those on the outside peered from a distance—often with disdain, if not hostility—at this ivory tower.

Consider *Breaking Away*, a 1979 movie that portrayed the gap between town and gown in Bloomington, Indiana. A group of freshly minted high school graduates struggled with their status as *cutters*—a derogatory term referring to their fathers' work cutting limestone from local quarries. Ironically, while the elite university students bestowed the second-class status of the fathers on their offspring, the very limestone the fathers cut built Indiana University, providing the students' classrooms, libraries and dormitories.

The movie won wide acclaim for depicting the tension between the young cutters and the elite college students. Although the university is in the same small, quaint Midwest town, it appears foreign, distant, and unattainable to the cutters. When one of the cutters begins a quiet romance with a college coed, the story takes on elements of *Romeo and Juliet*, with all of the tensions, rivalries, and fighting that exists between two distinct, rivaling and incompatible social groups. To obscure his unacceptable identity as a cutter, the hero pretends to be an exchange student from Italy. While *Romeo and Juliet* ends in death and tragedy,

Breaking Away concludes with mutual respect and acceptance on the part of both the cutters and the university students after the cutters win an unexpected victory in a dramatic bicycle race.

Both sides, one proudly and the other disdainfully, considered life outside the ivory tower to be the *real world*. For centuries, academics have considered the real world irrelevant, and businessmen have felt that there wasn't any serious or practical use for the ivory tower. The university was seen as providing a respite from the drudgery that took place outside its hallowed halls. If America's business was the business of doing business, there certainly didn't seem to be any serious business to be had within the hallowed gates of the university.

The view of the university as a refuge from the real world, albeit good-natured and innocent, is portrayed in the 1960 movie *High Time*. The actor Bing Crosby plays the character of an older returning college student studying at a university populated with the fun-loving, antic-seeking youth of postwar America. The university experience celebrated social rites and traditions like fish swallowing, coed serenading, and stuffing as many undergraduates as possible into telephone booths. Campus bonfires resembled church services. It was a charming but striking contrast to the real world of business, a respite from being too serious and focused. Professors were affable, incapable, and harmless, surviving in what appeared to be the sole sanctuary for the socially inept. The generations of students passing through the university's halls had a good-natured, if not condescending, affection for their professors, whose odd ramblings and eccentricities were part of the college experience.

However, to say that the university served as a haven from the real world after World War II is not to say that it didn't make a serious contribution to society. The opposite was true, in fact. The university made significant contributions to not just the most fundamental social and political values of America but also Western civilization. American universities had evolved from being extensions of religious institutions to being proud and independent institutions of higher learning by the twentieth century. The earliest colleges founded in America, Harvard being typical, had explicit ties to the church. The church played an instrumental role in establishing and financing higher education in America in its infancy. Such a connection, or even sponsorship of universities, between the church and the state was not at all unusual.

This had been established as the normal pattern for higher education in Europe.

This traditional connection between the church and the university was broken by Alexander Humboldt, a giant of a scholar and statesman during the early 1800s in Berlin. He shaped a new tradition for universities, with freedom of thought, learning, intellectual exchange, research, and scholarship as the cornerstone of the university. As the Humboldt tradition spread throughout Europe and later the United States, it had a profound impact. Universities broke free from parochial chains, becoming nonsecular, committed to fierce independent thinking, learning, scholarship, and research. Such independent thought and inquiry is valued deeply as the heart of America and Western civilization. Thus, throughout Europe and the United States, universities have emerged as an institution essential to the values needed for a free and democratic society. The university was the place where the young learned to think freely and independently, and were instilled with the values that underlie Western civilization and prepared them to carry them on.

However, people did not think that the universities contributed to the economy in a meaningful way. The university's role was to create well-rounded, reflective, and thoughtful citizens, equipped with the requisite appreciation of Western civilization and learning as well as respect for independence of thinking and inquiry, thus ensuring the basis of a democratic society. The Western, Humboldt-style university was obviously at odds with a totalitarian society. During communist and totalitarian revolutions, the first target, after the political elite, was the university and its professors. If you controlled the freedom to think, you were able to control society. Thus, the freedom of thinking and inquiry that served as the foundation of the modern Western Humboldt-style university was also the foundation of free society.

After the Potsdam Conference following the World War II, when Berlin was divided into sectors controlled by the Soviet Union and the victorious western Allies, the university named after Humboldt was located in Soviet-controlled East Berlin. The free universities proved incompatible with the goals of the postwar East German totalitarian regime, and one of the first steps the Soviet administrators took was to quickly eliminate the freedom of professors at Humboldt University by restricting and monitoring the professor's movement, teaching, and research. Humboldt University was no longer a university in the Humboldt tradition. It was no coincidence that one of the first steps the United States took in defending the viability and freedom of West Berlin was to establish a new university, the Free University of Berlin. This new university in West Berlin, created by a massive injection of funds, resources, and goodwill from the United States, presented a striking contrast to its famous emasculated counterpart in communist East Berlin. As the name reflected, thinking, expression, scholarly pursuit and research was *free*. It was deemed essential that such a free university serve as a beacon and catalyst for a free democratic society in West Berlin. Thirty years later, when the Berlin Wall fell, the Free University of Berlin maintained its course; and Humboldt University followed its path reverting to its earlier, prewar form.

Despite the university's contributions to the social and democratic principles underlying democracy, the university as an institution was seen as an economic drain or at best neutral in relation to the economy after World War II. As chapter 3 pointed out, the Nobel prize–winning Solow model in economics based economic growth on two factors: physical capital and the labor required to work it. What could the university contribute to these factors? The resources invested in the university could not be used to help production. Funds used to finance university education and research seemed like a diversion from doing business in the real world. In addition, labor in factories needed to be obedient, reliable, and to explicitly and exactly follow orders, something implicitly contrary to university freedom.

So while the contribution of universities might have been important and invaluable, America's factories didn't need or want thinking workers who would reflect and question. As I learned while working on the assembly line, the trick was not to think but simply to find a way into a mechanized zone beyond thinking, questioning, and challenging. In fact, the type of thinking, questioning, and challenging that is the goal of higher education in the United States and the West contradicts the behavior of the labor that powered America's factories during the managed economy.

Europeans felt that American universities were, on average, no better or worse than the ones in Europe.[1] Each country had universities consistent with its own history and institutions, appropriate for its own society. The United States developed an approach to higher education and research that was strikingly different from that in Europe. The first difference was the number of private universities in America. Many European countries have few, if any, private universities; instead they have exclusively public university systems, where the major decision-making and governance is carried out not by a board of trustees; as in the United States, but by high-level government ministries. In the 1990s, in response to a job offer to become a professor of economics at the University of Vienna, I was called on to negotiate not with university officials but rather with officials from the Austrian ministry of education. Even in the state universities of America, this would be unimaginable, but it remains the common mode of governance of European universities. In Europe, a professor is a civil servant and part of the state bureaucracy. In the United Kingdom, a country sitting between American and European cultures, the universities are overwhelmingly public. It must not be forgotten that the best British universities, Cambridge and Oxford, are first and foremost public institutions.

The strong presence of private universities in the United States also highlights a second striking difference—students pay tuition, covering a portion of the costs of their education. It is hard for parents to believe that the 2006 average annual tuition of $33,000 only partially covers the cost. Even today, tuition in Europe remains low, if not zero. Germany doesn't charge its students for university, while in the Netherlands a trivial tuition fee is charged. Not only can young people attend European universities at no cost, but in most countries, enrolling in college provides a myriad of state benefits. College students in Germany get free public transportation, including access to the trains. As I often commute back and forth between Weimar and Jena in Germany, I often think that I am the only one buying a ticket for the train. The hoards of students from around the region traveling to Jena's Friedrich Schiller University merely show their student ID cards.

A second distinction in the United States is the mix of institutions. While Europe, including the United Kingdom, has had mostly public universities, the United States also has a large number of public universities, usually referred to as state schools. Some of the United States' premiere universities, such as the University of California at Berkeley, the University of Michigan, and Indiana University, are state schools. While the tuition used to be relatively low, in recent years it has risen to a level that no one could maintain is trivial at most public state universities. For example, Indiana residents attending Indiana University paid $6,000 for 2005–2006, and out-of-state residents paid significantly more. This large chunk of change makes parents hope their kids need only four years to graduate. This is a great dividing point between Europeans and Americans. My friends in Europe find the $6,000 annual tuition incomprehensible—never mind the astronomical tuition at private colleges and universities.

And this leads to a key point concerning the mix of higher education institutions in the United States. Not only are there public and private schools, but they range from remarkably small and focused liberal arts colleges—with, in some cases, under fifteen hundred students—to the Ivy League schools, and beyond, including large, fully integrated state universities that offer just about every type of program possible. The role of research and creative activity varies considerably across these institutions. Smaller private colleges usually focus on the needs of a few highly selected undergraduates. Some of these four-year colleges include some research activities. At my first job teaching economics at Middlebury College, professors were required to do research in order to be promoted. However, Middlebury College, like most other small colleges, focuses on ensuring the best possible undergraduate experience. Larger private and state universities focus on and are dedicated to research. At the very best research universities, professors must focus on research in order to earn promotion and receive tenure.

Whether small four-year colleges or large state schools offer a better education for your child is beyond the scope of this book—both have their advantages and disadvantages. The main point here is that the diversity of options and institutions on the United States is unmatched in Europe. The homogenous experience found in Europe is that way by design. Germans deliberately designed their universities to be relatively equal of access, as part of their effort after World War II to ensure democracy and equality. Everyone who was qualified was entitled to an equal educational experience, a goal explicitly stated by the government.

Competition among American colleges and universities has been fueled by the variety of goals and sizes. This competition to be the best in one's area of expertise has driven American colleges and universities. For example, Rensselaer Polytechnic Institute is relentless in its efforts to be the best engineering school, while Julliard seeks to stay the best in music. The Thunderbird Business School in Arizona seeks to be the best at international business education, and the University of California at San Francisco is well known for research in the life sciences. This competition is not esoteric but rather to attain what matters in higher education—students and reputation, both of which are conducive to funding.

Thus, while the European universities spent decades equalizing their programs to ensure equal opportunities for all—so that that the diplomas of physics students in, say, Strasbourg, would represent the same experience and value as those of their counterparts in Paris—in America, colleges and universities were busy experimenting, creating new programs, finding new approaches and new ways to deliver education, and creating new opportunities for students and researchers, all spurred on by competition in the great race to attain an excellent reputation. Such experimentation took on various forms: evening programs; distance education; interdisciplinary studies; internships; overseas study programs; and the creation of new fields such as infomatics, telecommunications, women's studies, and sports management. It would be impossible to list all the innovations and changes spurred by competition; the list simply goes on and on.

Back in the 1980s when I lived in Berlin, I heard numerous complaints about the superficial nature and trendiness of American higher education, which resulted in an incomprehensible potpourri of programs, degrees, and standards. In trying to plan a conference and coordinate the event with American teaching schedules, European colleagues would typically ask "When does the semester start in the United States?" Europeans expected a single answer, because in European countries all the universities started and stopped on the same dates, a date centrally fixed. However, in typical American fashion, there isn't a single national answer. Much to the astonishment of my European colleagues, each American college and university sets its own calendar. The answer was, and continues to be, "It depends." It depends on not just the particular university but also the teaching schedule of the particular professor and program, because increasingly classes are being offered not only in the traditional fifteen-week semester format, but in a vast array of new alternatives, including blocked courses, intensive weekend seminars, and over the internet.

Even today, my European friends keep asking me questions about university life in the United States, questions they think have simple and easy standard answers. I still struggle to answer questions like "What is the teaching load in the United States?" and "How much do American professors earn?" My French, German, and Dutch friends have easy answers, as their governments dictate teaching load and pay. However, with the variety of schools in America, I frustrate my friends when I start answering their questions with "It depends." It depends on the university, the system, and the particular individual. On the other hand, I was able to find a quick answer to this question for France, where "most students are required to attend the universities closest to their high schools. Although certain universities excel in specific fields of study, the course offerings in, say, history or literature, are generally the same throughout the country."[2] In the European universities, the drive toward homogeneity and standardization means that every professor is expected to perform the same duties with standardized and predictable teaching loads, research expectations, and service contributions.

By contrast, competition in the United States has generated incredible diversity, flexibility, and individualization for professors. Europeans have a hard time understanding why a professor might move from the University of Virginia to the University of Wyoming. They think the professor is moving to be closer to his family, or perhaps fulfilling a lifelong desire to be a part-time cowboy. When I tell them "She got a better job," they are stunned. To them, professorial jobs are the same everywhere; but for Americans, the opportunity for a better research laboratory, better teaching opportunities, or better pay are powerful incentives.

In Europe, incentives for professors to move are limited and are focused on the office size and the number of graduate students supported, with trivial financial incentives thrown in. As the *New York Times* reports, in Europe, "professors lack the standing and the salaries of the private sector."[3] Thus, the primary reason for moving has typically been preference for a particular city. In a university system where parity rules and incentives are minimized, there is no pressure to change programs and recruit any given professor. By contrast, as *Time* magazine points out, the leading American universities "are more than ever caught up in competing with one another for faculty stars, whom they lure less with money and perquisites than with freedom to conduct research, which usually means light teaching loads and lots of graduate students to do scut work."[4]

A few years ago, Charlie Karlsson, the founding dean of Sweden's Jönkoping University, the country's first private university, visited Indiana University, seeking to make it one of his university's international partners. Upon learning from the dean of international programs, Patrick O'Meara, that Indiana University was a state university, Charlie wanted to know if all of its funding came from the state of Indiana. When Dean O'Meara shook his head and responded that only some 20 percent of the budget came from the state, Charlie was incredulous; "At Jönkoping University, which is proud to be Sweden's first private university, all of the budget comes from the state!" So while in Sweden the private university receives most of its funding from the state, in the United States, state universities are relying less and less on state funding. The University of Virginia and University of Michigan have a state share of their budgets that is so low that they are increasingly referred to as quasi-public institutions, which, in fact, they have been for many years.

So while early European universities were seminaries offering religion-based education, the rise of Humboldt-style universities shifted the focus to research and particularly research independent of the influence of church and state. The strong ties to the church were severed in favor of independent, autonomous universities more concerned with adherence to scientific and scholarly pursuits. American colleges and universities, though considerably younger, followed the European lead, with first the parochial, religion-based approach and somewhat later the Humboldt approach. During the first twenty years after World War II, the difference in the societal role of European and American universities was mostly cosmetic

At some point, the paths diverged. Colleges and universities in the United States became not just institutions promoting cultural and social values but engines of economic growth. Instead of being isolated in the ivory tower, professors and their research are now seen as a source of the knowledge and ideas driving economic growth. The shift away from the managed economy and the reliance on factories as the source of competitiveness, jobs, and growth drove this change in the role of universities. As long as the American economy used unskilled, unthinking labor with factory production, universities had little to contribute to the economy. In the knowledge economy, research skills learned at the university are the basis of economic growth.

As Michael Crichton observes in the opening pages of *Jurassic Park*, "the late twentieth century has witnessed a scientific gold rush of astonishing proportions: the headlong and furious haste to commercialize genetic engineering. This enterprise has proceeded so rapidly—with so little outside commentary—that its dimensions and implications are hardly understood at all."[5] Paul Romer formalized Crichton's observation in his new growth model in economics, showing that it is not just labor and capital that matters for economic growth and jobs but also knowledge and ideas. Once thinking and working with ideas, what scholars call knowledge, became important in the economy, the university's role changed. When knowledge and ideas became important for firms, they also became important for workers in those firms, and universities were the primary source of innovative knowledge and ideas based on research. Thus, toward the end of the twentieth century, universities such as MIT, Stanford, the University of California at San Diego, the University of North Carolina, and the University of Texas at Austin became key engines of regional economic growth and employment. New industries, based on new and potentially valuable research, sprang up around these universities. The source of the new economic growth and jobs was quickly identified, and universities were increasingly viewed as essential for economic reasons, not just the old traditional ones.

One major reason that American colleges and universities were predisposed toward applied science and commercialization was the passage of the Morrill Act and establishment of the land grant universities toward the end of the Civil War. The Morrill Act, more commonly known as the Land Grant Act, signed into law by Abraham Lincoln in 1862, granted to each state land that was to be used in perpetuity to fund agricultural and mechanical colleges benefiting the state.[6] The idea was to offer the opportunity for higher education to more people, not just those destined to sedentary professions. The Morrill Act proclaimed itself "an Act Donating Public Lands to the several States and Territories which may provide Colleges for the Benefit of Agriculture and Mechanic Arts." From the legislation, from its later amendments, and from Representative Justin Morrill's statements, it is clear that there were three principal reasons for the Act[7]. It was

1. A protest against the dominance of the classics in higher education
2. A desire to develop at the college level instruction relating to the practical realities of an agricultural and industrial society
3. An attempt to offer to those belonging to the industrial classes preparation for the "professions of life"

According to Representative Morrill,

> The land-grant colleges were founded on the idea that a higher and broader education should be placed in every State within the reach of those whose destiny assigns them to, or who may have the courage to choose industrial locations where the wealth of nations is produced; where advanced civilization unfolds its comforts, and where a much larger number of the people need wider educational advantages, and impatiently await their possession. . . . It would be a mistake to suppose it was intended that every student should become either a farmer or a mechanic when the design comprehended not only instruction for those who may hold the plow or follow a trade, but such instruction as any person might need—with the world all before them where to choose—and without the exclusion of those who might prefer to adhere to the classics.

In a speech before the Vermont legislature in 1888, Representative Morrill spoke of the need for knowledge to spill from the university to broader society.

> Only the interest from the land-grant fund can be expended, and that must be expended, first—without excluding other scientific and classical studies—for teaching such branches of learning as are related to agriculture and the mechanic arts— the latter as absolutely as the former. Obviously not manual, but intellectual instruction was the paramount object. It was not provided that agricultural labor in the field should be

practically taught, any more than that the mechanical trade of
a carpenter or blacksmith should be taught. Secondly, it was a
liberal education that was proposed. Classical studies were
not to be excluded, and, therefore, must be included. The Act
of 1862 proposed a system of broad education by colleges, not
limited to a superficial and dwarfed training, such as might
be supplied by a foreman of a workshop or by a foreman of
an experimental farm. If any would have only a school with
equal scraps of labor and of instruction, or something other
than a college, they would not obey the national law.

From these basic rules, a large system of colleges and universities,
managed by each state but conforming to the stipulations of federal
law, emerged. Although the universities were initially funded by land
grants, each state was expected to contribute to the institution's
continuing needs and to provide its buildings.

From this modest beginning, the federal government significantly
expanded its contributions to the land-grant universities. Recognizing
the need for research as a basis for developing agriculture, Congress
passed the Hatch Act in 1887, which authorized federal funding for the
universities to establish agricultural experiment stations. In 1914 the
Smith-Lever Act established the system of cooperative extension
services to spread the benefits of current developments in the fields of
agriculture, home economics, and related subjects to people across the
states, regardless of how far away they lived from the universities.
These land-grant institutions, designed to foster a program of education suited to the needs of the agricultural and industrial classes, came
to encompass a program of on-campus instruction, research, and off-
campus extension work. Since 1914, Congress has expanded the scope
and support of all three aspects of the program several times.[8] Now, in
addition to the income from the original land grants, federal funding of
more than $550 million annually aids state maintenance of land-grant
institutions.[9]

The establishment of the land-grant universities fostered the
diverging path of American colleges and universities, helping differ-
entiate them from the traditional Humboldt-style European university.
Over time, the land-grant universities developed an impressive and
effective set of institutional mechanisms that facilitated the spillover of

agricultural technology and knowledge from the university to the farm, a process that helped American farmers become the most productive and successful in the world. Thus, while the Humboldt-style university focused on the creation of new knowledge, land-grant universities had a dual purpose: to create new knowledge and to transfer it, through extension services, to those who could use it.

The Morrill Act and its subsequent amendments were "important in creating state institutions that would not only educate large numbers of Americans but would play an influential role in the development of research and technology programs with practical applications to industry."[10] In particular, American universities, particularly the land-grant institutions, earned a reputation for "hands-on problem solving"— "something that was lacking in British and European institutions."[11] Thus in the post-war era the United States, unlike its European allies, had a strong and vital tradition and institutions fostering not just basic research and fundamental science but also applied research with an orientation towards serving the community.

Another reason American colleges and universities diverged from European universities was their role in helping the United States win World War II. At that time, American universities were suddenly thrust into goal-oriented and directed research with specific concrete applications in mind. The partnership between the federal government and the universities was a key reason for the Allies' winning the war. This role played by the universities deeply impressed some, including Vannevar Bush, an American engineer who played a critical role in developing the nuclear bomb. Bush argued, in his 1945 book *Science: The Endless Frontier*, that the federal government needed to continue its massive investment in science, technology and research to ensure that the United States would not just win the war but also win the peace.[12]

However, the generous and unprecedented increases in university funding from both the states and the federal government came to a screeching halt with the mid-1970s oil crisis. Federal and state budgets were thrown into disarray, even as the universities were confronted with massive increases in energy costs. Universities, particularly state-funded ones, found it worthwhile to search for alternative sources of funding. These sources took many forms.

College sports became a major source of income, with lucrative television contracts. University team logos were put on T-shirts, baseball caps, and underwear, becoming a hot source of commercial revenue. The popularity of college sports, principally football and men's basketball, contributed to broad and enthusiastic support from large segments of the population who might otherwise have resented their tax dollars going to the university. Although some professors view the commercialization of the university as a betrayal of its core intellectual values, by recruiting the support, enthusiasm, and undying loyalty of large elements of the population who would never dream of attending the university themselves, these actions helped ensure a basic level of state support for the universities. Today state, and private, universities offer something for almost everyone. They provide entertainment, social connection, continuity, and a sense of place for alumni and sports fans in an otherwise rootless society. While the Raiders have moved from city to city and back, you know that the Ohio State Buckeyes in Columbus, Notre Dame's Fighting Irish in South Bend, and the UCLA Bruins in Los Angeles will always be there. Professional sports teams come and go. Ask any (by now gray-haired) fan of the Brooklyn Dodgers or New York Giants baseball teams. In contrast, universities cannot easily move their ivory towers.

Another source of funding for state universities came as they became the engines of economic development and jobs in the local economy. This orientation toward economic development and positively impacting the local community's economy is certainly inconsistent with the Humboldt-style university. While the agricultural extension services provided by the land-grant universities have always been committed to helping farmers in the state, it is important to remember that such agricultural and extension programs were typically looked down on as the weak stepsisters of academia. Pure science ruled and was disdainful of applied science and its real-world applications.

Ed Roberts, a pioneering scholar of innovation and entrepreneurship at MIT's prestigious Sloan School of Management, recalls that his university was not always so entrepreneurial or oriented toward commercial applications. After starting at MIT in 1961, Ed started his own company. Shortly thereafter, he was called into the office of his well-respected senior colleague, Jay Forrester, the author of the awe-inspiring *Limits to Growth*, and told in no uncertain terms that being an entrepreneur and founding his own firm was not just incompatible with being a professor at MIT, it was unacceptable.[13] It seems strange to think that at one of the world's premier business schools, starting a business was once considered *verboten*. Today MIT encourages and embraces its professors' commercialization efforts. But at the time, it sure wasn't obvious, at least not the way Ed tells it.

Another reason for the shift in American colleges and universities was a significant policy change that facilitated and encouraged the spillover of knowledge from universities to the community. The Bayh-Dole Act,[14] enacted into law by the United States Congress in 1980, was specifically designed to penetrate the knowledge filter by providing financial incentives to universities to commercialize research. Assessments of the impact of the Bayh-Dole Act on penetrating the knowledge filter and facilitating the commercialization of university research have bordered on the euphoric:[15]

> Possibly the most inspired piece of legislation to be enacted in America over the past half-century was the Bayh-Dole Act of 1980. Together with amendments in 1984 and augmentation in 1986, this unlocked all the inventions and discoveries that had been made in laboratories through the United States with the help of taxpayers' money. More than anything, this single policy measure helped to reverse America's precipitous slide into industrial irrelevance. Before Bayh-Dole, the fruits of research supported by government agencies had gone strictly to the federal government. Nobody could exploit such research without tedious negotiations with a federal agency concerned. Worse, companies found it nigh impossible to acquire exclusive rights to a government owned patent. And without that, few firms were willing to invest millions more of their own money to turn a basic research idea into a marketable product.[16]

An even more enthusiastic assessment by MIT's *Technology Review* said:

> The Bayh-Dole Act turned out to be the Viagra for campus innovation. Universities that would previously have let their intellectual property lie fallow began filing for—and getting patents at unprecedented rates. Coupled with other legal, economic and political developments that also spurred patenting and licensing, the results seems nothing less than a major boom to national economic growth.[17]

After the passage of the Bayh-Dole Act, the presence of Technology Transfer Offices (TTOs) on university campuses exploded. These offices facilitate the transfer of knowledge and the resulting commercialization of university scientists' research by acting as a repository for the intellectual property generated at the university. The American University Association of Technology Transfer Managers collects and reports a number of measures that reflect the intellectual property and commercialization of its member universities. A voluminous and growing body of research has emerged documenting the impact of TTOs on the commercialization of university research. By most accounts, their impact on facilitating the commercialization of university science is impressive.[18] For example, the percentage of patents registered by universities, as opposed to individuals and companies, has exploded since the passing of the Bayh-Dole Act in 1980 (see fig. 8.1).

As globalization and the emergence of knowledge replaced factories, knowledge sources were needed. But where is this knowledge meant to come from? While the research and development effort of private firms is important, universities also play a prominent role. Private industry accounts for about two-thirds of total R & D in the United States. The federal government accounts for another 28 percent.

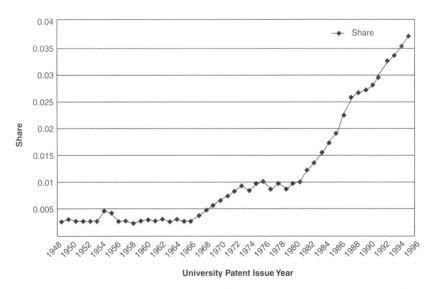

Figure 8.1 University patents as a share of all patents. Source: *Ivory Tower and Industrial Innovation*, by Mowery et al., 2005.

The remaining 6 percent is accounted for by universities, nonprofit organizations, as well as state and local governments.[19] In 1953, the federal government contribution to R & D accounted for 0.75 percent of the U.S. gross domestic product (GDP). This number varied over time, reaching a high of 1.98 percent in 1964, and falling to 0.76 percent in 2002.

As research and knowledge become an important component of the generation of economic growth and jobs in globally linked markets, universities emerge as a key to determining the country's future, especially since one of the most important university functions is to create new scientific knowledge. America's university system, which nurtures many of the most capable and creative scientists on the planet, is the envy of the world. However, the massive investment in university research can impact economic growth only if knowledge can be transformed into actual innovations and new and better products through the commercialization process—that is, the extent to which university research becomes commercialized. It matters for economic growth, for jobs, and for global competitiveness.

How exactly does knowledge created in university laboratories, institutes, classrooms, and discussions spill over, creating new products and innovations? Just having the universities patent intellectual property generated in research laboratories and then either license or sell the patents may not suffice. After all, if private corporations fall victim to the knowledge filter, why should universities be any different? As we learned in chapter 6, if it is tough for large corporations to separate the wheat from the chaff when bombarded by a plethora of ideas, suggestions, dreams, and insights, it is doubtful that universities would be any better positioned to avoid their own knowledge filters.

Thus, just as entrepreneurship became essential for harvesting ideas, hunches, and dreams generated in the private sector, it also became essential to harvest knowledge growing from the scientific seeds planted and nurtured at the university. It is even more important because universities are not in the business of business, even with all its recent changes, reorientations, reforms, and new directions. Universities remain committed to the basic business of education and research, no matter how entrepreneurially they behave. Since the only mechanism universities have for commercialization is patents and licenses, professors must now become entrepreneurs in order to pursue their dreams.

This is exactly what needs to happen in the entrepreneurial society. Steve Lohr writes in the *New York Times* that, "research funds often lead to start-ups."[20] Public policy in the entrepreneurial society must facilitate spillovers of its investments in science and research by encouraging and making it as easy as possible for university researchers and scientists to become entrepreneurs and to become involved with entrepreneurial startups.

In the managed economy, professors stayed in the classroom and research laboratory, hiding in the ivory tower that separated academia from the world. How can professors broach the tower to get their ideas out into the real world through entrepreneurship? Professors often face a formidable problem: they often have limited business experience, and their ideas are shrouded in uncertainty, hidden behind not just an unknown marketplace, but often behind obscure and perplexing academic language.

The myth that venture capital will finance scientist entrepreneurs is indeed . . . a myth. In reality, venture capital is focused on financing existing potential high-growth ventures. Few entrepreneurs, if any, receive venture capital to start their business. It is only once an idea has demonstrated market potential that might result in high growth that venture capitalists are willing to step in, putting a firm on the survival trajectory instead of the failure trajectory—two wholly different paths illustrated in figure 8.2. In the meantime, what's a scientist in a research laboratory, full of dreams, ideas, plans, and instinct, to do? Other than the three famous Fs of entrepreneurship—family, friends, and fools—where can scientists receive funding and other support to help them get going? The gap between getting the idea and when it starts to take off is called the Valley of Death. How can a scientist or researcher bridge the Valley? This is where the role of supportive public policy is so different, and important, in the entrepreneurial society.

Consider the dilemma confronted by Dr. Dick Peterson at the Indiana University School of Medicine.[21] In order to do his research, Peterson had developed a genetically biased diabetic rat model. Such rats are highly useful for medical researchers trying to cure or abate diabetes. Initially, Peterson only needed small breeding rooms to develop genetic reagents from rat antibodies. At first Peterson supplied his diabetic rats to interested colleagues at cost. However, as interest

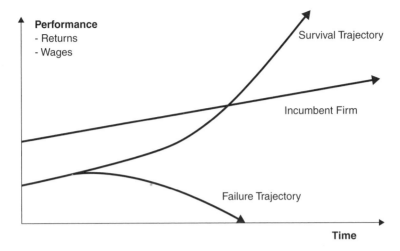

Figure 8.2 The entrepreneurial process.

and demand from other researchers grew, Peterson found that he needed to find a way to market his technology beyond what Indiana University could provide. With a team of five people, including Joe Persik, who had worked for Union Carbide, Peterson founded Genetic Models in 1991. The core product of Genetic Models consists of bred animal models, mainly rats and mice. The animals are bred with specific diseases, for example, obese male rats with diabetes. The animals are then sold to research laboratories that are testing disease cures. The highly specialized and developed laboratory rats were in high demand, and Peterson wanted to explore further business possibilities and expand to meet his anticipated demand, but it was unproven in the market. Peterson and his team were trying to bridge the Valley of Death.

Peterson and his team applied for financing from a bank. As a part of the process, Peterson recalls, the bankers asked him what his business experience was. He answered truthfully: "None." Then they asked about the demand for his laboratory rats and mice. Peterson's answer was speculative, and this, like his complete lack of business experience, was not encouraging to the bank. Next the bank asked about the company's assets, and Peterson answered truthfully: his idea and scientific knowledge were all there was. Peterson was facing a major problem: what bank would finance someone with no business experience, no clear product demand, and no physical assets? After he was turned down by bank after bank, Peterson was downright discouraged. He and his innovative product were prime candidates for the Valley of Death. Peterson would have given up on his dream of starting the firm, but fortunately, the federal government's Small Business Innovation Research (SBIR) program provided funding that enabled him to climb out of the Valley of Death. Peterson maintains that it was the SBIR program that provided the funding enabling his business to bridge the valley and to succeed and flourish.

The SBIR program is one of a host of policy initiatives and new institutions that have emerged to help create an entrepreneurial society and to facilitate science- and university-based startups. While the enactment of the Bayh-Dole Act was significant and consequential, it was in no way the only policy change that has facilitated America's shift from a managed economy to the entrepreneurial society. These policies have been implemented at the federal, state, and local levels, designed to enable academic and other knowledge-based entrepreneurs to bridge the Valley of Death.

The SBIR program was started in the early 1980s as a response to the loss of American competitiveness in global markets. Congress required each federal agency to allocate around 4 percent of its annual budget to funding innovative small firms in order to help restore America's international competitiveness.[22] The SBIR program invested nearly $2 billion in 2005. The program consists of three phases. During the first phase, businesses are given six months and up to $100,000 to determine the scientific and technical merit along with the feasibility of a proposed research idea. Forty percent of the projects are deemed successful enough to be advanced to the second phase. During the second phase, firms get up to two years and $750,000 to extend the technological idea and determine the possibilities for commercialization. The very best projects make it to the third phase, which is designed to help put the product on the market. At this stage, the businesses usually obtain additional private funding.

Josh Lerner, a finance professor at Harvard Business School, estimated that the SBIR program accounts for 60 percent of all public entrepreneurial finance programs.[23] Collectively, public financing of small businesses is only two-thirds the amount of privately invested venture capital, but that two-thirds amounted to $2.4 billion in 1995. The SBIR program, as well as other government programs, emphasizes early-stage financing, something private venture capitalists generally ignore. Apple, Compaq, and Intel are some of the companies that received early-stage financing under the SBIR program. While none would claim that these major companies wouldn't have existed without the SBIR program, there is a growing body of compelling evidence that the SBIR program has positively impacted the United State's economic performance.[24]

The goals established for the SBIR program were achieved when Indiana University professor Jeffrey Alberts established his firm Star Enterprises. Alberts was profiled in *Nature* magazine, which reported:

> Jeff Alberts, a psychology professor, was trained as a scientist, not an entrepreneur. But with the help of government funding, he turned his knack for designing animal cages and other experimental apparatus into a successful small business. Alberts made the move in the 1980s after working on part of a Soviet space project that involved developmental biology experiments using rats. The only problem was that Alberts knew little about business, so he turned to the recently established SBIR programme for help in getting his company off the ground.[25]

Alberts believes that his research would not have been commercialized without public policy such as the SBIR program. Alberts said:

> I would not have been involved in commercialization at all had it not been for the SBIR. The SBIR made it possible for me to develop and then build products for the space shuttle under NASA. In the absence of SBIR, I think all of my energy and efforts would be allocated towards basic research in the university laboratory and my administrative duties as Director of Research and Development Office at Indiana University.

Importantly, the SBIR program is not the only public policy designed to help knowledge-based entrepreneurs bridge the Valley of Death. Other programs abound at the state, regional, and local levels,[26] and include incubators, science and technology parks, startup programs, and entrepreneurial training programs. It would be safe to bet that in 1970, programs supporting entrepreneurs were few and far between, and those that existed were limited in scope, magnitude, and impact. Today virtually every state, region, county, and city supports at least one, if not many, such programs and policies. Nonexistent in the managed economy, these are standard instruments used to help create an entrepreneurial society.

The Indiana Venture Center, a public/private partnership, is a program designed to help emerging entrepreneurs with their businesses. The center, established in 2003, was started by Mike Hatfield, the inventor of key technologies that have made the broadband possible. The Center involves Indiana's five research universities and industry. Hatfield wanted to help his home state become entrepreneurial; he credits the values and education he received in Indiana with providing the basis for his dreams and ideas. But Indiana, lodged firmly in the declining Rust Belt of the managed economy, was not the right place to pursue those dreams. After graduating from the excellent engineering college Rose-Hulman, Hatfield immigrated to California's Bay Area to access the knowledge, ideas, and business connections he needed to realize his own vision—creating his own company to advance broadband transmission. But his love for his home state stayed with him. After his enormous entrepreneurial success, he provided financing for the Indiana Venture Center. As the old saying goes, "If you catch a fish for a man, he has a dinner. If you teach a man to fish, he has a livelihood." In "paying back" his home state for the values and education that later propelled him to create thousands of jobs and astonishing wealth, Hatfield sought to teach Indiana how to generate a livelihood in the entrepreneurial society with the creation of the Indiana Venture Center.

The president of the center, Steven Beck, had been in finance in New York City; he chose to become the center's president because of his passion and commitment to creating an entrepreneurial Indiana. The center helps entrepreneurs with the startup process, forcing them to validate their business idea and technology. Beck's program includes an internship that helps the entrepreneur develop a business plan and identify the market, and an "angel" program that matches investors with early-stage companies that have high growth potential but lack financing.[27]

Similarly, the state of Indiana's Twenty-First Century Research and Technology Fund was started to spur knowledge-based entrepreneurship, thereby facilitating the state's shift from the managed economy to the entrepreneurial society. Through this program, the Indiana government offers matching funds for academic/private partnerships.

These and other similar new policy initiatives, such as Biocrossroads, a statewide program intended to make Indiana a leading cluster in the life sciences, attest to increasing recognition within the state to the importance of an economic development strategy that is based on entrepreneurship. It is important to note that recent years have also been marked by a number of private efforts to boost Indiana's entrepreneurial society. These include creation of new funding sources, such as Indiana Futures Fund, Eli Lilly Ventures, and Spring Mill Ventures. These programs help individuals realize their entrepreneurial potential by increasing awareness of the viability and possibilities of entrepreneurship as a career option. These programs also act as resources for entrepreneurs, providing information to help them be successful.

When I moved to Indiana in 1998, I met with the head of the Indiana Economic Development Commission. As we discussed my interest in high-tech entrepreneurship and innovation, I was warned. "That's great, David, but high-tech entrepreneurship, that's for the coasts. Here in the Hoosier state, we have other traditions. It's all about manufacturing." Historically accurate—but the past stopped working in the mid-1970s, and it took close to thirty years for a new consensus to start to emerge: *It's not your father's Indiana anymore.* People like Mike Hatfield and Steve Beck along with institutions like the Indiana Venture Center are making sure that Indiana is a vital and dynamic place with a promising future that gives compelling reasons for bright, talented Hoosier kids to stay at home or come back home instead of seeking their fame and fortune elsewhere. These are the agents of change that are transforming the managed economy to an entrepreneurial Indiana.

San Diego is already transformed, but back in 1992 before Bill Clinton was first elected president, it wasn't. San Diego suffered from widespread unemployment and a questionable future, thanks to the massive layoffs and downsizing triggered by the closing of the U.S. Navy's San Diego bases and research facilities. Where others saw only resignation and dejection, Mary Walshok, a sociology professor at the University of California at San Diego, who now serves as the vice-chancellor of the university, saw opportunity. She knew that the science and research resources in San Diego were world-class quality. With the University of California at San Diego at the helm, the region was a global leader in life sciences research, but it lacked a regional identity. The scientists were isolated from both the private sector and the policy community. Mary resolved to change that with a plan to get everyone working together to build on their regional strength— biotechnology. She started the CONNECT program, which

> will provide entrepreneurs and startups in member regions access to global capital providers and financial markets, research opportunities, corporate partners, and new customer channels. International corporations, universities, and research institutions will have a powerful new resource to link with emerging companies for partnership and collaboration. Shared best practices and resources, improved assessment of innovation capacity, and strengthened university/industry interaction will bring the benefits of globalization to regions and entrepreneurs worldwide.[28]

In her now world-famous pioneering program, CONNECT San Diego, Mary succeeded in getting the region to change its identity, becoming an entrepreneurial city. It's not your father's San Diego, either.

Carolyn Lee, director of research for the Public Programs Office of Regional Innovations Studies at the University of California at San Diego, points out:

> If you can manage to find the funding to start your business you will pursue that idea . . . from what I can see from CONNECT entrepreneurs sometimes it [what stands in the way] is being unable to pursue this entrepreneurial idea within the context of your current work, be that as an academic within a university or as an engineer in an existing company or you know whatever the circumstances might be in your career.[29]

Lee believes that without CONNECT San Diego and other similar programs, many scientists would never have become entrepreneurs and, in fact, their research would never have been commercialized. She said she believes that the CONNECT program "can only heighten awareness that this is a career path you could pursue, if you had a great idea you ought to start a company. In the absence of programs like these, I don't see how you could possibly gain support." Thus, at least in these examples, public policy bridges the Valley of Death, enabling scientist entrepreneurs to penetrate the knowledge filter and commercialize research that otherwise would have remained locked in the ivory tower. This is how communities like San Diego and Indiana are creating new firms, industries, and jobs.

Bryan Renk, who serves as director of licensing at the Wisconsin Alumni Research Foundation at the University of Wisconsin, one of the nation's oldest and most prominent TTOs, makes it clear how public policy generates knowledge spillovers through entrepreneurship that might not otherwise have occurred. Referring to university scientists, he reports:

> from an academic standpoint, they can get that company formed, they can get an economic return themselves while at the same time maintaining their position within the university and . . . there are all levels of activity from partially running the company to running the company, taking a leave to get the company set up and running the company, to be on the scientific advisory board or be in the board of directors or not even be involved but be involved from a distance and just take equity and sit out. The other benefit is too if they felt in the past that their technology hasn't been used, or been commercialized appropriately and that they can do a better job of getting that technology out that's another benefit; it could be good, could be bad. It used to go both ways. The other issue is that sometimes the only way that that technology is going to be commercialized is by their entrepreneurial activity. It might be because of their knowledge base that that's the best way to go. It might be that it's not until somebody makes it from a company standpoint, nobody else will buy it. It might just fall in a category that that's the best way to do it.

Similarly, Tony Antoniadis, general manager of Georgia Tech University's Advanced Technology Development Center (ATDC), one of the nation's most successful collegiate university incubators, explains how public policy contributed to regional entrepreneurship capital by generating region-specific externalities.

> I think folks—they know we are here and we are a support
> organization and therefore they can start up a company a lot
> quicker and cheaper then if they were doing it on their own.
> And they have higher chances of success. So I think the fact
> that we are here and got this, have this support base might
> influence them and say there is a community I could go join
> or I could learn from others in there, I could get this thing up
> and running rather than stay in my basement, in my silo and
> try to figure it all out myself which might take a few years. I
> could go and join a program like ATDC and have the support
> base where I could get this off the ground much faster. And
> faster time to decision—is this a success or failure?

Support from ATDC has resulted in the creation of more than one hundred companies, including MindSpring Enterprises, which has since been bought by EarthLink. Support from ATDC includes connecting entrepreneurs to the resources they need to succeed, which includes funding sources like SBIR. The incubator reports:

> many entrepreneurs miss out on this funding because
> they're either unaware or have negative misperceptions. Yet
> companies in Georgia Tech's ATDC incubator that have won
> awards give the programs an enthusiastic thumbs-up.
> Orthonics Inc., which is developing new biomaterials for
> spinal disc repair, won an STTR [Small Business Technology
> Transfer] grant for $100,000 last fall from the National
> Institutes of Health (NIH). "Launching any new company is
> difficult, but biotech startups have particular challenges,"
> says Steve Kennedy, Orthonics' CEO. "It takes a long time to
> get to market—and a lot of money—so you can't bootstrap in
> traditional ways. This is no-strings-attached money from the
> federal government to do R & D."[30]

Thus, working in many cases hand in hand, the universities, the government, and the private sector, often in the form of private/public partnerships, are well on the way to creating entrepreneurial universities that support the entrepreneurial society.

However successful the entrepreneurial universities are, balancing the traditional roles of teaching, research, and service is a challenge not to be underestimated. Larry Summers, the former president of Harvard University, learned this lesson. As *Time* noted, "when Summers announced early on that he wanted to remake the undergraduate curriculum to ensure that Harvard graduates knew more, especially about science, he set off a direct conflict with the faculty, whose incentive is to spend as little time as possible designing and teaching undergraduate courses."[31] *Time* concludes: "the job is to make a successful but fragmented university cohere intellectually and educationally."[32] The challenge remains daunting; and former Princeton University president Harold Shapiro proclaims in his book *A Larger Sense of Purpose* that American universities don't appear to actually have a larger sense of purpose.

The darker side of the commercialization of universities is highlighted in an article by Stephen Budiansky in the *New York Times*, who describes

> how colleges prostitute themselves to improve their *U.S. News & World Report* rankings and keep up a healthy supply of tuition-paying students, while wrapping their craven commercialism in high-minded sounding academic blather. . . . [I] would keep coming up with what I thought were pretty outrageous burlesques of this stuff and then run them by one of my professor friends and he'd say, "Oh yeah, we're doing that."[33]

Budiansky's admonition about what has become of American universities and colleges triggered considerable resonance. For example, Richard Crepeau, a professor of history at the University of Central Florida, confirms that " 'Brand U.' precisely captures a cancer that has swept through academia in the last two decades. Somehow the business model captured the hearts and minds of university presidents looking for some way to leave their mark on higher education."[34] Similarly, Steve Lohr of the *New York Times* warns: "the entrepreneurial zeal of academics also raises concerns, like whether the direction of research is being overly influenced by the marketplace."[35] Harvard University business professor Toby E. Stuart questions whether "basic scientific questions [are] being neglected because there isn't a quick path to commercialization? No one really knows the answer to that question."[36] Thus, the role of the entrepreneurial university serving the entrepreneurial society is anything but simple, demanding entrepreneurial leadership.

Europeans are increasingly aware that one reason for the diverging economic growth and employment between the United States and Europe is the changing roles that universities play in society. While America's universities mutated and evolved to support the entrepreneurial society, European universities remain mired in the managed economy. Scholars and policy analysts typically attribute the divergence in economic performance to Europe's overregulation, an inflexible labor market, and a generous welfare state that discourages work. A simpler explanation is that Americans have harnessed their massive research and science investments while the Europeans have not. While the quiet, messy, and largely unnoticed revolution transformed American universities, European universities are barely out of the starting gate.

The gap between European and American universities has developed over time. Between 1901 and 1950, 73 percent of the Nobel Prizes awarded in science went to European scientists. More recently, between 1995 and 2004, European scientists have earned only 19 percent of the Nobel Prizes. According to the *Wall Street Journal*,

> officials are acutely conscious that Europe almost caught up economically with the U.S. by 1992, but that the U.S. leapt ahead during the tech boom, thanks in part to a more entrepreneurial culture and cutting-edge research at universities like Stanford, the University of California at Berkeley and MIT that acted as incubators for innovation.[37]

Claude Allegre, who served as minister of education in France, looked at the differences and told a group of visiting Americans that "in the United States your university system is one of the drivers of American prosperity. But here, we simply don't invest enough. Universities are poor. They're not a priority either for the state or the private sector. If we don't reverse this trend, we will kill the new generation."[38] One big obstacle facing European universities and research is a lack of funding. While the United States allocates 2.7 percent of its GDP to higher education, countries in the European Union invest only 1.1 percent.

In raw numbers, the United States spends $20,545 per student, while the United Kingdom spends only $11,621, and Germany $10,996.[39]

Something of a new consensus is emerging in Europe that they, too, need an entrepreneurial university system that is compatible with an entrepreneurial Europe. According to Josef Joffe, the publisher-editor of *Die Zeit*,

> a hundred years ago Humboldt University in Berlin was the model for the rest of the world. Today, Johns Hopkins, Stanford and the University of Chicago were founded in conscious imitation of the German university and its novel fusion of teaching and research. Today Europe's universities have lost their luster, and as they talk reform, they talk American. Indeed, America is one huge global "demonstration effect," as the sociologists call it.[40]

In response to this newly emerging consensus that their old university model, focused on fair and equal education, no longer suffices, Germany has introduced a bold new policy to move toward the entrepreneurial university. This new public policy approach is a striking rejection of the postwar policies of homogeneity and standardization, with its resulting curbing of cross-institutional competition. Rather, this new approach forces competition between universities through the introduction of a policy instrument called the *Exzellenzinitiative*, or Excellence Initiative. Over a five-year period, staring in 2005, the German government is investing €1.9 billion to create "elite universities." Funds will be awarded to universities that have developed the potential for excellence in research in particular specific fields.[41] After years of perhaps admiring the top American universities but writing them off as examples of elitism and exclusivity, the Germans have radically reversed direction. The Ludwig-Maximilians-University of Munich and the Technical University of Munich, along with eight others, are being groomed to become Germany's best.

Why did Germany change its policy toward higher education and research? The recognition that in the global economy the traditional Humboldt-style university is not sufficient was enough. According to Germany's minister of education, Annette Schavan, "the German Government needs to force scientific research and the economy to work together. The goal is to start a common innovation strategy to develop a science-based high-technology strategy."[42] Germany, like other European countries, is now committed to creating entrepreneurial universities.

Germany and other European countries spent too many years on the sidelines, saddled with a policy approach that inhibited not just state-of-the art research and scholarship, but its commercialization and application in the economy. As the *Wall Street Journal* reports, "political leaders and economists across the continent say that weak links to business, funding shortages and lack of competition for staff and students at universities are threatening to erode the technological edge the continent needs to compete globally."[43] Janez Potocnik, who serves as the European commissioner for science and research, concludes from looking across the Atlantic that "our universities must be able to respond to the demands of the market. We have fallen behind."[44] Accordingly, in May 2006 the European Commission identified not just increasing the funding of universities and research but also commercializing that research as a high priority for Europe. It has turned out that the United States' investment in universities and research was not an extravagant expenditure: it was the foundation for generating growth and competitiveness in the global economy.

Georg Winckler, president of the European Conference of University Presidents, emphasizes that in the twenty-first century,

> the higher is the level of education and human capital of citizens, the higher will be the standard of living. Human capital and education are the most important source of a high standard of living. Europe is suffering from a clear deficit of such human capital and education. . . . In contrast to the United States there is too low of a share of the European population with a degree in higher education.[45]

France's annual allocation of $8,500 per university student, 40 percent less than the investment made in each high school student, appears insufficient.[46] Whether France, Germany, and other European countries can catch up and compensate for years of passively watching the transformation of American universities remains to be seen. On the one hand, students complain about the quality of university courses and the inaccessibility of professors and the research process. On the other hand, as the *New York Times* reported, French students are unwilling to pay tuition because, they claim, "the university is a public service. The state must pay."[47] Despite student resistance, universities in Europe are starting to charge tuition. Starting in 2003, British universities began charging fees of £3,000, or $5,685, although exemptions were allowed for financially impoverished students. Meanwhile, a 2005 German court decision has allowed universities to start charging tuition, even if it is only €1,000 per year.[48]

One thing is becoming clear from the recent and startling revolution that is now beginning to shake up the sleepy European universities. The entrepreneurial university has emerged as a central institution and source of not just scientific research and knowledge but also cultural and social thinking and values in helping to create the entrepreneurial society. It's no longer your father's university.

9

Won't Get Fooled Again?

A central issue common to every era and confronting each generation is how best to move into the future. This issue confronts individuals, firms, organizations, cities, regions, states, and, in fact, entire societies. While the issue is known, the question remains—how?

It seemed like answering this question was simple in the era corresponding to the managed economy. In an economy where it was known what is to be produced, how it was to be produced, and who would be doing the producing, moving into the future did not seem all that complicated. The present simply needed to be more or less replicated to move into the future.

Certainly that pretty much described the strategy of people working in the automobile industry during its heyday. Of course, there was the annual new model, but this change, in its predictable annual cycle, was anticipated, marginal, and incremental. In the managed economy, public policy promoted investing in and building large factories—physical capital.

In terms of national policy, this meant first and foremost promoting and facilitating investment in plants and factories. When I started studying economics back in the 1970s, we were obsessed with interest rates as the key policy instrument that controlled economic growth. The interest rate was the cost for companies to borrow money, money used to build factories and buy equipment. Keynesian theory focused on generating growth from government spending as a mechanism for inducing firm investment in physical capital. The main thing was to get firms to invest in physical capital, which was the lifeblood of not just the firms and industry but also the nation's entire economy. What firms should invest their money in was so obvious and self-explanatory that it was never explicitly explained in any of my classes or textbooks. It was all about business as usual—just how to get more of it.

Of course, there were voices that questioned whether the managed economy and its corresponding institutional and social values had a positive effect on individuals. Writers like David Riesman, with *The Lonely Crowd*, Sloan Wilson, with *The Man in the Gray Flannel Suit*, and William H. Whyte, with *The Organization Man*, warned us about the erosion of the American soul, the loss of our traditional rugged, self-determined individualism. Though these voices were interesting, and received a lot of attention, few seriously considered changing what John Kenneth Galbraith called the "affluent society," fueled by the managed economy.[1] The affluent society was America's reward for its sacrifice on Omaha Beach and saving the world from fascism. There was no reason to doubt the expansion of America's affluent society.

Thus, feeding the capital-driven managed economy was not only essential to maintain and expand America's standard of living—ensuring economic growth and well-paid, secure, quality jobs—but also to stave off the communist threat: not just communist nuclear bombs but the massive Soviet industrial combines. John Kenneth Galbraith, William H. Whyte, and David Riesman were not alone in observing America's commitment to the managed economy. The focus on the large, successful corporations as the protectors of the American way of life received support and reinforcement from all of American's institutions and policies. Everything, not just education policy, but also family policy and cultural policy focused on supporting large companies, regardless of whether or not the impact on individuals or America's soul was positive or negative.

The only concern was on the fact that some industries, such as automobiles and steel, were too large and too powerful—this, it was thought, would be incompatible with America's decentralized democratic society. In the early 1960s—with inflation suddenly increasing, triggered by a round of price increases in the steel industry—President John F. Kennedy threatened the industry with serious repercussions if they did not cancel the price increases. Like the Soviets when confronted by that same American president in the missile crisis in Cuba and the face-off of tanks at Checkpoint Charlie in Berlin, the U.S. steel industry blinked. It was widely proclaimed that the president had *jawboned* the American steel industry, suggesting an important new policy instrument. The main point here is not the instrument but the target. The suspicion was widespread that, perhaps in terms of beating the feared Soviet Union, Charlie "Engine" Wilson had been right in proclaiming that General Motor's and America's interests were aligned, but when it came to preserving American democracy, large firms needed to be held in check.

Thus, in the 1970s, when the massive automobile and steel imports from Germany and Japan suddenly surged, America was stunned. As the imports spread to electronics, shoes, textiles, apparel, tires, and other manufactured goods, American industry was in a state of shock. How could it be that in these industries where American policy was seeking to restrain firms from having too much power and success, foreign companies were even more successful? General Motors, Ford, and U.S. Steel, with their highly efficient, productive, and successful factories, were actually weak and vulnerable to competition from countries that had been vanquished and defeated in World War II. The Achilles' heel of American manufacturing had been uncovered.

Certainly, first as a high school and later a college student, I had dutifully learned that American workers, especially in the all-important auto and steel industries, earned the highest wages in the world. Although they were no smarter than their foreign counterparts, they were luckier. They had the best factories and machinery to work with, which made them the most efficient workers and yielded the highest productivity in the world. Like *Mad* magazine's Alfred E. Newman, they had a "What, me worry?" philosophy.

In fact, the Japanese, Germans, and other Europeans had caught up. The premise driving the entire U.S. managed economy and certainly underlying Galbraith's affluent society was that America had an advantage, an almost natural, self-apparent, frankly an *American* advantage, based on capital—factories, machines, and equipment. America had more of it than the rest of the world. If America had accounted for half of the world's wealth, half of its output, and nearly two-thirds of the physical capital at the close of World War II, this was certainly no longer the case by the 1970s, as the British historian Robert

Payne noted. Not only had Germany and Japan more than caught up, in terms of investment in plants and factories, but they had policies and institutions designed to make the most of their investments. Generally, these policies revolved around superior training of workers through apprentice systems; cooperation among producers, trade unions and the government; and, in the case of Japan, explicit targeting of industries to ensure success in key export markets, principally the United States.[2] It all worked. By the 1970s and 1980s, the once mighty, proud American corporations, such as General Motors, Ford, and U.S. Steel, had been humbled, as floods of imports led to massive plant closings and downsizing, particularly in the Midwest.

The United States, that is, U.S. corporate, union, and political leaders, had duped themselves into arrogance and complacency. Their assumption that American superiority was natural, permanent, perhaps even God-given, had blinded them to how the world was changing. American superiority had been cut off at the knees by foreigners whom America had restored to life after World War II. How did the automobile industry fail to take advantage of any of the bright and daring ideas for advancing the automobile generated by their own young and passionate engineers? Not surprisingly, Detroit stuck with the status quo: "General Motors assaulted the new American market with ever bigger cars," and with what . . . the top auto designer in Detroit, termed "dynamic obsolescence."[3] If the strategy inherent in the managed economy was all about replicating the past, sticking to a strategy of incrementally larger and more ostentatious cars was consistent. Thus, it was not surprising that during the early 1970s OPEC embargo, when gas prices skyrocketed, smaller and more fuel-efficient cars came not from Detroit but from Japan and Germany.

Detroit never recovered. Similarly, the steel imports pouring into the United States from Germany and Japan were manufactured by state-of-the-art blast oxygen furnaces, something not found in Pittsburgh and Gary. What happened to America's superiority in capital investment and the supporting social and institutional systems? The failure lay in the assumption, the arrogance, and the complacency that the American advantage was somehow guaranteed. Bruce Springsteen captured the impact on American life in his song "The River":

> I got a job working construction for the Johnstown Company,
> But lately there ain't been much work on account of the economy,

Now all them things that seemed so important,
Well mister they vanished right into the air,
Now I just act like I don't remember,
Mary acts like she don't care.

David Halberstam recalled that back in those days, "GM was so mighty it knew it could simply pass on the burden of higher labor costs to the customers."[4] The scholars were hardly better prepared. Even after it had become clear that America had lost its capital advantage, academics focused on strategies to win back America's past glory in traditional manufacturing. It shouldn't be forgotten that as recently as 1992, when Bill Clinton ran for president, many scholars and policy-makers were still trying to find ways to imitate Japan and Germany's policies in order to help the flagging U.S. economy. This sentiment was generally mirrored in the influential study referred to in chapter 1, *Made in America*, which concluded that for the United States to restore its international competitiveness, it had to regain primacy in manufacturing plants and equipment, that is, its physical capital. To do this, America had to adopt policies like the ones in Japan and Germany that targeted specific industries and specific companies. In other words, if you couldn't beat them, you had to join them.

Similarly, W. W. Rostow, a Harvard economist and later American ambassador to Germany, predicted a revolution in economic policy, concluding: "the United States is entering a new political era, one in which it will be preoccupied by increased economic competition from abroad and will need better cooperation at home to deal with this challenge."[5] The message from leading American scholars was loud and clear: learn from the America's two leading competitors, Japan and Germany, and try to become more like them in order to gain economic growth and jobs. It still boiled down to building more factories.

Regional policy-makers were also fooled. Policies for communities, cities, states, and regions in the capital-driven managed economy had two general functions. First, if you had a major factory located nearby, the policy was to develop mechanisms to redistribute and share some of the profits within the local community or region. Such policy instruments went beyond taxation to include boosterism and philanthropy. Cities like Pittsburgh thrived on revenue from the Carnegie and Mellon foundations, Detroit from the Ford Foundation, and Indianapolis from the Lilly Foundation. Alternatively, if there wasn't a large manufacturing corporation in town, local policy focused on convincing a company to relocate. Policy instruments such as subsidies, interest-free loans, special training programs, and targeted public investment in infrastructure, such as highways or airports, were key to recruiting companies and their factories.

As the first wave of internationalization in the 1970s transformed the industrial heartland of the Midwest into the Rust Belt, communities and regions that were locked in to the traditional policy approach of the managed economy did not recover, and as the 1990s and pervasive globalization set in, Bruce Springsteen's song "My Hometown" seemed more apt than ever.[6] Certainly, communities that never weaned themselves from dependence on large factories, like Gary, Indiana, or East Lansing, Michigan, never recovered. The great manufacturing companies, like General Motors, Ford, US Steel, Bethlehem Steel, B. F. Goodyear, and RCA, hemorrhaged jobs, closing plants and downsizing remaining factories in response to the decreased demand that was resulting from the flood of imports.

American firms did not rest on their laurels as the world globalized. Companies fought back, some more successfully than others. One thing that nearly every large corporation did was eliminate factories and jobs in the United States. Michael Moore's documentary film *Roger and Me* shows an agitated Moore trying to ask Roger Smith, the CEO of General Motors, why his company was coldheartedly closing plants and eliminating factories that were profitable. Moore also wanted to know what had become of his beloved hometown, Flint, Michigan, which had been a thriving and vital community supporting middle-class families in his youth. His camera lens shows how Flint, like other Midwest communities, was devastated by the loss of factories and jobs during the 1980s, as factories moved to lower cost locations in Mexico and South America.

Moore accused the one-time great American manufacturing corporations, principally General Motors, of selling America out for profits. What Moore failed to grasp in *Roger and Me*, as well as his other documentaries, was the reality that his childhood world had vanished. Globalization had driven the nail deep into the capital-driven, managed economy. Communities that failed to realize and recognize the demise of the managed, factory-driven economy and devise new strategies to deal with the globalized economy were doomed to massive job losses, unemployment, low or negative growth, and the resulting social and personal suffering accompanying such devastation. It is no coincidence that the once thriving and rich city of Gary, Indiana, now registers the highest number of per capita murders in the United States. Detroit is not far behind now that its factories have closed. The cities and regions that fared better in the 1990s, such as Pittsburgh and Cleveland, clearly recognized the need to change strategies, and gave up seeking to attract and exploit large factories.

The bankruptcy of the local policy approach that revolved around large manufacturing plants is portrayed in a memorable scene from the movie *Primary Colors*, based on a bestselling book by Joe Klein. John Travolta plays the role of Jack Stanton, a young Bill Clintonesque presidential candidate. He is hard at work on the campaign trail, aspiring to his party's nomination in the 1992 primary. At a gathering of unionized textile workers facing imminent layoffs in a New Hampshire factory, Stanton is asked what he could do to help them. His answer was that although he'd like to paint them a happy future with secure jobs, he couldn't lie and gloss over the truth. Globalization was taking those jobs away, and they weren't coming back. Stanton advised the workers to get training and acquire skills for the new economy, and to ensure that their children did as well. Stanton, a character modeled closely on real-life candidate Bill Clinton, echoed Clinton's sentiments, feeling their pain as their jobs vanished from the United States.

Leaders of large companies, unions, and the government, as well as academics, weren't the only ones fooled by the managed economy's unexpected death. Individuals were caught off guard as well. Despite Bruce Springsteen's warning that "these jobs are going boys and they ain't coming back," many continued to fool themselves. Moore aside, the devotion to the culture of the large company with its patriarchal employee-boss relationship was remarkably slow to disappear. Despite the fact that certain aspects of large corporations, most notably their paternalism that made them eerily resemble the Soviet socialist combines, "the essential goodness of the corporation was never questioned."[7] General Motors was "regarded as, of all the many places to work, the best, because it was the biggest, the most respected."[8]

Values that made sense in the capital-driven managed economy, such as the redundancy of high school education, are to this day embedded in some midwestern communities, or at least in Indiana, where I live. The idea that a young person could either drop out of high school or end his or her education with a high school diploma is still alive and well in some communities. Back in the heyday of the managed economy, such young people would have left school to start their lifetime employment at their local auto plant. Today, a high school dropout can't get a good paying factory job, but the past values remain, reinforced by decades of family and community culture prevalent in towns, long after the reality has drastically changed.

A few years ago my son Alex was playing football in a league for ten- to twelve-year-olds. For me, it was a short drive across town to take my son to team practice and games. On the other hand, many of the kids came from small towns in the region. It was a sobering moment when I realized that several families drove some two hours from their homes to take their sons to not just the football games but also the daily practices. These families came from areas with high unemployment rates, with both Mom and Dad unemployed. However, getting their son to a two-hour practice was a priority. As a father, I respect family devotion. However, my inner economist wondered about the wisdom of such devotion to such an expensive sport. The hundreds of dollars I spent registering Alex and buying his equipment had not gone unnoticed, and this didn't even count the gas I bought and the rest of the family's commitment to support Alex. These were expensive for me, an employed professor, so I wondered if the unemployed parents might have made other financial and time choices that would have a better chance at improving their kid's future, such as helping with school. After all, their kids have to compete in a global economy, and I doubt football will take many of them far. The values of families and communities are exemplified by the passionate embrace of football and basketball for the boys, cheerleading for the girls. Meanwhile, academics are given lip service. People's values are reflected by how they choose to spend their time and money. Given the opportunity to put their money and their time where their priorities are, people do, but these priorities and values, which once led to prosperity and security, are now fraught with vulnerabilities. When these kids grow up, where will they find work? And if they do, what kind of jobs, paying what kind of salaries and benefits, will they be able to hold down? So in Indiana, the schools are filled with Hoosier kids aspiring to the NFL or NBA, cheered on by well-meaning parents who believe that opportunity lies in a million-dollar contract—or, one cringes to think, perhaps for the high school popularity those parents never quite achieved. Meanwhile, elsewhere in the world libraries are full of students studying. Don't foreign kids enjoy sports, too? Their families seem to have different priorities and values. Knowing how the world is changing and how best to take advantage of the coming entrepreneurial society, with the demise of the managed economy, and the emergence of the entrepreneurial economy, I surely hope the Hoosiers don't get fooled again.

It's not just about valuing education. It's also about *Weltanschauung*, or people's worldview. In the managed economy, a premium was assigned to fitting in, to conforming and being one of the crowd. Several years ago I found my report card from first grade in 1959. I was startled not just by how poor my grades were but also what I was graded on. The categories made it clear what was deemed important in the era of the managed economy for young children to be successful later in life: "Gets along well with others," "Does what he is told," "Obeys the rules," and "Is reliable." It was clear that, probably like most other grade school kids all across America, I was being groomed to fit in, with either the conformity required by white-collar corporate jobs in a large companies, if I earned a college degree, or the iron reliability and consistency required for an assembly-line job, if I did not.

Similarly, the founder and president of the National Foundation for Reaching Entrepreneurship, Steve Mariotti, looks back to his own upbringing and education at public school and reflects:

> people I grew up with in Flint, Michigan, in the 1960s, were not encouraged to consider the possibility that someday they could follow in Henry Ford's footsteps and start their own companies. My high school offered machine shop and auto repair, but not once were we encouraged to create new machines or taught how to run our own machine companies. Although my classmates and I would have been better off with the skills and know-how how to generate a livelihood emanating from our unique strengths, talents, and capacities, in my hometown we were taught to value security over risk taking. The weight of this bedrock security sapped the energy

and possibilities of a generation of dutiful employees who worked for the promise of a pension.[9]

The characteristics that were instilled in Mariotti and me reflected those that were imposed on a generation across the United States. These were the tried-and-true values that had proven to be a prerequisite for success. It was these values underlying the managed economy that caused William H. Whyte and David Riesman so much consternation. As David Halberstam explains in *The Fifties*,

> The culture was first and foremost hierarchical: An enterprising young executive tended to take all signals, share all attitudes and prejudices of the men above him, as his wife tended to play the sports and card games favored by the boss's wife, to emulate how she dressed and even to serve the same foods for dinner. The job of a junior executive was to know at all times what the senior executive wanted in his hotel room on the road, what his favorite meal at a favorite restaurant was in a given city.[10]

Does the entrepreneurial economy need a different kind of person from the managed economy? According to Mathew Stewart, who founded his own consulting firm, the characteristics required to thrive in the entrepreneurial society are the antithesis of those that were valued so highly during the era of the managed economy.

> According to all the experts, the enemy of the "new" organization was lurking in every episode of *Leave It to Beaver*. . . . If you believed our chief of recruiting, the consulting firm I helped to found represented a complete revolution from the Taylorist practices of conventional organizations. Our firm wasn't about bureaucratic control and robotic efficiency in the pursuit of profit. It was about love. . . . Many good things can be said about the "new" organization of the 1990s.[11] And who would want to take a stand against creativity, freedom, empowerment, and—yes, let's call it by its name—love?[12]

That the entrepreneurial society thrives on different human strengths and qualities than did the managed economy is not an exclusively American phenomenon. For example, in observing how much

Germany's current generation differs from past generations, *Der Spiegel* reports:

> For many young people, the flexibility demanded by studies, internships or years abroad is not a burden, but a vital part of becoming a well-rounded individual—in perfect accord with their parents' wishes. Rather than going to church on Sundays, these parents had elevated self-fulfillment to a calling and prescribed full appointment books for their offspring from the tender age of four onwards: Mondays meant music lessons, Tuesdays rhythmical gymnastics, and Wednesdays watercolor painting at the junior art school.

Does this sound familiar to American parents? The priority of giving our children the best opportunities, the most resources, the greatest advantages to develop themselves as individuals, to procure the talents, personality, experience, and perspective requisite for thriving in the globalized entrepreneurial society, is not a monopoly held by the United States. Rather, these values and capabilities are at least perceived to be the tools for success in the globalized entrepreneurial society that has spread across the developed world, including Europe. As *Der Spiegel* reports, " 'foster, promote, encourage' are the new watchwords: parents want to afford their children the opportunity they had been denied: the chance to discover and develop their own skills and talents."[13] According to the German sociologist Ulrich Beck "being an individual is what counts today. That is a core principle of our society."[14]

In the past, being an apprentice at a factory or earning a white-collar university degree was sufficient to guarantee lifetime employment in Germany, as was the case throughout Europe. However, in the globalized entrepreneurial society, there are no longer such guarantees.

> First and foremost, a broadly diversified resume is vital to success in the job market. Meeting requirements involves cloaking everything in the mantle of personality development. Whereas a basic degree with a moderate grade once ensured lifelong employment, today's recruits need numerous additional qualification—a German education alone no longer guarantees access to the globalized economy.[15]

In the managed economy, most work was a mechanical set of repetitive routines. This certainly was the case at the printing plant where I worked to pay my way through college. In repeating the movements required to pick each book up as it came rolling off the assembly line, nothing cerebral was needed; what was required was mastery of a physical routine and the ability to suppress thinking and imagination while lifting the books. In Whyte's *Organization Man*, it isn't that different for the white-collar workers. While they have to use their brains and not their brawn, the way they are supposed to use their brains is highly restricted and constrained to typically repetitive routines and calculations.

David Halberstam quotes George Walker, the head of styling at Ford Motor during the 1950s:

> the 1957 Ford was great, but right away we had to bury it
> and start another. We design a car, and the minute it's done,
> we hate it—we've got to do another one. We design a car to
> make a man unhappy with his 1957 Ford " 'long about the
> end of 1958."[16]

Of Harley Earl, General Motors' chief stylist in the 1950s, Halberstam observes: "it is possible that no one exerted as much influence on American style and taste in the fifties as [Earl], and no one reflected more accurately what the country had become."[17] Perhaps most telling was Earl's admission that "General Motors is in business for only one reason. To make money. In order to do that we make cars. But if we could make money making garbage cans, we would make garbage cans."[18] Earl was similarly quoted as admitting "Listen, I'd put smoke-stacks right in the middle of the sons of bitches if I thought I could sell more cars."[19]

However, as the managed economy was eclipsed, so was the premium of such values and personal character. Perhaps more than any other, IBM was the corporation that placed the highest premium on loyalty.[20] The relationship between IBM and its workers was reminiscent of the highly paternalistic relationships prevalent in socialist Eastern Europe and the Soviet Union. Workers at East German combines were provided with vacation facilities, recreational facilities, and even nurseries—services also provided by IBM to its employees. Because my father worked for IBM, I am a proud graduate of an IBM nursery school. One of my earliest memories is of a birthday party in my honor at the IBM country club. Since almost all of the fathers of my friends worked for IBM, most of us were IBM children. In the winter, we would sled on the slopes of the hills at the IBM park. In the summer, we would frolic in the IBM swimming pool. If an IBM worker stayed loyal to the company, IBM stayed loyal to the worker.

At least until the bottom fell out. By the 1980s, the IBM model of unquestioned loyalty to long-term loyal employees was no longer tenable. Interviewing the irate spouse of a laid-off IBM executive in the early 1990s, the *New York Times* reported:

> "To be an IBM executive was to have great significance," Mrs. Young said. Mrs. Young, a school social worker, did not lose a job at IBM; her husband did. It is a measure of the power of the cutbacks that her identity has also been unhinged. . . . "We were part of a great big family," said John Young, a tall, broad-shouldered man of 52. "The manager was a father figure. In exchange, workers put in long hours and the spouses dutifully did their part." "Their was no question what the wife did," Mrs. Young said, "The wife's primary role was enrolling the kids in a new school, redecorating the house, finding a new church, and entertaining the IBM employees." Mrs. Young said she felt a "sense of great betrayal" and was angry at her husband's "blind faith." "He was being crucified and he was still loyal."[21]

Of course, Mrs. Young's anger at her husband's sheeplike loyalty toward the very company that was betraying their social contract and leaving them out in the cold, belies the reality that both husband and wife were fooled. The times had changed; what once was very real in the IBM of the managed economy had simply disappeared on the eve of the entrepreneurial society. What was functional and valuable in the managed economy simply proved to be dysfunctional and counter-productive, in fact a hindrance, in the entrepreneurial society.

Of course, not everyone had been fooled. Some of IBM's best and brightest employees saw the writing on the wall and defected before the company could terminate them. Although the IBM motto had remained "Think" since it was instituted by Thomas J. Watson, a more accurate statement would be "Think—but only in the IBM way." In any case, there was never a shortage of voices—including those of Steve Jobs and Bill Gates—telling IBM that it needed to change. As the Princeton University social scientist Albert O. Hirschman argues in his proclaimed paradigm *Exit, Voice and Loyalty*, if "voice" fails, people will tend to resort to "exit," particularly as "loyalty" falters.[22] However, the communal, corporate, and personal values that were successful under the managed economy meant that not just IBM but its loyal employees were fooled. The *New York Times* reported: " 'Dutchess County has had this warm comfortable security blanket called IBM for decades,' said William R. Steinhaus, the county executive. 'People before me were very passive when it came to job diversification because they felt IBM was their meal ticket. That has come back to haunt us big time.' "[23]

My brother, Bruce, was fooled, too, and he didn't even work for IBM. During his stint as stage manager at the Bardavon, a local theater in the heart of IBM's hometown, Bruce witnessed people losing their jobs. The entire Hudson Valley area between New York City and Albany was decimated as ten thousand IBM employees lost their jobs. In Dutchess County, where we had grown up and my brother worked, IBM once provided 60 percent of the manufacturing jobs and 20 percent all jobs. Unemployment jumped from 3 percent in 1988 to nearly 12 percent in 1993. In surveying the economic, social, and psychological damage, the *New York Times* reported that very few, if any, of the middle-level managers who had been laid off would "ever make anywhere near the salaries of $80,000 or more that they once made, or keep their self-respect."[24] As the layoffs mounted, attendance at the Bardavon's music and theatre shows sagged. As Bruce's job security became doubtful, my brother followed many IBM refugees, including the computer and semiconductor entrepreneurs Gene Ahmdel and Ted Hoff, to California.

Poughkeepsie, Dutchess County, and the entire Hudson Valley between New York City and Albany had pretty much followed the classic economic development strategy of the managed economy by putting all of their eggs into one basket. And what a basket it was! IBM, the best of the best, or—as Peters and Waterman proclaimed—the most excellent corporation in the entire world.

The fallacy of this managed economy strategy for the Youngs, my brother Bruce, and the entire Hudson Valley was relying on one single

business, albeit the most successful one of its era, to always be successful and always be there. As we know, IBM has not disappeared, and
now thrives, but it does so in different industries, actually business services like its motto, "the Solution Company" suggests, and in different
places far from the Hudson Valley. Driving through my hometown,
Poughkeepsie, I am struck by the empty IBM plants and buildings, the
architecture of an earlier era. It reminds me of the managed economy
era that did not survive, with its set of economic development policy
goals that led to economic and social disaster for Poughkeepsie and the
entire region.

People like the Youngs, living in Poughkeepsie, surely ask themselves "Wasn't there anything that could have been done to prevent this
disaster? Surely, something could have been done." In fact, this is the
same question that is always posed when a great corporation or industry, once thought to be an unshakable source of jobs, prosperity, and
economic security, stumbles, falls, and starts hemorrhaging jobs. It is
the same question posed by countless citizens and businesses in the
once thriving textile towns of New England like Pawtucket and
Woonsocket, Rhode Island, and the devastated manufacturing communities like Gary and Detroit in the Rust Belt. It is the same question
posed by Michael Moore about his beloved hometown of Flint.
However, in his controversial films, Moore looks for solutions in the
wrong places, or at least in highly improbable places: in the companies
themselves, and in what government could have and should have done
to force the corporations to abstain from downsizing, outsourcing, and
offshoring. Maybe companies like IBM in Poughkeepsie or General
Motors in Flint could have been led to see the light and taken the
necessary steps to prevent the impending disasters triggered by global
competition from occurring in the first place. As governments around
the world have learned, it is not easy to force corporations into doing
something that lies outside their best interest. No amount of cajoling,
or industrial subsidies, was able to prevent massive job reductions and
plant closings in Germany's steel industry, located in the Ruhr Valley,
or in its shipbuilding industry, located in the Kiel region of Schleswig-
Holstein. This is the fatal flaw in the thinking underlying Moore's films
Roger and Me and *Downsize This*.

Rather, a better policy approach is to be proactive, considering
what can be done with the knowledge resources at hand. The Hudson

Valley was filled with well-educated scientists and engineers. However, virtually no effort was made to keep these people from moving away as they sought their fortunes not in the Hudson Valley but instead in Silicon Valley, where rich investments were being made to produce, say, another Hudson Valley full of scientists and engineers. There was no sense, at least back then, that a region, or even an entire country, could or should be trying to take advantage of its localized knowledge resources. One major difference between a managed economy policy regime and an entrepreneurial society policy regime is how knowledge resources are treated. A major point of chapter 4 was that in a globalizing economy, the existing corporations will probably not provide sufficient employment, generating the opportunities needed for growth. Large corporations typically respond to globalization by redeploying production to other places through outsourcing and off-shoring, thus resulting in unemployment. If companies don't outsource or offshore, then real (i.e., inflation-adjusted) wages will be pushed lower, unemployment will increase, or both. This is what happened in the midwestern United States, as well as throughout most of Europe. In the United States, it was a drop in real wages; in Europe, it was an increase in unemployment. This reflects the divergence between the competitiveness of businesses versus the competitiveness of communities.

Rather than rely on the status quo to deliver jobs, growth, and the desired standard of living in a globalizing economy, communities, cities, regions, and countries are realizing that they must take matters into their own hands. Rather than being passive victims of globalization, a new policy approach, the *strategic management of place*, has emerged as a local, regional, and national response to globalization. This approach focuses on taking advantage of the resource whose value is rising in a global economy: ideas and knowledge. As already explained in chapter 5, ideas are the gold standard in the globalized economy, and, as chapter 7 explained, communities, cities, regions, and countries can look to three sources to find people with ideas: existing businesses and organizations; universities and research laboratories; and investments made in education, culture, and experience. Some of these investments are made by society, such as education and university research, while others are made by private investors, such as corporations (although public funds may have been used to induce the corporation to locate in the first place). But this gold, in the form of knowledgeable, creative, and innovative people with potentially important ideas, may turn out to be only fool's gold if it is not converted into dollars, or economic growth. Rather, as chapter 6 emphasizes, the knowledge filter stands between people's ideas and knowledge and their ability to actually do something with them. If existing businesses are unwilling to pursue these ideas, then, as chapter 7 made clear, entrepreneurship can serve as the missing link between the most precious resource in a global era, knowledge and ideas, and their actual implementation and commercialization. As Heike Grimm, my colleague and friend who serves as director of the Erfurt School of Public Policy at Erfurt University in Germany, likes to say, entrepreneurs have emerged as the local heroes of the globalized economy.[25] According to Heike, "the entrepreneur is the local hero in the global village." The entrepreneur takes idle and unused investments in ideas, knowledge, and creativity and converts them into the thing society so desperately covets: new ventures that, if successful, will generate jobs, growth, and prosperity.

It's like trying to make lemonade with only one lemon. In the global economy, knowledge and ideas must be squeezed as much as possible to fully utilize the region's potential. But how can such knowledge and ideas be squeezed? If policy cannot force existing corporations to innovate, or solve a company's inherent problem with dealing with highly uncertain and asymmetric ideas, encouraging entrepreneurship is an effective policy alternative.

The most fundamental lessons for individuals and places in the entrepreneurial society is that targeting companies will not provide security and protection from a turbulent and globalized market. In an entrepreneurial society, companies are viewed by individuals as vehicles for gaining knowledge and valuable experience. Jack Harding picked IBM for his first job because he thought the training he would receive in sales would provide him with an understanding of how industry worked. His plan worked, and in due time he left the company. In the entrepreneurial society, companies are great sources of learning and augmentation of human capital and knowledge, but they no longer offer job security.

During the era of the managed economy, convincing a business to build a factory in your town was a promise of long-term job security for its employees. Having spent a lot of money building a factory, companies couldn't easily move, so employees and communities could take advantage of their dominant position. Globalization changed that. Suddenly factories could leave and choose different and faraway places with lower costs, building new factories. The message for communities, cities, states, and countries is that targeting specific companies is a poor idea. Focusing instead on investments in ideas, knowledge, and creative individuals will encourage people to start new and entrepreneurial firms. In the entrepreneurial society, policy needs to revolve around inputs and process, rather than the outputs and outcomes from firms that were the targets of the managed economy.

Indiana, like most other midwestern states, has had its share of plant closings and downsizings. As the state with the highest share of employment in manufacturing in the country, it has been especially vulnerable to the forces of globalization. Before 1970, during the era of the managed economy, inflation-adjusted real wages in Indiana were well above the national average. Since then, wages have fallen well below the national average. Indiana's best and brightest flee the state in what is called the Indiana brain drain. Several years ago I was at a meeting of many top government, industry, and university officials in Indiana. The focus of the meeting was how best to move the state into the future and centered on how to encourage spinoffs and other technology transfer from Purdue, Notre Dame, Indiana University, as well as other universities across the state. I imagine that these meetings had regularly taken place for some time, but I also realized that, until recently, these meetings had usually focused on how to attract and retain companies like General Motors and Ford because officials believed that this was where the jobs could be found. As I related earlier, after moving to Indiana in 1998, I was told by the Indiana Economic Development Commission, that while high technology and entrepreneurship was great and exciting, it was not for Indiana, or even the Midwest; Indiana and its neighbors were different: their strengths and advantages lay in traditional manufacturing. It was felt that Hoosiers needed to be patient and wait for the business cycle to pick up again. (This conversation took place at the end of the 1990s, the most prosperous decade since World War II! Could one really expect the business cycle to "pick up" any more?) I heard this message over and over again from a variety of people, including my own brethren, economists, who would shake their heads knowingly and lecture that under the law of comparative advantage, not every city, state, or region could be high tech, because somewhere there was somebody who would do the manufacturing. Unfortunately, they didn't realize that somewhere could easily be somewhere outside the borders of the United States.

But, as the Indiana meeting showed, something changed. Indiana is now looking to move into the future, and not by replicating the status quo but rather by creating something that doesn't exist or barely exists right now by focusing on entrepreneurship. Indiana needs to take advantage of its strong knowledge base, which includes not only the universities and the great research facility at Crane Naval Base (yes, Indiana has a naval base, and it's not located on Lake Michigan, it is in the heart of the state!) but also some of the great private corporations, such as Lilly Pharmaceutical, and Indiana's own home-raised and educated Hoosiers. Importantly, at that meeting, and countless others across the state, it has been recognized that just having the knowledge base is not sufficient. People with ideas, dreams, and visions must then act on them. Indiana, like many other states around the country, and other regions throughout the world, is on the verge of shifting from the managed economy to the entrepreneurial society. Early on, places like Indiana thought that they would only need to accentuate the knowledge, science, and engineering at research universities at that would be sufficient. However, it became apparent that knowledge alone was not enough—it was getting trapped in the knowledge filter. Trying to induce the innovation and subsequent economic growth and job creation happen by command, or wish, was about as successful as trying to make the science and technology commercialize by command or wish. It didn't happen.

This nonstarter happened not just in America but also in Europe. Germany declared 2005 the year of innovation. However, it didn't happen, and sitting chancellor Gerhard Schroeder was widely ridiculed for his empty rhetoric and wishful thinking, as if he could command Germany to be innovative because it would be good for the country. It was no different back in America's heartland, either, where states like Wisconsin, Michigan, Ohio, Illinois, Minnesota and Indiana committed themselves to developing knowledge-based growth.

What could be done? At a different meeting, then-governor of Indiana, Frank O'Bannon met with advisors from universities, industry, and government to consider whether the state should try to create a type of "Research Triangle" of knowledge-based entrepreneurship spanning the region between the location of the medical school at Indianapolis, Purdue University at Lafayette, and Indiana University at Bloomington. After hearing the proposal, modeled after North Carolina's Research Triangle Park, the governor shook his head, "I don't know," he wondered. "Those folks down in North Carolina are scientific and entrepreneurial. We Hoosiers have different traditions." I never found out who was sitting next to me at that meeting, but he whispered in my ear: "Hell, when I grew up in North Carolina, we were just a bunch of hicks."

Somehow North Carolina, through Research Triangle Park, had succeeded in changing itself from surviving on the production of furniture, textiles, and tobacco to being a thriving entrepreneurial society—a dramatic change, considering the state's past. The traditional public policy instruments failed to preserve employment, and international competitiveness in the traditional industries in North Carolina—furniture, textiles, and tobacco—had all lost international competitiveness, resulting in declines in employment and stagnated real incomes. In 1952, only Arkansas and Mississippi had lower per capita incomes. According to two of my friends and colleagues, University of North Carolina at Greensboro economics professor Al Link and Dartmouth College economics professor John Scott, a movement encouraging the use of the region's rich knowledge base emerged. Based on the three major universities (Duke University, the University of North Carolina at Chapel Hill, and North Carolina State University),[26] this movement of businesspeople, politicians, and academics looking to improve industrial growth ultimately fell into the hands of the governor, who not only had a vision to create Research Triangle Park but championed the creation of an entrepreneurial society. In 1959 North Carolina announced the formation of Research Triangle Park, claiming four thousand acres of pine forest west of Raleigh. The transformation has been amazing: Who can forget the portrayal of a sleepy, slightly seedy, but in no way dynamic or high-tech Durham in the movie featuring Susan Sarandon and Kevin Costner, *Bull Durham*. Visiting today, it's hard to imagine the Durham portrayed in that movie.

Empirical evidence shows that Research Triangle Park has fundamentally changed the region. Link and Scott document the growth in the number of research companies in the Park, going from none in 1958 to fifty in the mid-1980s and over one hundred in 1997.[27] At the same time, employment zoomed from zero in 1958 to over forty thousand in 1997. Michael Lugar of the University of North Carolina at Chapel Hill attributes to Research Triangle Park the direct and indirect generation of one-quarter of all jobs in the region between 1959 and 1990, and the shifting of the nature of those jobs toward high-value-added knowledge activities.[28] The industries range from software development to pharmaceuticals and biotechnology. As Tim Gray observes, "the vision has yielded greater benefits than anyone probably could have imagined. Today, Research Triangle Park . . . is the hard-thumping heart of one of the nation's most prominent technology centers."[29] At the heart of this success story in North Carolina is its transformation into an entrepreneurial society. It wasn't easy in the early days, but, with the cultural diversity injected by having three high-quality universities within a short drive, the region has become one of the most creative in the country, according to Richard Florida.

John McConnell, the founder of Medic Computer Systems, which makes software for doctors, points out: "when we started Medic, there was no venture capital. You went to the bank or you bootstrapped."[30] The situation is far different today, with local and national sources of investment easily available. Similarly, the region has become a Mecca for Angel Capital. Combined with the technical prowess of North Carolina State University and the entrepreneurial society created by Research Triangle Park, the state has created what the rest of the world wants—growth, good jobs, and a high standard of living with an enviable quality of life.

Indiana took a good look at what North Carolina had created and decided it wanted that, too. In a time of downsizing, outsourcing and offshoring, rather than being victimized by globalization, North Carolina had found a way to take advantage of the opportunities afforded by globalization. The solution lay in creating the entrepreneurial society. Indiana was not alone in wanting to shift away from the managed economy by doing so. Most places also want an entrepreneurial society. This policy goal comes not from any sort of political or ideological conviction but is inspired by the pragmatic observation that it works. Even more striking, it is about the only thing working in the globalized economy.

It hasn't been just Research Triangle Park in North Carolina. Before that, there was the mother of the entrepreneurial society, Silicon Valley, followed by Boston's Route 128. Since then more and more entrepreneurial clusters have sprung up, ranging from Austin to San Diego to Madison and beyond, including Boise, Idaho, and Salt Lake City, Utah. What these places have in common is the economic performance that everyone covets—jobs, economic growth, and a high standard of living—created with knowledge and entrepreneurship.

Back in the 1980s, our first sighting of the entrepreneurial economy was in California, what we now call the Silicon Valley. As Gordon Moore—cofounder of Intel and one of Silicon Valley's founding fathers—and Kevin Davis, an economic historian, put it, "we hold that the central element in the history of Silicon Valley is the founding of a previously unknown type of regional dynamic, high-technology economy."[31] Before Silicon Valley, innovative new technology was usually only associated with the large flagship companies like IBM, Kodak, and AT&T, which seemed invincible, with their armies of engineers and scientists. These scientists demonstrated undying loyalty to their employers forged from lifetime contracts and their generally paternalistic stance toward their employees.

In Peters and Waterman's bestseller *In Search of Excellence*, which documented the top fifty U.S. corporations, these characteristics not only placed IBM at the top of the list, but made it as a shining example for corporate America to learn from and imitate. The incipient entrepreneurial economy of Silicon Valley provided a striking contrast, a place where people were quick to leave their jobs in order to start new firms and even entirely new industries. While IBM was large and bureaucratic, with rules and hierarchical decision-making, the emerging Silicon Valley thrived on spontaneity, participation, openness, and a general disdain for rules and hierarchy. While obedience and conformity were trademarks of the capital-driven economy, corresponding to the Solow model, the entrepreneurial economy values, above all, creativity, originality, independence, and autonomy.

It's important to realize that the entrepreneurial economy involves more than just starting a number of businesses and hoping for the best. Too many cities, regions, and entire countries have tried this and failed. Rather, creating entrepreneurial attitudes, action, and values requires creating an entrepreneurial society. The flagship institutions and policies in an entrepreneurial society must have an entirely different focus than their counterparts did in the managed economy. The entrepreneurial society institutions are a departure from the managed economy stalwarts: unions, big government programs, and corporate hierarchy.

As already discussed, by the end of the Reagan and Bush era and at the start of the Clinton era, many of the top policy analysts and business leaders had written off American economic leadership. In the title of his bestseller, Paul Krugman, the *New York Times* columnist, mourned *The Age of Diminished Expectations*.[32] In another bestseller, Paul Kennedy warned of *The Rise and Decline of Great Nations*.[33] The gloom and doom of the prophecies for America's future as we headed into the last decade of the twentieth century was pervasive. It was a continuation of the pessimism that America had felt since the 1970s stagflation, as expressed by Lester Thurow's title *The Zero Sum Society*.[34] Thurow argued that the only point of most transactions in the post-OPEC American economy was to reallocate resources and wealth. One person's gain was another's loss, hence the zero sum society. Thus it came as something of a surprise when in the 1990s, to paraphrase Mark Twain, it turned out that reports of America's economic demise had been greatly exaggerated. What had saved America from what most experts and leading scholars predicted as an inevitable economic decline? The emergence of the entrepreneurial society.

No doubt this society first emerged in what today is referred to as Silicon Valley. But it didn't stop there. It diffused outward, first to Boston's Route 128, then to North Carolina's Research Triangle Park, and later to even less likely places like San Diego, Madison, and Austin. A world desperate for the performance that the managed economy had churned out year after year—that is, jobs—good jobs—and a growing prosperity—couldn't help but notice that those places, the entrepreneurial places, had exactly that.

Starting in the mid-1970s, the Europeans knew that their European model provided a high standard of living, complete with an array of social benefits, including job security. However, America proved resurgent and, after 1993, started to look better and better. The country, anchored by the emergence of the entrepreneurial society, turned into a job machine. Growth and job creation were at record levels. Meanwhile, back in Europe, tepid growth resulted in stubborn levels of unemployment. The Europeans seemed unable to create jobs and generate economic growth.[35] A divergence was taking place between the opposite sides of the Atlantic. The U.S. economy, fueled by an entrepreneurial society, was leaving the anemic European economy, still burdened by the chains of the managed economy, in the dust. Most telling, for all of their coveting of job security, Europeans couldn't help but notice the irony that job security was actually greater in Silicon Valley than in their highly regulated and protected economies. It was true that a particular job in a particular firm was not especially secure, but it was easy to find another. By contrast, in the highly regulated and protected Europe, finding a new job was becoming increasingly difficult as downsizing became rampant. The whole world was watching the U.S. growth miracle. It came unexpectedly, and was unanticipated, but certainly welcome. Perhaps Paul Krugman's admonition about "the age of diminished expectations" would ultimately prove true, and David Kennedy was right to warn of the "rise and decline of great powers," but the American growth miracle of the 1990s was more about the rise, while the concept of decline seemed more applicable to the Europeans, still saddled with a managed economy.

America had transformed itself from Lester Thurow's zero sum society into a job and growth machine unmatched in history. Job opportunities abounded, the stock market skyrocketed to record highs, and real estate prices soared. These were heady times. The rest of the world looked enviously on. America seemed to have something that eluded the awed onlookers. What America had, and they did not, was an entrepreneurial society.

America had in ten years transformed itself from a self-doubting society to one of self-celebration. America had it, and the rest of the world did not. At a Capitol Hill conference on globalization and entrepreneurship, the final panel was asked to consider future challenges.[36] Having spent considerable time in Europe and Asia observing recent efforts to create their versions of an entrepreneurial society, I wondered, "What will the United States do when the rest of the world catches up?" My friend Chuck Wessner, head of the Science, Technology and Economic Policy Division of the National Academy of Sciences, constantly reminds me how the panel of experts literally laughed me off the stage. "What, catch up?" responded one outraged colleague, "That will never happen in a thousand years! The Europeans are far too bureaucratic and regulated to become entrepreneurial. The Asians lack the necessary creativity." Apparently experts believed that only the Americans have the right stuff for an entrepreneurial society. This was America's destiny, its shining moment in history—after all of the doubts and detours of the second half of the twentieth century, such as Vietnam, the 1970s stagflation, the humility of watching President George Bush grovel before the Japanese after more than a decade of having the manufacturing backbone in automobiles and steel wiped out by Japanese imports, the increasing smugness of the Europeans shaking their head at the hollowing out of the U.S. manufacturing corporations—America was back, and back with a vengeance. America was back because it had the one thing that mattered in a rapidly globalizing economy—an entrepreneurial society that generated not just the glamorous success stories of Bill Gates's Microsoft and Michael Dell's Dell Computer but also a massive army of people who, armed with entrepreneurial values and capabilities, had embraced the entrepreneurial economy.

When I left my teaching position at Middlebury College in 1984, none of my students had ever thought about starting their own business. I spent the next twelve years in Berlin, isolated from the changing mores of American culture and society. In 1997, when I returned to the United States, I was shocked by the change in college students. Not only did many of my students talk openly about an entrepreneurial career, a number of them had already experienced working with an entrepreneurial startup. My home, America, had changed. With it, American preeminence and leadership, which had shined so brightly in the years following World War II, was again unavoidable. There was again a sense of inevitability and destiny regarding the capacity and gift for entrepreneurship that was uniquely American. Twenty percent of the largest firms (that did not grow large as a result of mergers) in the world in 2002 are new companies founded in the US after 1960. There is only one European startup included in the list of the largest enterprises in the world—SAP, which ranked number 73.[37] As Lester Thurow concludes, "Europe is falling behind because it doesn't build the new big firms of the future."[38]

Increasingly, the rest of the world has realized that the root cause of the divergence in economic growth is due to the emergence of the American entrepreneurial society. This awareness and response has evolved through five distinct phases: denial, recognition, envy, acceptance, and attainment. If these five phases sound reminiscent of how psychology tells us we deal with loss, there was a loss to be dealt with: the bell tolled for the managed economy. However, with loss comes the potential for regeneration, and it is the entrepreneurial society that the other countries of the world now believe will allow them to become successful anew.

In the first stage, *denial*, prior to the fall of the Berlin Wall in 1989, most people looked to Silicon Valley with skepticism and doubts. People either denied the existence of the entrepreneurial society or they denied its effectiveness. For example, writing in 1988 in the eminent *Harvard Business Review*, the MIT scholar Charles Ferguson, in an article entitled "From the People who Brought You Voodoo Eeconomics," provided a scathing critique of the entrepreneurial society that had emerged in Silicon Valley:

> fragmentation, instability, and entrepreneurialism are not signs of well-being. In fact, they are symptoms of the larger structural problems that afflict U.S. industry. In semiconductors, a combination of personnel mobility, ineffective property protection, risk aversion in large companies, and tax subsides for the formation of new companies contribute to a fragmented *"chronically entrepreneurial"* industry. U.S. semiconductor companies are unable to sustain the large, long-term investments required for continued U.S. competitiveness. Companies avoid long-term R & D, personnel training, and long-term cooperative relationships because these are presumed, often correctly, to yield no benefit to the original investors. Economies of scale are not sufficiently developed. An elaborate infrastructure of small subcontractors has sprung up in Silicon Valley. Personnel turnover in the American merchant semiconductor industry has risen to 20 percent compared with less than 5 percent in IBM and Japanese corporations. . . . Fragmentation discouraged badly needed coordinated action—to develop process technology and also to demand better government support.[39]

The old saying "If you're a hammer, then everything else looks like a nail" applies. If you are a scholar raised and educated with the primacy of capital and manufacturing in the managed economy as your gold standard, every deviation, such as a *chronically entrepreneurial* industry, looks like a problem and not a solution.

The view from the Europe was not any different. After all, this was the continent where in 1968 statesman Jean Jacques Servan-Schreiber warned Europeans to beware the "American Challenge" in the form of the "dynamisms, organisation, innovation, and boldness that characterize the giant American corporations." Because gigantic corporations were needed to amass the requisite resources for innovation, Servan-Schreiber advocated a European policy designed to create large companies that would compete with American businesses in a global economy.

Europe was used to looking across the Atlantic and facing a competitive threat from large multinational corporations like General Motors, US Steel, and IBM, not nameless and unrecognizable startup firms in exotic industries such as software and biotechnology. In fact, the Cecchini Report to the European Commission in 1988 documented the economic gains in terms of the scale economies to be achieved from the anticipated European integration. Emerging firms like Apple, Microsoft, and Intel were interesting but thought to be irrelevant compared to the mainstay businesses in the automobile, textile, machinery, and chemical industries, Europe's engines of economic growth and employment. The high performance of Silicon Valley was thought to be short term, as Ferguson pointed out in the *Harvard Business Review*: it was seen as a place where long-term investments and commitments were being sacrificed for short-term profits. It was exactly this short-termism that the authors of *Made in America* criticized in favor of the long-term approach prevalent in Japan and Germany. Thus, in the first stage, the existence, or at least viability, of the entrepreneurial society was simply denied.

In the second stage, *recognition*, which occurred subsequently to the fall of the Berlin Wall, Europe and the rest of the world recognized that the high performance exhibited by the entrepreneurial society in Silicon Valley did, in fact, deliver economic growth and jobs. However, along with this recognition also came recognition of what economists call the law of comparative advantage. This meant that while the United States—or rather a few pinpoints such as Silicon Valley, Research Triangle Park, and Boston's Route 128—might have the high-tech advantage, Europe had a comparative advantage in high-quality manufacturing. It was felt that Americans could produce computers, microprocessors, and software, and Europe would provide automobiles, textiles, and machine tools. It seemed like a lot more people needed those products than the high-tech gadgets coming out of Silicon Valley, Route 128, and Research Triangle Park. Each continent would specialize in its comparative advantage and then trade with the other, just as the law and history dictated. Thus, Europe was secure holding onto the mainstay institutions of the managed economy that had made it so successful after World War II.

In the third stage, *envy*, the rest of the world became envious of the American capacity to shift from the managed economy to an entrepreneurial society. The envy stage took place in the mid-1990s, when the European managed economy fell apart. The German model of a social market economy had generated a standard of living that created not only the material wealth found in America but also provided the social services and security found elsewhere on the European continent. The German economic model demonstrated that capitalism could generate a high and equitable standard of living and also have a friendly face. The realization that this social market economy could collapse sent shock waves throughout the country and across Europe. Early in 1998, the unemployment rate had reached nearly 13 percent,[40] representing, the highest level of unemployment since before the Nazi era.[41] Germans, remembering how high unemployment had once helped Hitler take control, became increasingly skittish and concerned about their country's inability to create jobs and generate economic growth. One of Germany's newsweekly magazines, *Stern*, warned—with the headline "Germany before the Crash?"—of unemployment levels exceeding five million people.[42]

Unemployment of such proportions threatened the once solid economic basis on which postwar German democracy had been built, ultimately threatening the stability of the country. The public's confidence in the economy and the government's ability to manage the crisis was eroded. In the September 1998 election, this shaken confidence led to the defeat of the Christian Democratic Union and the reigning chancellor, Helmut Kohl, and the election of the Social Democratic challenger Gerhard Schroeder. As economic growth stalled and unemployment ratcheted upward in the early 1990s, German reunification was frequently cited as the culprit. However, it was clear that the burden that had been imposed on the West German managed economy by its absorption of 18 million people from the former communist German Democratic Republic was not singularly responsible for Germany's current problems. At the heart of the crisis was an outdated economic model, one that, though no longer viable, was being imposed on the states of the former East Germany that had rejoined West Germany. However, other European countries that were not burdened with reunification, most noticeably France, Spain, and Sweden, also experienced economic stagnation and rising unemployment. This suggests that the core problem was not Germany's reunification but an inability to adjust to the new globalized economy. Perhaps had the unification taken place a decade earlier, prior to the advent of globalization, and while the managed economy was still viable, the unified Germany would have had a much easier time of it. In any case, that is not what history had in store for Germany.

As unemployment in countries such as Germany, France, and Spain soared into double digits and economic growth stagnated, the capacity of the entrepreneurial society in Silicon Valley to generate economic growth and jobs was envied. The United States and Europe were on diverging trajectories. The *separate but equal* doctrine, from the concept of comparative advantage, yielded to the *different but better* doctrine of dynamic competitive advantage.[43] This was reflected by diverging rates of economic growth and unemployment rates between the two sides of the Atlantic during the 1990s. At the start of the decade, in 1991, per capita GDP barely differed between the United States and her leading European counterparts. For example, GDP per capita was only $1,000 higher in the United States than in France. The gap was somewhat higher, $2,000, with Italy and Germany, and $5,000 with the United Kingdom.[44]

However, by 2001, the transatlantic gap in GDP had exploded to $11,000 with the United Kingdom, $12,000 with Germany, $13,000 with France, and $16,000 with Italy. Taken as a whole, the transatlantic gap in the standard of living, as measured by GDP per capita, was greater at the turn of the century than it had been in the forty years after World War II.[45] The transatlantic gap in economic growth was also reflected in diverging unemployment rates. Even as unemployment sank to the lowest levels since the 1960s in the United States, unemployment skyrocketed in Europe to postwar highs. The United States saw 22 million net new jobs created, while no new net jobs were created in Europe.

As the entrepreneurial society continued to spread across the United States, most policy-makers despaired that European traditions, institutions, culture, and values were seemingly inconsistent and incompatible with the entrepreneurial society. For example, Joschka Fischer, a member of the Green Party who would later become the foreign minister of Germany, mourned in 1995 that "a company like Microsoft would never have a chance in Germany."[46] Envy was evident in *Der Spiegel*'s admission that

> global structural change has had an impact on the German economy that only a short time ago would have been unimaginable: Many of the products, such as automobiles, machinery, chemicals and steel are no longer competitive in global markets. And in the industries of the future, like biotechnology and electronics, the German companies are barely participating.[47]

Part of the reason for envy was the political gridlock created by the system that had generated Germany's economic miracle in the first place—the core institutions serving as the cornerstones to the managed economy. None of the people involved—not industry, labor, or government—was interested in championing individuals' ability to move outside established companies and start new firms. New firms posed a threat to established firms by generating not just new competition in product markets but also competition for the best employees. Similarly, new firms in new industries might generate new employment, but those jobs might not be compatible with established labor practices. Thus, part of the envy associated with this stage emanated from what could be characterized as the industry-union-government cartel.[48] The highly profitable German companies and the highly paid unionized workers shared a common interest in blocking the deregulation that was needed to trigger the startup and growth of new firms in knowledge-based industries. As Machiavelli had observed centuries earlier, "The innovator has for enemies all who have done well under the old, and lukewarm defenders in those who may do well under the new law."

Envy gave way to the more positive stage of *consensus* in the final years of the twentieth century. European policy-makers reached a consensus and commitment to creating a European entrepreneurial society. Inherent in this stage is the recognition that the entrepreneurial society is a viable strategy for growth, jobs, and prosperity in the globalized economy. Rather than despairing that the United States had what Europe could not attain, European policy-makers instituted a broad set of policies intended to make Europe entrepreneurial. They looked across the Atlantic and realized that if places like North Carolina, Austin, and Salt Lake City could implement very conscious and targeted policies to create the entrepreneurial economy, cities like Munich, Helsinki, Stockholm, and Rotterdam could as well. After all, Europe had a number of assets and traditions, such as a highly educated and skilled labor force and the existence of world-class research institutions. Europe also had a long tradition of government-industry-worker partnerships that, if redirected, could be well suited for the entrepreneurial society. Perhaps most important, Europe had traditions dating back to the Enlightenment focusing on creativity, originality, and independence of thinking and action.

Thus, following the decade of Europe's worst economic performance since World War II, it might not have been surprising when a bold new strategy to spur economic growth was unveiled. However, the focus of this new approach would have seemed unimaginable just a few years earlier. With the 2000 Lisbon Proclamation, Romano Prodi, then president of the European Commission, committed Europe to becoming the knowledge and entrepreneurship leader in the world by 2020 in order to ensure prosperity and a high standard of living throughout the continent. According to Prodi, "our lacunae in the field of entrepreneurship need to be taken seriously because there is mounting evidence that the key to economic growth and productivity improvements lies in the entrepreneurial capacity of an economy."[49]

Europe has no shortage of ideas or entrepreneurs, but the European story has two endings, both discouraging. People with ideas will encounter the knowledge filter, at which point they either give up—and nothing will ever come of their idea—or they will find their opportunity outside Europe. Either way, Europe loses. Society may invest in universities, research institutes, in culture and education, developing people who are well educated and incredibly creative; and what we call the knowledge filter can block existing firms from implementing their ideas in the market. And, of course, the citizens of Europe, the taxpayers, are growing impatient. They have made substantial investments creating a knowledge society, but the return in terms of jobs and growth has remained elusive. Society may make wonderful and inspiring investments in knowledge and culture—but it also wants a return, especially a return in terms of jobs, growth, and competitiveness.

As the president of the Max Planck Society, Peter Gruess, reminded his audience at a 2005 meeting, "it was a wonder that Columbus discovered America. It would have been an even greater wonder if America had never been discovered."[50] Gruess's point was that many of the best ideas, like the idea that there was something out there if you set sail in a westward direction from Spain, will ultimately come to fruition. Just as the question of discovering America was more in terms of when than if, so, too, is the issue of implanting ideas, pursuing dreams, and acting on insights also more a question of when rather than if. Also who. Gruess's reminder was that if we don't do it, someone else likely will—which may not be so bad for the world, and is actually great for the institution and country where the idea is commercialized. But it may not be very good for the society investing in and creating that knowledge in the first place.

Communities, regions, and countries want ideas to be commercialized, and they want the ideas to be commercialized at home in their communities. They want their jobs, growth, and standard of living to be created at home. This is why the SAP story is so important; the ideas would have been lost forever, or at least lost by Europe, had the entrepreneurs founding SAP never penetrated the European knowledge filter. Investment in knowledge—research, universities, and education—is not sufficient. Entrepreneurship is needed. Entrepreneurship serves as the missing link to growth and jobs. If the existing great corporations cannot supply the desperately needed jobs, there is little accomplished by cajoling or by appealing to duty or social responsibility. Businesses find themselves in the midst of a race for competitiveness in global markets and are likely to focus on accessing workers around the world and not necessarily at home. Instead, look to what Europe has generated—highly creative, innovative and talented workers. If the great European companies can no longer supply the needed jobs, set the talents of Europeans free. Let entrepreneurship make use of ideas to create new firms and new jobs for Europeans.

The fifth and final stage will be *attainment*. While Europe and most of the rest of the world may not be there quite yet, there are definite stirrings of an entrepreneurial society emerging in Europe. Consider the cover story in *Der Spiegel* that proudly proclaimed: "Cell Phones, Hightech and Reform: Good Morning, Europe—How the Old Continent Is Attacking the Economic Power USA."[51] Whether the glass creating the European entrepreneurial society is still half empty or now half full is open to debate, but the direction is undeniable. Of course, other parts of the world, such as China and India, seem to have skipped over the first three phases entirely. They are well along in creating their own versions of the entrepreneurial society.

Jack Harding, founder and CEO of eSilicon, warns,

> if there's a weak spot in the Silicon Valley innovation cluster, it's in state government. Roads, taxes, energy prices and school systems can be addressed by insightful and courageous government policies. But it's a tough, unenviable job dominated during the past decade by partisan agendas. However, the performance of state government has been poor long enough for its shortcomings to be accommodated by the economic model of the region: It can only get better. . . . The factors that we hear will bring down Silicon Valley are not threats to the culture of innovation and won't pierce the heart of what makes Silicon Valley the U.S. high-tech capital. Traffic, housing prices and even high taxes are critical quality-of-life metrics but are not predictive of how innovation is being nurtured, encouraged and financed locally. And it is innovation that is the core of Silicon Valley's place in the world, not our roads and housing.
>
> Indeed, if we look at what threatens Silicon Valley's decades long status as tech leader, it isn't Boston, but Beijing; not Seattle, but Seoul. The real threat to Silicon Valley lies beyond our borders, not within them. Here, again, government on all levels not could, but must, do a better job of building and maintaining infrastructure, creating affordable energy and, most importantly, improving schools on a national basis. We are in the midst of a grave international challenge that requires immediate action. That must be the focus of future policy.[52]

Similarly, the president of the Ewing Marion Kauffman Foundation, Carl Schramm,[53] worries that "universities are becoming too bureaucratic in their approach to intellectual property, creating a new bottleneck in the transfer of technology to startups."[54]

Will the United States once again be fooled by the deadly cocktail of complacency mixed with arrogance? In the 1990s, the nation had a virtual monopoly in terms of the entrepreneurial society, just as it had a virtual monopoly on plants and factories at the close of World War II. Monopoly breeds complacency and arrogance. It was exactly this complacency and arrogance that led to the American downfall of the 1970s and 1980s. As the rest of the world recovered, America lost its assumed monopoly on capital.

Fast-forwarding to the twenty-first century, there are already signs that America is rapidly losing, if it hasn't already lost, its monopoly on the entrepreneurial society. Will America be fooled again, or will it react wisely, with a measured response to develop and nurture its entrepreneurial society? Just as in those heady years following World War II, in the 1990s, growth, jobs, and prosperity seemed never ending. Scholars and policy-makers wondered if the business cycle had come to an end, for the new economy seemed to have put an end to what had been seen as the inevitability of downturns.

Things have not gone quite as smoothly in this new century. While there are a number of contributing factors, such as the escalating prices of oil and other energy sources, America has lost its innocence, and it must now compete in a world where partners increasingly are committed to creating their own entrepreneurial society. The first decade of the new century has been more problematic than the last decade of the old.

This book started by showing how different today's entrepreneurial society is from the managed economy I grew up with. I will close with a similarity. The 1950s and 1990s stand out as two golden eras of recent American history. Both were eras of prosperity, growth, and confidence. Both were American decades, and both bred complacency and arrogance. In the case of the managed economy, such arrogance and complacency ultimately contributed to the demise of American leadership and economic supremacy. Will the era of the entrepreneurial society prove to be the same? Will America be fooled again? As George Santayana warned, "those who cannot remember the past are condemned to repeat it."

Notes

Chapter 1

1. David Halberstam, *The Fifties* (New York: Villard Books, 1993), p. 118, corrects the record of this famous quotation. What Wilson actually said was "We at General Motors have always felt that what was good for the country was good for General Motors as well."

2. Tom Brokaw, *The Greatest Generation* (New York: Random House, 1998).

3. William H. Whyte, *The Organization Man* (New York: Simon and Schuster, 1956).

4. Betty Friedan, in *The Feminine Mystique* (New York: Norton, 1963), makes it very clear that the prevalent and expected role of women in the postwar era was in the home, preferably as a housewife, and certainly not in the workplace, and most definitely not in a position of leadership or decision-making. Material from *The Feminine Mystique* by Betty Friedan. Copyright © 1983, 1974, 1973, 1963, by Betty Friedan. Used by permission of W.W. Norton & Company, Inc.

5. Sloan Wilson, *The Man in the Gray Flannel Suit* (New York: Simon and Schuster, 1955).

6. David Riesman, *The Lonely Crowd: A Study of Changing American Character* (New Haven: Yale University Press, 1950).

7. Friedan, *The Feminine Mystique*.

8. The term *managed economy* was introduced together with my colleague and friend Roy Thurik of Erasmus University Rotterdam, in "What's New about the New Economy? Sources of Growth in the Managed and Entrepreneurial Economies," *Industrial and Corporate Change* 19 (2001): 267–315.

9. See, for example, David B. Audretsch, *The Market and the State: Government Policy towards Business in Europe, Japan and the USA* (New York: New York University Press, 1989).

10. Copyright © 1963 by Warner Bros. Inc. Copyright renewed 1991 by Special Rider Music. All rights reserved. International copyright secured. Reprinted by permission.

11. "Can America Compete?" *Business Week*, April 27, 1987, pp. 45–69.

12. "Can America Compete," p. 45.

13. See for example, Audretsch, *The Market and the State*.

14. Audretsch, *The Market and the State*.

15. Thomas Friedman, *The World Is Flat* (London: Lane, 2005).

16. Lester Thurow, "Losing the Economic Race," *New York Review of Books*, September 27, 1984, (v 31, n 14) pp. 29–31.

17. Lester Thurow, "Healing with a Thousand Bandages," *Challenge* 28 (1985), p. 23.

18. Paul Kennedy, *The Rise and Decline of Great Powers* (New York: Random House, 1989).

19. Michael L. Dertouzos, Richard K. Lester, and Robert M. Solow, *Made in America: Regaining the Productive Edge* (Cambridge, Mass.: MIT Press, 1989).

20. See Whyte, *The Organization Man*, and Wilson, *The Man in the Gray Flannel Suit*.

21. Alan Bloom, in *The Closing of the American Mind* (New York: Simon and Schuster, 1987), argues that the 1960s marked the beginning of the decline of the quality of higher education in the United States.

22. It is interesting to note that this same generation of the 1960s played the same rebellious and antiestablishment role in Europe as did their counterparts in the United States. In Germany they are still referred to as *Die 68er*.

23. Personal recollection.

24. I observed one of my master's students proudly wearing this T-shirt in the spring of 2004.

25. Craig Wilson, "Cirque Ignites 'The Spark,'" *USA Today*, May 10, 2006. Last retrieved January 9, 2007, from http://www.usatoday.com/educate/college/firstyear/articles/20060514.htm.

26. For an analysis of the American deregulation movement and its sweeping scope, see Audretsch, *The Market and the State*.

27. Alexis de Tocqueville, *Democracy in America*, Project Gutenberg. Translated by Henry Reeve, Released January 21, 2006. Last retrieved January 9, 2007, from http://www.gutenberg.org/files/816/816-h/816-h.htm.

28. Speech by George W. Bush, November 4, 2004. Last retrieved January 10, 2007, from http://www.whitehouse.gov/news/releases/2004/11/20041104-5.html.

29. Steven Davis, John Haltiwanger, and Scott Schuh, "Small Business and Job Creation: Dissecting the Myth and Reassessing the Facts," *Small Business Economics* 8, no. 4 (1996): 298.

30. Representative Robert Michel, House minority leader, in the Republican response to the 1993 State of the Union address; Davis et al., "Small Business and Job Creation," p. 298.

31. Elaine Sciolino, "Higher Learning in France Clings to Its Old Ways," *New York Times*, May 12, 2006, p. A1.

32. Sciolino, "Higher Learning in France Clings to Its Old Ways," p. A1.

Chapter 2

1. Robert J. Samuelson, "The Politics of Make-Believe," *Newsweek*, April 3, 2006, p. 29. Also Robert J. Samuelson, "The French Denial," *Washington Post*, March 28, 2006, p. A23.

2. Samuelson, "The Politics of Make-Believe," p. 29. Also Samuelson, "The French Denial," p. A23.

3. "Wo das Glück zu Hause ist," *Der Stern*, April 20, 2004, pp. 48–54.

4. David Halberstam, *The Best and the Brightest* (New York: Random House, 1972).

5. It must be noted that not all scholars and policy-makers were persuaded by Keynesian economic policy. For example, Milton Friedman, in *Free to Choose*, clearly rejected the Keynesian policy approach embraced by both Democrats and Republicans alike, at least by the end of the 1960s and early 1970s.

6. Thomas Friedman, *The World Is Flat* (London: Lane, 2005).

7. Strictly speaking, it is referred to as *Sektstimmung*, "sparkling wine mood"; "Angst vor Aufschwung ohne Jobs," *Süddeutsche Zeitung*, February 1, 2006, p. 1.

8. "Angst vor Aufschwung ohne Jobs."

9. "Merkel ist Gewarnt," *Die Welt*, February 1, 2006, p. 8.

Chapter 3

1. Alfred Chandler, *The Visible Hand: The Managerial Revolution in American Business* (Cambridge, MA: Belknap Press, 1977).

2. Michael Piore and Charles Sabel, *The Second Industrial Divide* (New York: Basic Books, 1984).

3. Robert Reich, *The Next American Frontier* (New York: Times Books, 1983), p. 26.

4. Steven C. Wheelwright, "Restoring Competitiveness in U.S. Manufacturing," *California Management Review* 27 (1985), p. 26.

5. Frederick W. Taylor, *Principles of Scientific Management* (New York: Harper, 1911), quoted in Matthew Stewart, "The Management Myth," *Atlantic*, June 2006, p. 81.

6. David Halberstam, *The Fifties* (New York: Villard Books, 1993), p. 116.

7. Halberstam, *The Fifties*, p. 117.

8. This section is adapted from David B. Audretsch, *The Market and the State: Government Policy towards Business in Europe, Japan and the USA* (New York: New York University Press, 1989).

9. Piore and Sabel, *The Second Industrial Divide*.

10. Halberstam, *The Fifties*, p. 119.

11. Quoted in David Halberstam, *The Fifties* (New York: Villard Books, 1993), p. 119.

12. Quoted in Halberstam, *The Fifties* (New York: Villard Books, 1993), p. 119.

13. Piore and Sabel, *The Second Industrial Divide*.

14. Gabriel Kolko, *The Triumph of Conservativism* (New York: Macmillan, 1963), pp. 30–31.

15. See Ralph Nelson, *Merger Movements in American Industry 1895–1956* (Princeton: Princeton University Press, 1959).

16. Kolko, *The Triumph of Conservativism*, p. 27.

17. *U.S. v. US Steel Corp.*, 251, US 417 (1920).

18. Karl Marx, *Capital*, vol. 3 (Moscow: Progress Publishers, 1894), quoted in Nathan Rosenberg, "Economic Experiments" *Industrial and Corporate Change* (1992), 1:197.

19. *Munn v. Illinois*, 94 US 113, 1877.

20. Jesse Markham, "Mergers: The Adequacy of the New Section 7," in A. Phillips (ed.), *Perspectives on Antitrust Policy* (Princeton: Princeton University Press, 1965), p. 166.

21. *U.S. v. Aluminum Co. of America*, 148 F. 2d 416 (1945) p. 8. Note that in this case the Second Circuit Court served as a "court of last resort," or substitute for the U.S. Supreme Court, because several of the justices, who had previously worked with the prosecution, had to disqualify themselves, and the Supreme Court was unable to meet the necessary quorum of six justices to hear the case.

22. *Brown Shoe Co. v. U.S.*, 370 US 294 (1962).

23. See for example *U.S. v. General Dynamic Corp.*, 415 US 486 (1973).

24. *Brown Shoe Co. v. U.S.*, 370 US 294 (1962), p. 345.

25. See *FTC v. Consolidated Foods Corp.*, 380 US 592 (1965); *US v. Falstaff Brewing Corp.*, 410 US 526 (1973); and *FTC v. Proctor & Gamble Co.*, 386 US 568 (1967).

26. Federal Trade Commission, complaint against Kellogg, General Mills, General Foods, and Quaker Oats, docket no. 8883, filed April 26, 1972. Quaker Oats Company was subsequently dropped from the complaint.

27. *U.S. v. Arnold Schwinn & Co. et al.*, 388 US 365 (1967).

28. *Continental TV Inc. et al. v. GTE Sylvania, Inc.*, 433 US 36 (1977).

29. Todd Gitlin, *The Sixties: Years of Hope, Days of Rage* (New York: Bantam Books, 1993) p. 13.

30. Gitlin, *The Sixties*, p. 13.

31. Halberstam, *The Fifties*, p. 116.

32. This meant families earning at least $5,000 annually after taxes.

33. Halberstam, *The Fifties*, p. 587.

34. Halberstam, *The Fifties*, p. 496.

35. Halberstam, *The Fifties*, p. 496.

36. Quoted in Halberstam, *The Fifties*, p. 496.

37. Halberstam, *The Fifties*, p. 496.

38. Halberstam, *The Fifties*, p. 497.

39. See two of the most prominent articles by Robert Solow, "A Contribution to Theory of Economic Growth," *Quarterly Journal of Economics* 70 (1956): 65–94, and "Technical Change and the Aggregate Production Function," *Review of Economics and Statistics* 39 (1957): 312–320.

40. John H. Moore. "Measuring Soviet Economic Growth: Old Problems and New Complications." *Journal of Institutional and Theoretical Economics* 148(1) (1992): 72–92.

41. James Noren, "Soviet Industry Trends in Output, Inputs, and Productivity." In *New Directions in the Soviet Economy*. (Washington: Subcommittee Foreign Econ. Policy Join Econ. Committee, U.S. Congress, 1966).

42. What was known as the Gaither report—"Deterrence and Survival in the Nuclear Age," which was leaked from the Security Resources Panel of the Science Advisory committee of the Office of Defense Mobilization—made a strong case that the United States was "slipping in our nuclear capacity while the Soviets were becoming stronger all the time." The report concluded that the Soviet buildup "clearly indicates an increasing threat which may become critical"; quoted in Halberstam, *The Fifties*, pp. 699–700.

43. Quoted in Halberstam, *The Fifties*, pp. 701–702.

44. Quoted in F. M. Scherer, "The Posnerian Harvest: Separating Wheat from Chaff," *Yale Law Journal* 86 (April 1977): 980.

45. According to the Robinson-Patman Act, "It shall be unlawful for any person engaged in commerce, in the course of such commerce, either directly or indirectly, to discriminate in price between different purchasers of commodities of like grade and quality"; U.S. Code, title 15, chap. 1, sec. 13. For example, A & P was found in violation of the Robinson-Patman Act for direct purchases from suppliers and from performing its own wholesale functions. While these activities resulted in lower distribution costs, the gains in efficiency were seen as being irrelevant because small business was threatened.

46. Richard A. Posner, *Antitrust Law: An Economic Perspective* (Chicago: University of Chicago Press, 1976), p. 196.

47. Robert H. Bork, *The Antitrust Paradox: A Policy at War with Itself* (New York: Basic Books, 1978), p. 382.

48. U.S. Code, title 15, chap. 14A, sec. 631; www.sba.gov/aboutsba/sbahistory.html.

49. F. M. Scherer, *Industrial Market Structure and Economic Performance* (Chicago: Rand McNally), 1970.

50. Oliver Williamson, "Economies as an Antitrust Defense: The Welfare Tradeoffs," *American Economic Review* 58 (March 1968): 18–36.

51. With a decided focus on the role of large corporations, oligopoly, and economic concentration, the literature on industrial organization yielded a number of key insights concerning the efficiency and impact on economic performance associated with new and small firms: (1) Small firms were generally less efficient than their larger counterparts. Studies from the U.S. in the 1960s and 1970s revealed that small firms produced at lower levels of efficiency. (2) Small firms

provided lower levels of employee compensation. Empirical evidence from both North America and Europe found a systematic and positive relationship between employee compensation and firm size. (3) Small firms were only marginally involved in innovative activity. Based on R & D measures, small firms accounted for only a small amount of innovative activity. (4) The relative importance of small firms was declining over time in both North America and Europe. See David B. Audretsch, 2003 "Entrepreneurship Research: A Review of the Literature," Commission of the European Community, Director General for the Enterprise. Brussels, Belgium.

52. Scherer, *Industrial Market Structure and Economic Performance*, p. 44.

53. Zoltan J. Acs and David B. Audretsch (eds.), *Small Firms and Entrepreneurship: An East-West Perspective* (Cambridge: Cambridge University Press, 1993).

54. Nielson Research, ATS/Nielsen Automotive Industry Survey; www. advancedtech.com/survey.

55. Halberstam, *The Fifties*, p. 487.

56. Gitlin, *The Sixties*, p. 21.

57. Halberstam, *The Fifties*, p. 488.

58. William H. Whyte, *The Organization Man* (New York: Simon and Schuster, 1956), p. 129.

59. Gitlin, *The Sixties*, p. 16.

60. Halberstam, *The Fifties*, p. 295.

61. Halberstam, *The Fifties*, p. 591.

62. Betty Friedan, *The Feminine Mystique* (New York: Norton, 1963), p. 15.

63. Friedan, *The Feminine Mystique*, pp. 15–16.

64. Halberstam, *The Fifties*, p. 143.

65. Gitlin, *The Sixties*, p. 15.

66. Friedan, *The Feminine Mystique*, p. 37.

67. Friedan, *The Feminine Mystique*, p. 37.

68. Nora Johnson, "Desperate Housewives," *The Atlantic Monthly*, June 1961, pp. 123–128; http://www.theatlantic.com/ideastour/women/johnson-full .mhtml

69. Quoted in Halberstam, *The Fifties*, p. 512.

70. Halberstam, *The Fifties*, p. 118. In contrast, Halberstam observed, "its primary competitor, the Ford Motor Company hovered near bankruptcy after the war, thanks to the madness and paranoia of its founder."

71. Halberstam, *The Fifties*, p. 295.

72. Arlo Guthrie, "The City of New Orleans." (©1970, 1971 EMI U Catalogue, Inc and Turnpike Tom Music (ASCAP)).

73. Halberstam, *The Fifties*, p. 296.

74. Halberstam, *The Fifties*, pp. 300–301.

75. The title of Kris Kristofferson's song was "Me and Bobby McGee." In J. Joplin, Pearl Album, 1971. Me and Bobby McGee. Words and music by Kris Kristofferson and Fred Foster © 1969 (Renewed 1997) TEMI Combine Inc. All rights controlled by Combine Music Corp. and administered by EMI Blackwood Music Inc. All rights reserved. International copyright secured. Used by permission.

76. As David Halberstam notes of the beatniks, "if much of the rest of the nation was enthusiastically joining the great migration to the suburbs, they consciously rejected this new life of middle-class affluence and were creating a new, alternative life-style; they were pioneers of what would eventually become the counterculture." *The Fifties*, p. 295.

Chapter 4

1. Copyright © 1963 by Warner Bros. Inc. Copyright renewed 1991 by Special Rider Music. All rights reserved. International copyright secured. Reprinted by permission.

2. Tom Brokaw, *The Greatest Generation* (New York: Random House, 1998).

3. Studs Terkel, *Hard Times* (New York: Pantheon Books, 1974).

4. David Halberstam, *The Fifties* (New York: Villard Books, 1993), p. 214.

5. Julia Bonstein and Merlind Theile, "The Global Generation," *Der Spiegel Special International Edition* 4 (2005): 130–135.

6. Bonstein and Theile, "The Global Generation," p. 130.

7. Bonstein and Theile, "The Global Generation," p. 130.

8. Bonstein and Theile, "The Global Generation," p. 130.

9. Bonstein and Theile, "The Global Generation," p. 131.

10. Bonstein and Theile, "The Global Generation," pp. 131–132.

11. Robert Wright, "They Hate Us, They Really Hate Us," *New York Times Review of Books*, May 14, 2006, p. 28.

12. Julia A. Sweig, *Friendly Fire: Losing Friends and Making Enemies in the Anti-American Century* (New York: PublicAffairs, 2006), and Andrew Kohut and Bruce Stokes, *America against the World: How We Are Different and Why We Are Disliked* (New York: Times Books, 2006).

13. Wright, "They Hate Us," p. 28.

14. Josef Joffe, "The Perils of Soft Power: Why America's Cultural Influence Makes Enemies, Too," *New York Times Magazine*, May 14, 2006, p. 15.

15. Joffe, "The Perils of Soft Power," p. 16.

16. Wright, "They Hate Us," p. 28.

17. Quoted in Wright, "They Hate Us," p. 28.

18. For an excellent analysis of how the institutions of postwar Germany combined to create a more effective and productive managed economy than that in the United States, see Wolfgang W. Streeck, "On the Institutional Conditions of Diversified Quality Production," in *Beyond Keynesianism: The Socio-Economics of Production and Full Employment* (Aldershot, England: Elgar, 1991), pp. 21–61.

19. Thomas L. Friedman, *The World Is Flat* (London: Lane, 2005).

20. "The River" by Bruce Springsteen. Copyright © 1980 Bruce Springsteen (ASCAP). Reprinted by permission. International copyright secured. All rights reserved.

21. "Special Report: Rise of a Powerhouse," *Business Week*, European ed., December 12/19, 2005, p. 44.

22. Lester Thurow, *Fortune Favors the Bold* (New York: HarperCollins, 2002), pp. 25–26.

23. Thurow, *Fortune Favors the Bold*, pp. 38–39.

24. The data are adopted from Michael Jensen, "The Modern Industrial Revolution, Exit, and the Failure of the Internal Control Systems," *Journal of Finance* 48 (1993): 831–880.

25. "Special Report: Rise of a Powerhouse," p. 56.

26. "Special Report: Rise of a Powerhouse," p. 54.

27. Alexander Jung, "A New Economic Age," *Der Spiegel Special International Edition*, 4 (2005): 107.

28. "Bye-Bye 'Made in Germany,' " *Der Spiegel* 44 (2004): 94.

29. "Bye-Bye 'Made in Germany,' " p. 101.

30. "Bye-Bye 'Made in Germany,' " p. 94.

31. "Bye-Bye 'Made in Germany,' " p. 94.

32. Sharon Silke Carty, "GM Offers Buyouts to 126,000," *USA Today*, March 23, 2006, p. 1.

33. Philip Stephens, "A Future for Europe Shaped by Museums and Modernity," *Financial Times*, April 28, 2006, p. 11.

34. Jung, "A New Economic Age," p. 103.

35. Josef Hofmann, "VW Greift nur im Ausland Durch," *Handelsblatt*, May 5, 2005, Number 87, p. 15.

36. Hofmann, "VW Greift nur im Ausland Durch," p. 15.

37. Hofmann, "VW Greift nur im Ausland Durch," p. 15.

38. Bundesministerium für Wirtschaft und Technologie, *Annual Report 2000*.

39. "Wenn der Profit zur Pleite fuehrt: Mehr Gewinne—und mehr Arbeitslose: Wo bleibt die soziale Verantwortung der Unternehmer?" *Die Zeit*, February 2, 1996, p. 1.

40. "Wenn der Profit zur Pleite fuehrt," p. 1.

41. "The Downsizing of America," *New York Times*, March 3, 1996, p. 1.

42. Nils Klawitter, "The Faceless Factory," *Der Spiegel Special International Edition* 4 (2005): 120.

43. Jung, "A New Economic Age," p. 121.

44. Jung, "A New Economic Age," 120.

45. Stephens, "A Future for Europe Shaped by Museums and Modernity," p. 11.

46. Klawitter, "The Faceless Factory," p. 120.

47. "Special Report: Rise of a Powerhouse," p. 44.

48. "Special Report: Rise of a Powerhouse," p. 44.

49. "Research and Development: Looking for Innovation in the East, Where the Engineering Pool Is Deep," *Business Week European Edition*, December 12/19, 2005, p. 58.

50. "Research and Development: Looking for Innovation in the East," p. 58.

51. "Research and Development: Looking for Innovation in the East," p. 58.

52. "Research and Development: Looking for Innovation in the East," p. 58.

Chapter 5

1. The introduction of knowledge into macroeconomic growth models was formalized by Paul Romer, "Increasing Returns and Long-Run Growth," *Journal of Political Economy* 94 (1986): 1002–37; "Endogenous Technological Change," *Journal of Political Economy* 98 (1990): 71–102; and "The Origins of Endogenous Growth Theory," *Journal of Economic Perspectives* 8 (winter 1994): 3–22. Romer's critique of the Solow approach was not of the basic model of the neoclassical production function but of its omission of the role of knowledge. Romer, along with Robert E. Lucas and others, argued not only that knowledge was an important factor of production, along with the traditional factors of labor and capital, but also that because it was endogenously determined as a result of externalities and spillovers, it was particularly important.

2. It would be a mistake to think that knowledge was not considered as a factor influencing economic growth prior to the "new endogenous growth theory." As already explained, one of the main conclusions of the Solow model was that the traditional factors of capital and labor were inadequate in accounting for variations in growth performance. Indeed, it was the residual, which was thought to reflect technological change, that typically was thought to account for most of the variations in economic growth. As Richard Nelson concludes, the research "provided evidence that neoclassical variables do not account for all of the differences among firms in productivity"; "Research on Productivity Growth and Productivity Differences: Dead Ends and New Departures," *Journal of Economic Literature* 19 (1981): p 1063 .

3. For example, Richard Florida, *Rise of the Creative Class* (New York: Basic Books, 2002), argues that creativity is the key factor.

4. "Da muss man powern," *Managermagazin* 2 (2005): 88.

5. Lyn Heward and John U. Bacon, *The Spark: Igniting the Creative Fire That Lives within Us All* (New York: Currency, 2006).

6. "The Death of Distance," *Economist*, September 30, 1995, Survey Section, p 3.

7. Personal recollection.

8. Craig Wilson, "Cirque Ignites 'Spark,' " *USA Today*, May 10, 2006, p. 8B.

9. Wilson, "Cirque Ignites 'Spark,' " p. 8B.

10. Upton Sinclair, *The Jungle* (New York: Doubleday, 1906).

11. *Focus*, October 19, 2004, p. 118.

12. Edward Glaeser, H. Kallal, J. Scheinkman, and A. Shleifer, "Growth in Cities," *Journal of Political Economy* 100 (1992): 1127.

13. Personal communication.

14. There is systematic empirical evidence linking the success of entrepreneurial startups to the nature of the parent corporation of the entrepreneur. See, for example, Rajshree Agarwal, R. Echambadi, A. Franco, and M. Sarkar, "Knowledge Transfer through Inheritance: Spin-Out Generation, Development and Performance," *Academy of Management Journal* 47 (2004): 501–522; and Steven Klepper, "Spinouts," paper presented at the first annual Ewing Marion

Kauffman–Max Planck Conference, entitled "Entrepreneurship and Economic Growth," Tegernsee, Germany, May 7–9, 2006.

15. Lester Thurow, *Fortune Favors the Bold* (New York: HarperCollins, 2002), p. 25.

16. "Special Report: Rise of a Powerhouse," *Business Week European Edition*, December 12/19, 2005, p. 56.

17. "Research and Development: Looking for Innovation in the East Where the Engineering Pool Is Deep," *Business Week: European Edition*, December 12/19, 2005, p. 58.

18. "The Best Cities for Knowledge Workers," *Fortune*, November 15, 1993, p. 44.

19. The survey was carried out in 1993 by the management consulting firm of Moran, Stahl & Boyer of New York City.

20. "The Best Cities for Knowledge Workers," p. 44.

21. Personal communication with Jack Harding.

Chapter 6

1. Birch Bayh, statement to Association of University Technology Managers, September 13, 1978, in *Recollections: Celebrating the History of AUTMs and the Legacy of Bayh-Dole*. (Northbrook, Ill.: Association of University Technology Managers, 2004), p. 5.

2. The first references to the term *knowledge filter* was Zoltan J. Acs, David B. Audretsch, Pontus Braunerhjelm, and Bo Carlsson, "The Missing Link: The Knowledge Filter and Entrepreneurship in Endogenous Growth," Centre for Economic Policy Research, discussion paper 4783 (London: Centre for Economic Policy Research, 2004); and David B. Audretsch, Max Keilbach, and Erik Lehmann, *Entrepreneurship and Economic Growth* (New York: Oxford University Press, 2006).

3. Birch Bayh, statement on the approval of S.414 (Bayh-Dole) by the U.S. Senate on a 91–4 vote, April 13, 1980, quoted in Association of University Technology Managers, *Recollections*, p. 16.

4. "Konzeption eines Innovationsfonds der Deutschen Forschung (IFDF) zur Stärkung des Technologietransfers," *Garching Information*, January 2006, pp. 27

5. SAP, Annual Report, 2005, p. 25.

6. Kenneth Arrow identified greater uncertainty as a key characteristic distinguishing economic activity based on knowledge from that based on the traditional factors of physical capital, raw materials, or unskilled labor; Arrow K.J., (1962), Economic Welfare and the Allocation of Resources for Invention, in Nelson, R.R. ed., *The Rate and Direction of Inventive Activity*, Princeton University Press, Princeton.

7. Asymmetries are explained in the famous article by George Akerlof, "The Market for Lemons," *Quarterly Journal of Economics* 84 (1970): 488–500.

8. For an excellent analysis of the large organization and its functions see Alfred Chandler, *The Visible Hand: The Managerial Revolution in American Business* (Cambridge, Mass.: Belknap Press, 1977).

9. David Halberstam, *The Fifties* (New York: Villard Books, 1993), p. 127.

10. Halberstam, *The Fifties*, p. 127.

11. Stephen Klepper related this view in "Spinouts," paper presented at the first annual Ewing Marion Kauffman–Max Planck Conference, "Entrepreneurship and Economic Growth," Tegernsee, Germany, May 7–9, 2006.

12. William H. Whyte, *The Organization Man* (New York: Simon and Schuster, 1956), p. 205.

13. "System Error," *Economist*, September 18, 1993, p. 99.

14. Paul Carrol, "Die Offene Schlacht," *Die Zeit*, September 24, 1993, p. 18.

15. Daniel Ichbiah and Susan I. Knepper, *The Making of Microsoft: How Bill Gates and His Team Created the World's Most Successful Software Company* (Rocklin, Calif.: Prima, 1991).

16. Tom Peters and Robert H. Waterman Jr., *In Search of Excellence* (London: HarperCollins, 1995).

17. Lester Thurow, *Fortune Favors the Bold* (New York: HarperCollins, 2002).

18. Richard Florida, *The Rise of the Creative* Class (New York: Basic Books, 2002).

19. According to Jeremy Rifkin, *The European Dream* (New York: Penguin, 2004), Europe is the model of the future.

Chapter 7

1. Robert X. Cringley, "Accidental Empires: How the Boys of Silicon Valley Make Their Millions, Battle Foreign Competition, and Still Can't Get a Date" (New York: Harper Business, 1993), p. 39.

2. Jon Palfreman and Doron Swade, *The Dream Machine: Exploring the Computer Age* (London: BBC Books, 1991), p. 108.

3. Frank Rose, *West of Eden: The End of Innocence at Apple Computer* (New York: Viking Press, 1989).

4. Paul Carrol, "Die Offene Schlacht," *Die Zeit*, September 24, 1993, p. 18.

5. Tom Peters and Robert H. Waterman Jr., In *Search of Excellence* (London, HarperCollins, 1995)

6. For example, Saras D. Sarasvathy, Nicholas Dew, S. Ramakrishna Velamuri, and Sankaran Venkataraman, Part III Chapter 7, "Three Views of Entrepreneurial Opportunity", pages 141–160 in Zoltan Acs and David B. Audretsch (eds), *Handbook of Entrepreneurship Research* (Dordrecht: Kluwer Academic Publishers, 2003), p. 142, suggest that entrepreneurship is unbounded by organizational context: "an entrepreneurial opportunity consists of a set of ideas, beliefs and actions that enable the creation of future goods and services in the absence of current markets for them." By contrast, William B. Gartner and Nancy M. Carter "Entrepreneurial Behaviour and Firm Organizing Processes", pages 195–221,in Zoltan Acs and David B. Audretsch (eds), *Handbook of Entrepreneurship Research* (Dordrecht: Kluwer Academic Publishers, 2003) constrain the context for entrepreneurship to the creation of a new firm or organization: "entrepreneurial behavior involves the activities of individuals

who are associated with creating new organizations rather than the activities of individuals who are involved with maintaining or changing the operations of on-going established organizations"; p. 195. .

7. "Ein Mann, ein Brett," *Focus*, February 6, 2006, p. 106.

8. "Ein Mann, ein Brett," p. 106.

9. "Ein Mann, ein Brett," p. 106.

Chapter 8

1. According to Kent Hill, "Universities in the U.S. National Innovation System," unpublished manuscript, Center for Business Research, L. William Seidman Research Institute, W. P. Carey School of Business, Arizona State University, March 2006, p. 8, "by 1940 American universities were regarded as equal to or better than the best universities in Europe."

2. Elaine Sciolino, "Higher Learning in France Clings to Its Old Ways," *New York Times*, May 12, 2006, pp. A1, A14.

3. Sciolino, "Higher Learning in France Clings to Its Old Ways," pp. A1, A14.

4. "What Harvard Taught Larry Summers," *Time*, March 6, 2006, p. 64.

5. Michael Crichton, *Jurassic Park* (New York: Ballantine Books, 1990).

6. The Morrill Act provided for "the endowment, support, and maintenance of at least one college where the leading object shall be, without excluding other scientific and classical studies, and including military tactics, to teach such branches of learning as are related to agriculture and the mechanic arts, in such manner as the legislatures of the states may respectively prescribe, in order to promote the liberal and practical education of the industrial classes in the several pursuits and professions in life." Under this Act, each state was granted thirty thousand acres of public land for each senator and representative then in office. Thus the minimum amount of land granted is ninety thousand acres: two senators and one representative. Most states received much more land for their new universities.

7. Material about the Morrill Act was taken from several helpful websites, including the University of Kentucky's (Last retrieved February 20, 2007: http://www.uky.edu/CampusGuide/land-grant.html); US Department of State (Last retrieved February 20, 2007: http://usinfo.state.gov/usa/infousa/facts/democrac/27.htm); and the Higher Education Resource Hub's helpful site on the subject of Land Grant Institutions (Last retrieved February 20, 2007: http://www.higher-ed.org/resources/morrill_acts.htm).

8. Because the 1890 land grants do not receive Hatch Act or Smith-Lever funds, special programs have been created to help finance agricultural research and extension at these institutions. The Evans-Allen program supports agricultural research with funds equal to at least 15 percent of Hatch Act appropriations. Another program funds extension activities at the 1890 land grants with an emphasis on reaching socially and economically disadvantaged people.

9. These funds are distributed to the states on several different bases. Some funds go in equal amounts to all states; some go to the states on the basis of their farm population, or of their total population in relation to the total population of the United States. The United States Department of Agriculture (USDA) plays a key role in the administration of federal land-grant funds and the coordination of land-grant activities at the national level. The USDA's Cooperative State Research Service, for example, administers both Hatch Act and Morrill-Nelson funds. The Extension Service of the USDA administers Smith-Lever funding, though it cooperates with state governments—which provide additional funding for extension—in setting priorities and sharing information nationally.

10. Hill, "Universities in the U.S. National Innovation System," p. 10

11. Claudia Goldin and Larry Katz, "The Shaping of Higher Education: The Formative Years in the United States, 1890 to 1940," *Journal of Economic Perspectives*, 13, 1 (winter 1999): 37–62.

12. Vannevar Bush, *Science: The Endless Frontier* (Washington, D.C.: Government Printing Office, 1945). This book can be found on the web at www.nsf.gov/about/history/vbush1945.htm

13. Ed Roberts, personal communication, December 7, 2005.

14. Public Law 98–620.

15. David Mowery, "The Bayh-Dole Act and High-Technology Entrepreneurship in U.S. Universities: Chicken, Egg, or Something Else?" in Gary Liebcap (ed.), *University Entrepreneurship and Technology Transfers* (Amsterdam: Elsevier, 2005), argues that such a euphemistic assessment of the impact on Bayh-Dole is exaggerated. "Although it seems clear that the criticism of high-technology startups that was widespread during the period of pessimism over U.S. competitiveness was overstated, the recent focus on patenting and licensing as the essential ingredient in university-industry collaboration and knowledge transfer may be no less exaggerated. The emphasis on the Bayh-Dole Act as a catalyst to these interactions also seems somewhat misplaced"; p. 42.

16. "Innovation's Golden Goose," *Economist*, December 12, 2002, Special "Technology Quarterly" p 15.

17. Rebecca Zacks, "The TR University Research Scorecard 2000," *Technology Review*, January 11, 2002. Last retrieved February 19, 2007 from http://www.technologyreview.com/Biztech/12149/.

18. See for example Scott Shane, *Academic Entrepreneurship* (Cheltenham, England: Elgar, 2004); David C. Mowery, Richard R. Nelson, Bhaven N. Sampat, and Arvids A. Ziedonis, *Ivory Tower and Industrial Innovation: University-Industry Technology Transfer before and after the Bayh-Dole Act* (Stanford: Stanford University Press, 2004), and Marie Thursby and Richard Jensen, *Patent Licensing and the Research University*, National Bureau of Economic Research working paper no. W10758 (Washington, D.C.: National Bureau of Economic Research, September 2004).

19. Hill, "Universities in the U.S. National Innovation System," p 8.

20. Steve Lohr, "U.S. Research Funds Often Lead to Start-Ups, Study Says," *New York Times*, April 10, 2006.

21. The interview with Dick Peterson was carried out for preparation of and reported in David B. Audretsch, Juergen Weigand, and Claudia Weigand, "Does the Small Business Innovation Research Program Foster Entrepreneurial Behavior? Evidence from Indiana," in Charles W. Wessner (ed.), *The Small Business Innovation Research Program: An Assessment of the Department of Defense Fast Track Initiative* (Washington, D.C.: National Academies Press, 2000), pp. 166–185.

22. Wessner, *The Small Business Innovation Research Program (SBIR): An Assessment*, and David B. Audretsch, Albert N. Link, and John T. Scott, "Public/Private Technology Partnerships: Evaluating SBIR-Supported Research," *Research Policy* 31 (2002): 145–158.

23. Joshua Lerner, "The Government as Venture Capitalist: The Long-Run Impact of the SBIR Program," *Journal of Business* 72, no. 3 (1999): 285–318.

24. Wessner, *The Small Business Innovation Research Program (SBIR): An Assessment*.

25. Eugene Russo, "Making the Switch from Science to Business," *Nature*, October 30, 2003, pp. 988–989. Reprinted by permission from Macmillan Publishers Ltd: *Nature*, copyright 2003.

26. For an excellent survey of entrepreneurship policies in an international context, see Anders Lundstrom and Lois Stevenson, *Entrepreneurship Policy: Theory and Practice* (New York: Springer, 2005), and David B. Audretsch, Isabelle Grillo, and A. Roy Thurik, (eds.) *The Handbook of Research on Entrepreneurship Policy* (London: Elgar, 2007).

27. Interview with Steven Beck, president of Indiana Venture Center, February 24, 2005.

28. Press release by the University of California, San Diego, "UC San Diego Launches Global CONNECT to promote technology enterprises and regional innovation worldwide." July 18, 2003 Last retrieved January 16, 2007 from http://ucsdnews.ucsd.edu/newsrel/general/Global%20Connect.htm.

29. Personal interviews.

30. "Help with R & D Costs: SBIR Funding Pays Off in a Variety of Ways for ATDC Companies," July 12, 2005; www.atdc.org/news_details.asp?NewsID= 700. This website is operated and maintained by the Advanced Technology Development Center.

31. "What Harvard Taught Larry Summers," *Time*, March 6, 2006, p. 64.

32. "What Harvard Taught Larry Summers," p. 64.

33. Stephen Budiansky, "Brand U.," *New York Times*, April 26, p. A23.

34. Richard Crepeau, "Colleges Try to Sell Themselves," *New York Times*, April 30, 2006, p. 13.

35. Lohr, "U.S. Research Funds Often Lead to Start-Ups, Study Says."

36. Quoted in Lohr, "U.S. Research Funds Often Lead to Start-Ups, Study Says."

37. John W. Miller, "Europe's Flat Learning Curve: Innovation Wants for Funding, Tighter University-Business Ties," *Wall Street Journal*, May 16, 2002, pp. A7–A9, A8. Material from *The Wall Street Journal*, copyright © 2002

Dow Jones & Company, Inc. All rights reserved worldwide. License number 1546561487864.

38. Sciolino, "Higher Learning in France Clings to Its Old Ways," pp. A1, A14.

39. Miller, "Europe's Flat Learning Curve," p. A7.

40. Josef Joffee, "The Perils of Soft Power: Why America's Cultural Influence Makes Enemies, Too," *New York Times Magazine*, May 14, 2006, p. 15. Material from *The New York Times*, copyright © 2006, by The New York Co. Reprinted with permission.

41. "Der Triumph des Südens," *Focus*, January 30, 2006, pp. 48–49.

42. "Ministerin Schavan: Dialog Zwischen Wissenschaft und Wirtschaft forcieren," *Deutschland Nachrichten*, May 22, 2006.

43. Miller, "Europe's Flat Learning Curve," p. A7.

44. Miller, "Europe's Flat Learning Curve," p. A7.

45. "Entscheidend ist die Bereitschaft neues Wissen anzunehmen," *Frankfurter Allgemeine*, March 11, 2006, p. 12.

46. Sciolino, "Higher Learning in France Clings to Its Old Ways," pp. A1, A14.

47. Sciolino, "Higher Learning in France Clings to Its Old Ways," pp. A1, A14.

48. Miller, "Europe's Flat Learning Curve," p. A7.

Chapter 9

1. John Kenneth Galbraith, *The Affluent Society* (Boston: Houghton Mifflin, 1958).

2. For an analysis of public policy in Europe and Japan that facilitated the catch-up and overtaking the U.S. in a broad array of manufacturing industries see David B. Audretsch, *The Market and the State: Government Policy in Europe, Japan and the USA* (New York: New York University Press, 1989).

3. Halberstam, *The Fifties*, p. 127.

4. Halberstam, *The Fifties*, p. 119.

5. W. W. Rostow, "Here Comes a New Political Chapter in America," *International Herald Tribune*, January 2, 1987.

6. "My Hometown" by Bruce Springsteen. Copyright © 1984 Bruce Springsteen. Reprinted by permission. International copyright secured. All rights reserved.

7. Halberstam, *The Fifties*, p. 489.

8. Halberstam, *The Fifties*, p. 489.

9. Steve Mariotti, "Opening the Door of Entrepreneurial Possibility," *Kauffman Thoughtbook* (Kansas City, Missouri: Kauffman Foundation, 2005), p. 66.

10. Halberstam, *The Fifties*, p. 489.

11. Mathew Stewart, "The Management Myth," *Atlantic*, June 2006, points out that "one thing that cannot be said of the 'new' organization . . . is that it is new"; p. 85.

12. Stewart, "The Management Myth," pp. 84–85.

13. Julia Bonstein and Merlind Theile, "The Global Generation," *Der Spiegel Special International Edition* 4 (2005): 131.

14. Bonstein and Theile, "The Global Generation," p. 131.

15. Bonstein and Theile, "The Global Generation," p. 131.

16. Halberstam, *The Fifties*, p. 127.

17. Halberstam, *The Fifties*, p. 123.

18. Halberstam, *The Fifties*, p. 127.

19. Halberstam, *The Fifties*, p. 127.

20. Tom Peters and Robert H. Waterman Jr., *In Search of Excellence* (London, HarperCollins, 1995).

21. "The Pain of Layoffs for Ex–senior IBM Workers," *New York Times*, December 7, 1993, pp. B1, B5. Material from *The New York Times*, copyright © 1993, by The New York Times Co. Reprinted with permission.

22. Albert O. Hirschman, *Exit, Voice and Loyalty* (Cambridge, Mass.: Harvard University Press, 1970).

23. "The Pain of Layoffs for Ex–senior IBM Workers," p. B5.

24. "The Pain of Layoffs for Ex–senior IBM Workers," pp. B1, B5.

25. Heike Grimm, "Assessment of Entrepreneurship Policies Across Nations and Regions." In David Audretsch, Heike Grimm, and Charles W. Wessner (eds.), *Local Heroes in the Global Village: Globalization and the New Entrepreneurship Policies* (New York: Springer, 2005).

26. Albert Link and John Scott, "The Growth of Research Triangle Park," *Small Business Economics* 20 (March 2003): 167–175.

27. Link and Scott, "The Growth of Research Triangle Park".

28. See Michael Lugar, "The Research Triangle Experience," in Charles Wessner (ed.), *Industry-Laboratory Partnerships: A review of the Sandia Science and Technology Park Initiative* (Washington, D.C.: National Academy Press), 2001, pp. 35–38; and Michael Lugar and H. Goldstein, *Technology in the Garden: Research Parks and Regional Economic Development* (Chapel Hill: University of North Carolina Press, 1991).

29. Tim Gray, "From Tobacco to Tech: How the City of Raeigh Planted the Seeds for a New Economy," *US Airways*, April 2006, p. 228.

30. Gray, "From Tobacco to Tech," p. 230.

31. Stanford Institute For Economic Policy Research SIEPR Discussion Paper No. 00–45 "Learning the Silicon Valley Way," Gordon Moore and Kevin Davis, July 15, 2001. Last retrieved January 16, 2007, from http://www-cepr.stanford.edu/papers/pdf/00-45.pdf, p. 3.

32. Paul Krugman, *The Age of Diminished Expectations* (Cambridge, Mass.: MIT Press, 1997).

33. Paul Kennedy, *The Rise and Decline of Great Powers* (New Haven: Yale University Press, 1989).

34. Lester Thurow, *The Zero-Sum Society: Distribution and the Possibilities for Economic Change* (New York: Basic Books, 1980).

35. One important exception was Ireland.

36. The papers from the conference have been published in a special issue, "The Invisible Part of the Iceberg: Research Issues in Industrial Organization and Small Business" *Small Business Economics*, February 2001, v. 16, n.1.

37. "Fortune Dared to Touch Hot Topic," *International Harold Tribune*, May 10, 2002, p. 1.

38. Lester Thurow, *Fortune Favors the Bold* (New York: HarperCollins, 2002) p. 35.

39. Charles Ferguson, "From the people who brought you voodoo economics." *Harvard Business Review* (1988): 66:3 p 55–62. Quote on page 61.

40. "Schroeder Tries for Consensus in Fight to Cut Jobless Rate," *New York Times*, December 8, 1998, p. A8.

41. "Deutschland vor dem Absturz?" *Stern*, February 13, 1997.

42. "Recession Looms in Germany," *International Harold Tribune*, November 22, 2001, p. 1.

43. For a distinction between the concepts of comparative advantage and competitive advantage see Michael Porter, *The Competitiveness of Nations* (New York: Free Press, 1990).

44. "Recession Looms in Germany," p. 1.

45. These figures are from Thurow, *Fortune Favors the Bold*, p. 35.

46. "Those German Banks and Their Industrial Treasures," *The Economist*, January 21, 1995, 75–76.

47. "Strukturwandel in Deutschland" *Der Spiegel* 5 (February 6, 1994): 82–83.

48. David B. Audretsch, "Can Schroeder Break the Industry-Union-Government Cartel?" *Wall Street Journal Europe*, January 12, 1999. p. 10.

49. Romano Prodi, "For a New European Entrepreneurship," public speech delivered at Instituto de Empresa, Madrid, February 7, 2002.

50. Adapted from Mark Twain [Samuel Langhorne Clemens], *Pudd'nhead Wilson* (Mineola, New York: Dover, 1999 (1894)), p. 121.

51. "Handys, Hightech und Reformen, Guten Morgen Europa: Wie der alte Kontinent die Wirtschaftsmacht USA attackiert, " *Der Spiegel* May 29, 2000, p. 110.

52. Personal Communication with Jack Harding.

53. Carl Schramm has written an excellent book, *The Entrepreneurial Imperative: How America's Economic Miracle Will Reshape the World (and Change Your Life)*, (New York: Collins, 2006).

54. "The Evangelist of Entrepreneurship," *The Economist*, November 5, 2005, p. 76.

Works Cited

Acs, Zoltan. (1984). *The Changing Structure of the U.S. Economy: Lessons from the U.S. Steel Industry*. New York: Praeger Publishers.

Acs, Zoltan and Catherine Armington. (2006). *Enterpreneurship, Geography and American Economic Growth*. New York: Cambridge University Press.

Acs, Zoltan J., and David B. Audretsch (eds.). (1993). *Small Firms and Entrepreneurship: An East-West Perspective*. Cambridge, U.K.: Cambridge University Press.

Acs, Zoltan J., David B. Audretsch, Pontus Braunerhjelm, and Bo Carlsson. (2004). "The Missing Link: The Knowledge Filter and Entrepreneurship in Endogenous Growth." Centre for Economic Policy Research discussion paper no. 4783. London: Centre for Economic Policy Research.

Akerlof, George. (1970). "The Market for Lemons." *Quarterly Journal of Economics* 84: 488–500.

Agarwal, Rajshree, R. Echambadi, A. Franco, and M. Sarkar. (2004). Knowledge Transfer through Inheritance: Spin-out Generation, Development and Performance. *Academy of Management Journal* 47: 501–522.

Arrow K.J., (1962). Economic Welfare and the Allocation of Resources for Invention. In Nelson, R.R. (ed.), *The Rate and Direction of Inventive Activity*, Princeton University Press: Princeton, pp. 609–626.

Association of University Technology Managers. (2004). *Recollections: Celebrating the History of AUTM and the Legacy of Bayh-Dole*. Northbrook, Ill.: Association of University Technology Managers.

ATDC. (2005, July 12). Help with R & D Costs: SBIR Funding Pays Off in a Variety of Ways for ATDC Companies. Last retrieved January 16, 2007, from www.atdc.org/news_details.asp?NewsID=700.

Audretsch, David B. (2003). "Entrepreneurship: A Survey of the Literature."
   Brussels, Belgium: Commission of the European Union.

Audretsch, David B. (1999, January 12). "Can Schroeder Break the Industry-
   Union-Government Cartel?" *Wall Street Journal Europe*, p. 10.

Audretsch, David B. (1989). *The Market and the State: Government Policy towards
   Business in Europe, Japan and the USA*. New York: New York University Press.

Audretsch, David B., Isabelle Grillo, and A. Roy Thurik. (eds.). (2007). *The
   Handbook of Research on Entrepreneurship Policy*. London: Elgar.

Audretsch, David B., Heike Grimm, and Charles Wessner. (eds.). (2005). *Local
   Heroes in the Global Village*. New York: Springer.

Audretsch, David B., Max Keilbach, and Erik Lehmann. (2006). *Entrepreneurship
   and Economic Growth*. New York: Oxford University Press.

Audretsch, David B., Albert N. Link, and John T. Scott. (2002). Public/Private
   Technology Partnerships: Evaluating SBIR-Supported Research. *Research
   Policy* 31: 145–158.

Audretsch, David B., and Roy Thurik. (2001). What's New about the New
   Economy? Sources of Growth in the Managed and Entrepreneurial
   Economies. *Industrial and Corporate Change* 10, no. 1: 267–315.

Audretsch, David B., Juergen Weigand, and Claudia Weigand. (2000). Does the
   Small Business Innovation Research Program Foster Entrepreneurial
   Behavior? Evidence from Indiana. In Charles W. Wessner (ed.), *The Small
   Business Innovation Research Program (SBIR): An Assessment of the Department
   of Defense Fast Track Initative*. Washington, D.C.: National Academies Press,
   pp. 166–185.

Auerswald, Philip and Lewis Branscomb. (2003). "Valleys of Death and
   Darwinian Seas: Financing the Invention to Innovation Transition in the
   United States," *Journal of Technology Transfer*, 28, pp. 227–239.

Bloom, Alan. (1987). *The Closing of the American Mind*. New York: Simon and
   Schuster.

Bonstein, Julia, and Merlind Theile. (2005). The Global Generation. *Der Spiegel
   Special International Edition* 4: 130–135.

Bork, Robert H. (1978). *The Antitrust Paradox: A Policy at War with Itself*. New York:
   Basic Books.

Brokaw, Tom. (1998). *The Greatest Generation*. New York: Random House.

Budiansky, Stephen. (2006, April 26). Brand U. *New York Times* p. A23.

Bundesministerium für Wirtschaft und Technologie (German Federal Ministry
   of Economics and Technology). (2000). *Annual Report 2000*. Berlin:
   Bundesministerium für Wirtschaft und Technologie.

Bush, George W. (2004, November 4). Press conference, the White House [Speech].
   Last retrieved January 16, 2007, from http://www.whitehouse.gov/news/
   releases/2004/11/20041104-5.html.

Bush, Vannevar. (1945). *Science: The Endless Frontier*. Washington, D.C.:
   Government Printing Office.

Bye-Bye 'Made in Germany '. (2004). *Der Spiegel* 44, p. 94.

Carrol, Paul. (1993, September 24). "Die Offene Schlacht." *Die Zeit*, pp. 17–20.

Carty, Sharon S. (2006, March 23). GM Offers Buyouts to 126,000. *USA Today*, p. 23.

Chandler, Alfred. (1977). *The Visible Hand: The Managerial Revolution in American Business*. Cambridge, Mass.: Belknap Press.

Crepeau, Richard. (2006, April 30). Colleges Try to Sell Themselves. *New York Times*, p. 13.

Crichton, Michael. (1990). *Jurassic Park*. New York: Ballantine Books.

Cringley, Robert X. (1993). *Accidental Empires: How the Boys of Silicon Valley Make Their Millions, Battle Foreign Competition, and Still Can't Get a Date*. New York: Harper Business.

Da muss man powern. (2005). *Managermagazin* 2: 88.

Davis, Steven, John Haltiwanger, and Scott Schuh. (1996). Small Businesses and Job Creation: Dissecting Myth and Reassessing the Facts. *Small Business Economics* 8, no. 4: 297–315.

The Death of Distance. (1995, September 30). *The Economist*, Special Section, p. 3.

Der Triumph des Südens. (2006, January 30). *Focus*, pp. 48–49.

Dertouzos, Michael L.; Richard K. Lester, and Robert M. Solow. (1989). *Made in America: Regaining the Productive Edge*. Cambridge, Mass.: MIT Press.

Deutschland vor dem Absturz? (1997, February 13). *Stern*, pp. 48–50.

Ein Mann, ein Brett. (2006, February 6). *Focus*, p. 106.

Florida, Richard. (2002). *Rise of the Creative Class*. New York: Basic Books.

Friedan, Betty. (1963). *The Feminine Mystique*. New York: Norton.

Friedman, Milton, and Rose Friedman. (1980). *Free to Choose*. New York: Harcourt Brace Jovanovich.

Friedman, Thomas L. (2005). *The World Is Flat*. London: Lane.

Ferguson, Charles. (1988). From the people who brought you voodoo economics. *Harvard Business Review* 66:3 pp. 55–62.

Galbraith, John Kenneth. (1958). *The Affluent Society*. Boston: Houghton Mifflin.

Gartner, William B. and Nancy M. Carter. (2003). Entrepreneurial Behaviour and Firm Organizing Processes. In Zoltan Acs and David B. Audretsch (eds.), *Handbook of Entrepreneurship Research*. Dordrecht: Kluwer Academic Publishers, pp. 195–221.

Gitlin, Todd. (1993). *The Sixties: Years of Hope, Days of Rage*. New York: Bantam Books.

Glaeser, Edward L., Hedi D. Kallal, Jose A. Scheinkman, and Andrei Shleifer. (1992). Growth in Cities. *Journal of Political Economy* 100: 1126–1152.

Goldin, Claudia, and Larry Katz. (1999, Winter). The Shaping of Higher Education: The Formative Years in the United States, 1890 to 1940. *Journal of Economic Perspectives* 13: 37–62.

Gray, Tim. (2006, April). From Tobacco to Tech: How the City of Raleigh Planted the Seeds for a New Economy. *US Airways*, p. 228.

Grimm, Heike. (2005). Assessment of Entrepreneurship Policies Across Nations and Regions. In David Audretsch, Heike Grimm, and Charles W. Wessner (eds.), *Local Heroes in the Global Village: Globalization and the New Entrepreneurship Policies*. New York: Springer.

Halberstam, David. (1972). *The Best and the Brightest*. New York: Random House.

Halberstam, David. (1993). *The Fifties*. New York: Villard Books.

Handys, Hightech und Reformen, Guten Morgen Europa: Wie der alte Kontinent die Wirtschaftsmacht USA attackiert. (2000, May 29). *Der Spiegel*, p. 110.

Heward, Lyn, and John U. Bacon. (2006). *The Spark: Igniting the Creative Fire That Lives within Us All*. New York: Currency.

Hofmann, Josef. (2005, May 5). VW Greift nur im Ausland durch. *Handelsblatt*, p. 15.

Hill, Kent. (2006). *Universities in the U.S. National Innovation System* [Unpublished manuscript]. Center for Business Research, L. William Seidman Research Institute, W. P. Carey School of Business, Arizona State University.

Hirschman, Albert O. (1970). *Exit, Voice and Loyalty*. Cambridge, Mass.: Harvard University Press.

Ichbiah, Daniel, and Susan I. Knepper. (1991). *The Making of Microsoft: How Bill Gates and His Team Created the World's Most Successful Software Company*. Rocklin, Calif.: Prima.

Innovation's Golden Goose. (2002, December 12). *The Economist*, Technology Quarterly Special Section, p. 15.

Jensen, Michael (1993). The Modern Industrial Revolution, Exit, and the Failure of the Internal Control Systems. *Journal of Finance* 48: 831–880.

Joffe, Josef. (2006, May 14). The Perils of Soft Power: Why America's Cultural Influence Makes Enemies, Too. *New York Times Magazine*, pp. 15–16.

Johnson, Nora (2006, June). Desperate Housewives. *The Atlantic Monthly*, pp. 51–54.

Jonas, Norman (1987, April 20). Can America Compete? *Business Week*, pp. 45–69.

Jung, Alexander. (2005). A New Economic Age. *Der Spiegel Special International Edition* 4: 102–109.

Kennedy, Paul (1989). *The Rise and Decline of Great Powers*. New Haven: Yale University Press.

Keck, Otto. (1993). The National System for Technical Innovation in Germany. In Richard R. Nelson (ed.), *National Innovation Systems: A Comparative Analysis*. Oxford: Oxford University Press, pp. 115–157.

Kennedy, Paul. (1989). *The Rise and Decline of Great Powers*. New York: Random House.

Kerouac, Jack. (1957). *On the Road*. New York: Penguin Books.

Klawitter, Nils. (2005). The Faceless Factory. *Der Spiegel Special International Edition* 4: 120–129.

Kleppter, Steven. (2006, May 7–9). "Spinouts." Paper resented at the first annual Ewing Marion Kauffman-Max Planck Conference, "Entrepreneurship and Economics Growth" Tegernesee, Germany.

Kohut, Andrew, and Bruce Stokes. (2006). *America against the World: How We Are Different and Why We Are Disliked*. New York: Times Books.

Kolko, Gabriel. (1963). *The Triumph of Conservativism*. New York: Macmillan.

Konzeption eines Innovationsfonds der Deutschen Forschung (IFDF) zur Stärkung des Technologietransfers. (2006, January). Garching Information, pp. 27–29. Last retrieved January 16, 2007, from http://www.max-planck-innovation.de/share/newsletter/Newsletter_01_2006_en.pdf.

Kristofferson, Kris. (1971). Me and Bobby McGee. In J. Joplin, Pearl Album.

Krugman, Paul. (1997). *The Age of Diminished Expectations*. Cambridge, Mass.: MIT Press.

Lerner, Joshua. (1999). The Government as Venture Capitalist: The Long-Run Impact of the SBIR Program. *Journal of Business* 72, no. 3: 285–318.

Link, Albert, and John Scott. (2003, March). The Growth of Research Triangle Park. *Small Business Economics* 20: 167–175.

Lohr, Steve. (2006, April 10). U.S. Research Funds Often Lead to Start-Ups, Study Says. *New York Times*, p. C2.

Lugar, Michael. (2001). "The Research Triangle Experience." In Charles Wessner (ed.), *Industry-Laboratory Partnerships: A review of the Sandia Science and Technology Park Initiative*. Washington, D.C.: National Academy Press, pp. 35–38.

Lugar, Michael and H. Goldstein. (1991). *Technology in the Garden: Research Parks and Regional Economic Development*. Chapel Hill: University of North Carolina Press.

Lundstrom, Anders, and Lois Stevenson. (2005). *Entrepreneurship Policy: Theory and Practice*. New York: Springer.

Mariotti, Steve. (2005). "Opening the Door of Entrepreneurial Possibility," *Kauffman Thoughtbook*. Kansas City, Mo: Kauffman Foundation.

Markham, Jesse. (1965). Mergers: The Adequacy of the New Section 7. In A. Phillips (ed.), *Perspectives on Antitrust Policy*. Princeton: Princeton University Press, pp. 164–188.

Miller, John W. (2002, May 16). Europe's Flat Learning Curve: Innovation Wants for Funding, Tighter University-Business Ties. *Wall Street Journal*, p. A7.

Mills, C. Wright. (1951). *White Collar: The American Middle-Classes*. New York: Oxford University Press.

Ministerin Schavan: Dialog Zwischen Wissenschaft und Wirtschaft forcieren. (2006, May 22). *Deutschland Nachrichten* [German e-newsletter]. Last retrieved January 17, 2007, from http://www.germany.info/relaunch/info/publications/d_nachrichten/2006/060522/pol1.html.

Moore, Gordon and Kevin Davis. (2001, July 15). Learning the Silicon Valley Way. Stanford Institute for Economic Policy Research SIEPR Discussion Paper no. 00–45. Last retrieved January 16, 2007, from http://www-cepr.stanford.edu/papers/pdf/00-45.pdf.

Moore, John H. (1992). "Measuring Soviet Economic Growth: Old Problems and New Complications." *Journal of Institutional and Theoretical Economis* 148(1): 72–92.

Mowery, David (2005). The Bayh-Dole Act and High-Technology Entrepreneurship in U.S. Universities: Chicken, Egg, or Something Else? In Gary Liebcap (ed.), *University Entrepreneurship and Technology Transfers*. Amsterdam: Elsevier, pp. 38–68.

Mowery, David C., Richard R. Nelson, Bhaven N. Sampat, and Arvids A. Ziedonis. (2004). *Ivory Tower and Industrial Innovation: University-Industry Technology Transfer before and after the Bayh-Dole Act*. Stanford: Stanford University Press.

Nelson, Ralph. (1959). *Merger Movements in American Industry 1895–1956*. Princeton: Princeton University Press.

Nelson, Richard. (1981). Research on Productivity Growth and Productivity Differences: Dead Ends and New Departures. *Journal of Economic Literature* 19: 1029–1064.

Noren, James. (1966). "Soviet Industry Trends in Outputs, Inputs, and Productivity." *In New Directions in the Soviet Economy*. Washington: Subcommittee Foreign Econ. Policy, Join Econ. Committee, US Congress.

Odagiri, Hiroyuki, and Akira Goto. (1993). The Japanese System of Innovation: Past, Present, and Future. In Richard R. Nelson (ed.), *National Innovation Systems: A Comparative Analysis*. Oxford: Oxford University Press, pp. 76–114.

Palfreman, Jon, and Doron Swade. (1991). *The Dream Machine: Exploring the Computer Age*. London: BBC Books.

Peters, Tom, and Robert H. Waterman Jr. (1995). *In Search of Excellence*. London: HarperCollins.

Piore, Michael, and Charles Sabel. (1984). *The Second Industrial Divide: Possibilities for Prosperity*. New York: Basic Books.

Porter, Michael. (1990). *The Competitiveness of Nations*. New York: Free Press.

Posner, Richard A. (1976). *Antitrust Law: An Economic Perspective*. Chicago: University of Chicago Press.

Prodi, Romano. (2002, February 7). *For a New European Entrepreneurship*. Instituto de Empresa, Madrid [Speech].

Reich, Robert. (1983). *The Next American Frontier*. New York: Times Books.

Research and Development: Looking for Innovation in the East, Where the Engineering Pool Is Deep. (2005, December 12–19). *Business Week* [European edn.], p. 58.

Riesman, David. (1950). *The Lonely Crowd: A Study of Changing American Character*. New Haven: Yale University Press.

Rifkin, Jeremy. (2004). *The European Dream*. New York: Penguin.

Romer, Paul. (1986). Increasing Returns and Long-Run Growth. *Journal of Political Economy* 94: 1002–37.

Romer, Paul. (1990). Endogenous Technological Change. *Journal of Political Economy* 98: 1–102.

Romer, Paul. (1994, Winter). The Origins of Endogenous Growth Theory. *Journal of Economic Perspectives* 8: 3–22.

Rose, Frank. (1989). *West of Eden: The End of Innocence at Apple Computer*. New York: Viking Press.

Rosenberg, Nathan. (1992) Economic Experiments. *Industrial and Corporate Change* vol. 1: 181–203.

Rostow, W. W. (1987, January 2). "Here Comes a New Political Chapter in America" *International Herald Tribune*.

Russo, Eugene. (2003, October 30). Making the Switch from Science to Business. *Nature*, pp. 988–989.

Samuelson, Robert J. (2006, March 28). "The French Denial." *Washington Post.* p. A23.

Samuelson, Robert J. (2006, April 3). "The Politics of Make-Believe" *Newsweek.* p. 29.

Sarasvathy, Saras D., Nicholas Dew, S. Ramakrishna Velamuri, and Sankaran Venkataraman. (2003). Three Views of Entrepreneurial Opportunity. In Zoltan Acs and David B. Audretsch (eds.). *Handbook of Entrepreneurship Research.* Dordrecht: Kluwer Academic Publishers, pp. 141–160.

Scherer, Frederick M. (1970). *Industrial Market Structure and Economic Performance.* Chicago: Rand McNally.

Scherer, Frederick M. (1977, April). The Posnerian Harvest: Separating Wheat from Chaff. *Yale Law Journal* 86: 974–1002.

Schramm, Carl. (2006). *The Entrepreneurial Imperative: How America's - Economic Miracle Will Reshape the World (and Change Your Life).* New York: Collins.

Sciolino, Elaine. (2006, May 12). Higher Learning in France Clings to Its Old Ways. *New York Times*, pp. A1, A16.

Shane, Scott. (2004). *Academic Entrepreneurship.* Cheltenham, England: Elgar.

Sinclair, Upton. (1906). *The Jungle.* New York: Doubleday Page.

Solow, Robert. (1956). A Contribution to Theory of Economic Growth. *Quarterly Journal of Economics* 70: 65–94.

Solow, Robert. (1957). Technical Change and the Aggregate Production Function. *Review of Economics and Statistics* 39: 312–320.

Special Report: Rise of a Powerhouse. (2005, December 12–19). *Business Week* [European edn.], p. 44.

Stephan, Paula. (2006). "Wrapping It Up in a Person: The Location Decision of New PhDs," Innovation, Policy and the Economy, National Bureau of Economic Research, Washington, D.C.

Stephens, Philip. (2006, April 28). A Future for Europe Shaped by Museums and Modernity. *Financial Times*, p. 11.

Stewart, Mathew. (2006, June). The Management Myth. *The Atlantic Monthly*, pp. 80–86.

Streeck, Wolfgang W. (1991). On the Institutional Conditions of Diversified Quality Production. In *Beyond Keynesianism: The Socio-Economics of Production and Full Employment.* Cheltenham, England: Elgar, pp. 21–61.

Strukturwandel in Deutschland. (1994, February 6). *Der Spiegel* 5: 82–83.

Sweig, Julia A. (2006). *Friendly Fire: Losing Friends and Making Enemies in the Anti-American Century.* New York: PublicAffairs.

System Error. (1993, September 18). *The Economist*, p. 99.

Terkel, Studs. (1974). *Hard Times.* New York: W. W. Norton.

The Best Cities for Knowledge Workers. (1993, November 15). *Fortune*, p. 44.

The Evangelist of Entrepreneurship. (2005, November 5). *The Economist*, p. 76.

The Invisible Part of the Iceberg: Research Issues in Industrial Organization and Small Business. (2001, February). *Small Business Economics* [Special Issue] vol. 16, no. 1.

Those German Banks and Their Industrial Treasures. (1995, January 21). *The Economist*, pp. 75–76.

Thurow, Lester. (1984, September 27). Losing the Economic Race. *New York Review of Books*, pp. 29–31.

Thurow, Lester. (1985). Healing with a Thousand Bandages. *Challenge* 28: 19–28. Last retrieved January 16, 2007, from http://siteresources.worldbank.org/WBI/Resources/wbi37180.pdf.

Thurow, Lester. (2002). *Fortune Favors the Bold*. New York: HarperCollins.

Thursby, Marie, and Richard Jensen. (2004, September). *Patent Licensing and the Research University*. National Bureau of Economic Research working paper no. W10758. Washington, D.C: National Bureau of Economic Research.

de Tocqueville, Alexis. *Democracy in America*. Last retrieved January 17, 2007, from Project Gutenberg http://www.gutenberg.org/files/816/816-h/816-h.htm.

Twain, Mark (Samuel Langhorne Clemens). (1999, 1894). *Pudd'nhead Wilson*. Mineola, New York: Dover.

University of California, San Diego. (2003, July 18). UC San Diego Launches Global CONNECT to promote technology enterprises and regional innovation worldwide. Last retrieved January 16, 2007, from http://ucsd-news.ucsd.edu/newsrel/general/Global%20Connect.htm

Wessner, Charles (ed.). (2000). *The Small Business Innovation Research Program (SBIR): An Assessment of the Department of Defense Fast Track Imitative*. Washington D.C.: National Academies Press.

What Harvard Taught Larry Summers. (2006, March 6). *Time*, p. 64.

Wheelwright, Steven C. (1985). Restoring Competitiveness in U.S. Manufacturing. *California Management Review* 27, no. 3: 26–42.

Whyte, William H. (1956). *The Organization Man*. New York: Simon and Schuster.

Williamson, Oliver. (1968). Economies as an Antitrust Defense: The Welfare Tradeoffs. *American Economic Review* 58, no. 1: 18–36.

Wilson, Craig. (2006, May 10). Cirque Ignites 'The Spark.' *USA Today*, pp. 7B–8B.

Wilson, Sloan. (1955). *The Man in the Grey Flannel Suit*. New York: Simon and Schuster.

Wright, Robert. (2006, May 14). They Hate Us, They Really Hate Us. *New York Times Review of Books*, p. 28.

"Wo das Glück zu Hause ist," (2004, April 20) *Der Stern*, pp. 48–54.

Zacks, Rebecca. (2002, January 11). "The TR University Research Scorecard 2000." *Technology Review*. Last retrieved February 19, 2007, from http://www.technologyreview.com/Biztech/12149/.

Index